Springer Series on
REHABILITATION

Editor: Thomas E. Backer, Ph.D.
Human Interacion Research Institute, Los Angeles

Advisory Board: Carolyn L. Vash, Ph.D., Elizabeth L. Pan, Ph.D.,
Donald E. Galvin, Ph.D., Ray L. Jones, Ph.D., James F. Garrett, Ph.D.,
Patricia G. Forsythe, and Henry Viscardi, Jr.

Paul R. Sachs, Ph.D., is in private practice in the Philadelphia area. He also serves as consultant to New Medico Rehabilitation Center of Philadelphia, Suburban General Hospital and Northwestern Institute. Dr. Sachs received his B.A. with honors from Trinity College and his M.A. and Ph.D. in clinical psychology from Vanderbilt University. Since 1981, he has worked in the field of brain-injury rehabilitation for acute and post-acute rehabilitation treatment facilities. From 1984–1986 he was Program Director of a transitional living program for brain-injury survivors. He has contributed articles to rehabilitation journals on brain-injury rehabilitation and rehabilitation psychology.

Treating Families of Brain-Injury Survivors

Paul R. Sachs, Ph.D.

Springer Publishing Company
New York

No part of this publication may be reproduced, stored in a
retrieval system, or transmitted in any form or by any means,
electronic, mechanical, photocopying, recording, or otherwise,
without the prior permission of Springer Publishing Company, Inc.

Springer Publishing Company, Inc.
536 Broadway
New York, NY 10012-3955

91 92 93 94 95 / 5 4 3 2 1

Library of Congress Cataloging-in-Publication Data

Sachs, Paul Reid.
    Treating families of brain-injury survivors / Paul R. Sachs.
        p.   cm.
    Includes bibliographical references.
    ISBN 0-8261-6920-1
    1. Brain—Wounds and injuries—Patients—Family relationships.
    2. Adjustment (Psychology) 3. Counseling. I. Title.
    [DNLM: 1. Brain Injuries—psychology. 2. Family Therapy. WL 354
S121t]
RD594.S23   1991
155.9′16—dc20
DNLM/DLC
for Library of Congress   91-4612
                                                               CIP
                                                               Rev.

Printed in the United States of America

To Janet, Daniel, and Rachel;
and to my parents, Herbert and Claire Sachs

Contents

Preface

This book was written during a transitional period of my life. It was begun several weeks before I left a full-time job as director of a post-acute residential program for traumatically brain-injured adults. At that time, I had been married for almost four years and my first child was a month old. I left the security of full-time employment for the flexibility of private practice. I was dissatisfied and disenchanted with administrative work and looked forward to doing direct clinical work again.

Over the next five years this book was written and completed. The work was done on my own time, sandwiched between consultation projects, part-time jobs, and time with my family. Writing has always been a way for me to make sense out of events and to express my feelings. From the beginning, work with brain-injury survivors and families presented me with an especially difficult experience to comprehend. Rarely did a day pass that I did not see images of myself or my wife as a brain-injury survivor, or myself as a parent, sibling, or child of a survivor. When I became a father, I was moved by the experiences of family members of survivors even more intensely. It is perhaps no surprise then that writing this book coincided with the changes in my life brought about by fatherhood.

Thus, I am writing first for myself. The best way I have found energy and inspiration for professional work with traumatic brain-injury survivors is to create some aspect of the work that is satisfying for me alone. For this reason, I am writing this book.

I also write for other professionals in the hope that my own experiences and insights will be helpful to them in learning how to work effectively with brain-injury survivors and their families. Finally, I write for the families of survivors. Writing makes connections between experiences. Connections between family and professionals are essential to effective rehabilitation outcome from traumatic brain injury. I hope that this book helps to create some of those connections.

Acknowledgements

First to thank for this project are all of the traumatic brain-injury survivors and families with whom I have had the opportunity to work and to learn from their experiences. In particular I am very grateful to Judy, Robert, Rona, and Susan for their willingness to share their personal experiences in this book. Each of these personal statements is eloquent and powerful. I also wish to thank the following brain-injury rehabilitation facilities where I have had the opportunity to work with brain-injury survivors and their families: Bryn Mawr Rehabilitation Hospital, Genesis Head Injury program at Hartefeld, and New Medico Rehabilitation Center of Philadelphia. I am indebted to Sue Apter, M.S.W., Terri Patterson, R.N., M.S.N., and Jed Yalof, Psy.D. for taking time to read drafts of the book and offer such helpful comments on the manuscript. Thanks to Dr. Tom Backer and Kathleen O'Malley of Springer Publishing Company for their astute editorial comments which helped me to refine my ideas. Thanks also to Pat Gladstone who typed portions of an early draft of this book. My most special thanks are reserved for my wife, Janet Sandell Sachs, for her suggestions and editing, but moreso for her love and support. Without her encouragement I feel certain that this book would not have been completed.

Introduction

No more than five or ten years ago, books and articles on traumatic brain injury began with an acknowledgment of the advances in emergency medical care and the possibilities rehabilitation held for brain-injury survivors. Today, emergency medical care and acute rehabilitation facilities for traumatic brain-injury survivors are numerous and well-established. There is a wide range of rehabilitation techniques available to handle the survivor's medical, cognitive, physical, and emotional impairments. An active National Head Injury Foundation (NHIF) creates public awareness of traumatic brain injury as a unique condition (Brody, 1983; Chance, 1986; Clark & Zabarsky, 1981; Freudenheim, 1987; Lasden, 1982) and advocates for relevant legislation.

Greater attention in the field is now focused on treatment specifically for families of brain-injury survivors. A recent issue of the *Journal of Head Trauma Rehabilitation* (Bond, 1988) was devoted exclusively to family treatment issues. Families of the survivors are recognized as playing a major role in decision-making regarding choice of rehabilitation treatment institution for the survivor, treatment modalities, and implementation of treatment. Jacobs (1985) noted that, "families (constitute) the major source of support, socialization and assistance to the head injury survivor" (p. 429). Furthermore, families may take on more responsibility for these support activities than any community agency or facility (Kozloff, 1987) particularly over the lifetime of the survivor after institutional care is no longer provided.

Rehabilitation professionals generally agree that the family must be included in treatment planning and implementation if rehabilitation is to be effective for the survivor. In order to involve families in treatment, a strong working relationship between the rehabilitation professionals and families must be established. Effective techniques should be developed for incorporating the family into rehabilitation treatment as soon as possible after the trauma (Durgin, 1989). In addition, family involvement in treatment should be maintained by continually addressing the family's needs throughout the long course of the survivor's rehabilitation.

In terms of psychological intervention with families, treatment strategies must be comprehensive. The strategies must include an understanding of family structure, family coping strategies, and how these interact with the condition of the brain-injury survivor. The following areas are important components of a comprehensive program of family treatment.

ASSESSING FAMILY STRUCTURE AND INCORPORATING THIS ASSESSMENT INTO TREATMENT INTERVENTIONS

Each family can be understood in terms of its structure or organization. The nature of the family structure and the roles and responsibilities of each family member within that structure will have an impact on the family's emotional adjustment to the traumatic brain injury of a family member. Psychological treatment must include an assessment of family structure, family history, and the family's strengths and weaknesses. Psychological treatment interventions for the family should be derived, in part, from an understanding of family structure and how the structure has been stressed by the trauma. The goal of treatment intervention should be to strengthen the family structure in order to help family members function effectively as individuals and as a family unit in the face of the trauma.

PREPARATION OF THE FAMILY FOR PSYCHOLOGICAL TREATMENT

Families of brain-injury survivors are involuntary participants in psychological and rehabilitation treatment. They did not choose to have the trauma occur to their family member. Therefore, part of the intervention process should be a means of preparing the family for subsequent rehabilitation treatment. This preparation is accomplished by educating the family about the brain injury, its effects on the survivor and family, and the goals and techniques of rehabilitation care. The practitioner should not presume that the family is informed about and willing to cooperate with treatment before they have been properly prepared for what treatment entails.

FLEXIBILITY IN DESIGNING TREATMENT

In addition to preparing the family adequately for psychological treatment, the practitioner must be flexible in designing treatment. Treatment should be tailored to the level of motivation and emotional state of the family and the needs of the rehabilitation treatment situation. Limiting oneself to one theoretical orientation or technique greatly decreases the clinician's effectiveness in engaging the family in psychological and general rehabilitation treatment. Family treatment must encompass several methods of intervention that can be used judiciously over the course of rehabilitation treatment.

RELATING FAMILY TREATMENT TO THE SURVIVOR'S COURSE OF RECOVERY

The survivor's recovery from a severe traumatic brain injury is measured in years and spans several treatment settings. The needs of the family will change over the course of recovery. As the survivor recovers, or when recovery falters, the family will present different questions and emotional difficulties to the professional. Moreover, when the survivor is transferred from one treatment site to the next, the professional in each treatment setting must be prepared to handle the needs of the family for that particular treatment setting. A psychological treatment program for families must be closely linked to the milieu in which rehabilitation treatment for the survivor is provided.

GUIDELINES FOR SPECIFIC TREATMENT TECHNIQUES

Each family will present the professional with a unique constellation of problems and behaviors. Some presenting problems, however, will affect all families in one form or another. Treatment guidelines for such problems as behavioral dyscontrol in the survivor, sexual behavior of the survivor, and discharge planning should be specified so that they can be used consistently by the professional, taught to other professionals, and subjected to empirical investigation.

WORKING WITHIN A TRANSDISCIPLINARY TREATMENT PROGRAM

Treatment for the traumatic brain-injury survivor involves a team of professionals with different areas of specialty. The emotional adjustment difficulties that the family members may present will not be confined to an occasional contact with a psychologist or social worker but rather will be expressed in their interactions with each professional. Thus, treatment techniques should be flexible enough that each professional working with the family has some means of dealing with the family's presenting problems. Such techniques should also take into consideration how the professionals come together as a team to help the family and the survivor in the course of recovery.

WORKING WITH SELF-HELP AND ADVOCACY GROUPS

The National Head Injury Foundation assists families with educational information about brain injury and information about head injury programs. NHIF also is an active political group working with local, state, and national governments. Because of its high standing in the field of head injury rehabilitation, NHIF and its support groups for families must be incorporated into a psychological treatment program for families of brain-injury survivors. Rehabilitation professionals working with families should also be able to work with the NHIF as a partner in assisting families to cope with the demands of the rehabilitation process. Thus, a psychological treatment program should specify how the interaction between professionals and brain injury advocacy and self-help groups can be accomplished.

TRAINING PROFESSIONALS IN THE FIELD

As the field of brain-injury rehabilitation grows, greater numbers of professionals are needed to provide services to survivors and their families. The unique needs of brain-injury survivors and their families requires that psychologists be adequately trained to provide the needed services effectively. A comprehensive treatment program for families of survivors is important as a clinical tool and should suggest areas of training for professionals who are entering the field.

This book is written to address the aforementioned issues in psychological treatment for families of traumatic brain-injury survivors. It is designed to be a gateway to the development of effective working relationships between rehabilitation professionals, particularly rehabilitation psychologists, and families of traumatic brain-injury survivors. The book offers strategies for developing assessment and treatment within the transdisciplinary rehabilitation setting.

To accomplish these goals the book is written with several restrictions in mind. One, the emphasis in this book is on family adjustment and treatment rather than traumatic brain-injury's effects on the survivor. Though some overview of brain-injury sequelae will be provided, this information will be discussed in terms of the family rather than the survivor. The reader should refer to cited texts for detailed information about traumatic brain injury and its effects on the survivor. Two, practical treatment intervention will be discussed more than theory, although at certain points the relationship between theoretical understanding of the family and clinical intervention will be highlighted. Again, the reader is encouraged to consult the references cited for more information specific to family theory. Three, it is assumed that the reader has experience with the basic principles of psychotherapy. This book is not a guide to family psychotherapy. It is hoped that the book will provide the reader with a framework for applying psychotherapy principles to work with the family of a traumatic brain-injury survivor. Four, the focus of the family evaluation and treatment is on families of severe traumatic brain-injury survivors. Recently, increased professional attention has been given to the survivors of mild traumatic brain injury (Alves *et al.*, 1986, Kay, 1986). In addition, individuals who have experienced other brain impairing conditions (e.g., cerebrovascular accident, brain tumors, anoxia) may be treated in traumatic brain-injury rehabilitation facilities. The reader should be cautious about generalizing the issues raised in this book to families of individuals with these other conditions.

A basic premise of this book is that traditional psychotherapy intervention for families needs to be modified for the families of traumatic brain-injury survivors. It is also felt that the role and tasks of the mental health professional are broader in a brain-injury rehabilitation center than in other mental health treatment settings. For this reason, the term "psychological treatment" rather than "psychotherapy" is used throughout this book when referring to the interventions that the professional provides to families.

In general, this book is directed toward mental health professionals who work in a brain-injury rehabilitation setting. Other rehabilitation professionals may find the information here of interest to their work with brain-injury survivors and families. In order to address the widest group of readers, terms such as "rehabilitation professional" and "practitioner" are used to refer to the individual providing psychological treatment. Occasionally the term "psychologist" is used to refer to the specific role of the psychologist as opposed to other professionals within the rehabilitation setting.

Rehabilitation professionals zealously guard their areas of professional expertise even while working together on a rehabilitation team. It is not the author's intention to debate whether rehabilitation psychologists should be the sole providers of family evaluation and treatment services described here or that they provide such services more or less effectively than other mental health professionals. That is a question for empirical research to answer.

Interspersed between the chapters of this book are four personal statements from family members of traumatic brain-injury survivors. These statements were written by the family members themselves describing their actual experiences. The author of this book gave them no direction other than to describe their relationship with the survivor before the trauma and how this relationship was changed by the trauma. At the request of several of these family members, their names and the names mentioned in the statements have been changed. In the context of the book, these statements are a reminder that the professional must address traumatic brain-injury rehabilitation as both a clinical condition and a personal life experience for the survivor and the family.

1

Overview of Traumatic Brain-Injury Rehabilitation and Its Implications for the Family

A cornerstone of evaluation and treatment strategies for families of traumatic brain-injury survivors is a thorough understanding of the effects of the injury on the survivor. The family's emotional adjustment to the injury will be determined in large part by their reactions to the difficulties that they observe in the survivor. Therefore, the professional working with the family must, in addition to being a skilled clinician, be familiar with the nature of traumatic brain injury, the course of recovery and major sequelae of the injury in order to be truly effective as a facilitator of the family's adjustment (Rosenthal, 1989).

Many excellent publications, all written within the last decade, detail the medical, physical, and psychological sequelae of the traumatic brain-injury survivor (Brooks, 1984; Jennett & Teasdale, 1981; Levin et al., 1982; Prigatano, 1987; Rapp, 1986; Rosenthal et al., 1990; Ylvisaker, 1985). In addition, the National Head Injury Foundation (NHIF) maintains a library of educational materials on brain-injury rehabilitation.

As mentioned in the Introduction, it is not the purpose of this book to present a detailed discussion of traumatic brain injury. The focus in this chapter will be to discuss some of the major sequelae of traumatic brain injury in terms of their implications for the family of a brain-injury survivor. This discussion will provide a framework for understanding family adjustment. The psychological treatment that is provided to the family will be elaborated from this framework in subsequent chapters.

EPIDEMIOLOGY

The tragic incident that results in a traumatic brain injury appears to the outsider to be a random event. In an effort to reduce anxiety about the injury, one might wish to believe that the survivor was in some way to blame

1

for the injury. The fact is that a traumatic brain injury can occur to individuals of any age, sex, race or nationality.

One of the most uncomfortable moments for a professional working in the traumatic brain injury field is the realization that happy, well-adjusted, productive and promising individuals can be cut down by the trauma for no apparent reason. Being a "good person" does not necessarily minimize one's chance of suffering a traumatic brain injury or any other life trauma. (see Kushner, 1981).

Nevertheless, it has been determined that some people are more likely than others to be victims of traumatic brain injury. Young men under 30 years of age of are more at risk for traumatic brain injury (Kalsbeek et al., 1980), particularly if they are involved in certain types of physically challenging or risky occupations (Rimel et al., 1990).

Preexisting personality and life adjustment problems have been documented with greater frequency among survivors of traumatic brain injury than among the general population (Adamovich et al., 1985; Haas et al., 1987; Levin et al., 1982; Malec, 1985; Rimel et al., 1990). These problems include history of disrupted family life, learning difficulties, treatment for emotional maladjustment, and history of drug and alcohol use. The individual may have also engaged in dangerous work or leisure activities thereby increasing his or her chance of experiencing physical injury.

Epidemiological studies also show that severe traumatic brain injuries are overwhelmingly caused by motor vehicle accidents (Jennett & Teasdale, 1981). The majority of these involve some drug or alcohol use (Rimel et al., 1990; Sparadeo & Gill, 1989). Injuries are also caused by falls, assaults, or machinery-related accidents. Drug and alcohol use may be a contributing factor in these latter groups of injuries.

Rapid medical intervention after a severe injury can result in greater rates of survival and can reduce the deleterious effects of medical complications after the injury (Levin et al., 1982). The progress in techniques for ensuring the individual's survival from a traumatic brain injury is the major reason for the growth in traumatic brain-injury rehabilitation centers and treatment services.

Implications for the Family

This epidemiological information about brain-injury survivors has implications for the projected emotional reactions and subsequent psychological treatment of families. Specifically, this information suggests that family emotional conflicts and psychological treatment will center on three main themes: independence, control, and personality change.

Independence

The identified at-risk group for traumatic brain injury, young men in their teens and twenties, are at a transitional stage in their development. They are just becoming independent from their families. The older members of this group may be recently married, without children or with very young children. The youngest members of this group may be living alone or with their parents. The men in this group are usually in academic and vocational transition. They may be in the middle of an academic or vocational training program or they may have just become established in a job without much experience or seniority.

The transition to independence is also an important issue in the life of the families of such young men. Parents of the survivor may have been looking ahead to having an independent child who requires less time and financial obligations from them as parents. A young wife of a survivor may have been getting to know her husband and beginning to establish a life independent from her family of origin. Suddenly the trauma throws a dependent individual with a brain-injury into these families' lives.

This general scenario, admittedly simplified, points out the basic theme of independence with which the family of a brain-injury survivor must struggle. The brain-injury survivor is struggling to regain independence that was lost as the result of the trauma. The family must come to terms with how much independence can be expected for themselves and for the survivor. The professional working with the family will need to assess the manner in which the family experiences these conflicts. Psychological treatment will consist in part of assisting the family in understanding their feelings and values about independence, resolving conflicts about it that may occur during the course of rehabilitation, and helping the family and survivor to make appropriate decisions for the future with respect to independence in daily life.

Control

Epidemiological studies point out the variety of incidents that can result in a traumatic brain injury. Regardless of the types of injuries and who or what is to blame for the injury, families and survivors usually experience the injury as a loss of control. The degree to which they feel this loss of control will have an effect on their emotional reaction to the injury. For example, some causes of injury, such as those that occur at home, may be perceived as more within the family's ability to control than others. Family members may feel in some way responsible for the injury and express this feeling in their emotional reaction to the injury. In the case of work-related injuries, the family may feel that the situation was not in their power to control.

They may place responsibility on the survivor's employer or co-workers, feeling anger toward these people in order to alleviate the family's own distress over not preventing what happened.

The family's sense of control and responsibility for the injury is also likely to be affected by the geographic location where the injury occured. The injury may have occured near or far from home, in a place frequently or less frequently traveled by the survivor. Each of these sites may evoke a slightly different reaction from the family in terms of their feelings of control over the injury.

The relationship between the family's attribution of responsibility, the sense of loss of control and the family's emotional reaction is one that should be evaluated by the rehabilitation professional. Psychological treatment will seek to help families understand the events of trauma and their interpretation of these events in order to regain feelings of control and to function effectively in everyday life.

Indeed, the relationships between people's attributions about events in their lives and their attitudes and emotions has been extensively studied in the social psychological field (Jones et al., 1977) and in the field of health psychology (Strickland, 1978). This relationship has not been empirically investigated in the traumatic brain injury field but presents an interesting avenue for research that would have implications for the professional's understanding of the family's posttrauma reaction and subsequent treatment planning.

Personality Change

As noted above, certain preexisting adjustment patterns or personality characteristics among traumatic brain-injury survivors have been identified. In addition, the traumatic brain injury itself will often result in changes in the survivor's emotional and social behavior. These changes will be discussed later in this chapter. During the course of rehabilitation the family will be trying to make sense out of these changes and how they will affect the survivor's long-term adjustment (Oddy et al., 1978).

The discussion of the survivor's preexisting personality and injury-related personality changes is apt to be an important theme in psychological treatment. The family's expectations for rehabilitation will be affected by their understanding and feelings about the survivor's functioning prior to the injury. The behavioral changes in the survivor and the uncertainty about the permanence of these changes will force the family to adjust to a person in the family who may look the same as before the injury but act quite differently. This adjustment will affect the organization and functioning of the family as a whole.

The family and the professional will need to work together to differentiate the pre-morbid personality of the survivor from the behavioral changes that have occured to the survivor post-injury. In psychological treatment, the professional will need to help the family to understand the changes in behavior that occur as the result of the brain injury, and guide the family in handling such behavior in an appropriate manner.

THE INJURY AND ITS SEQUELAE

"The lesions in head trauma are multifacted and no two head traumas are identical" (Signoret, 1985, p. 179). Individual differences must be considered in planning and implementing psychological treatment for the traumatic brain-injury survivor. There are, however, general anatomical similarities in brain structure across individuals and similarities in the body's physiological response to trauma that can be described (Alexander, 1984; Friedman, 1983; Narayan et al., 1990; Pang, 1985; Teasdale & Mendelow, 1984). In this section, some of the sequelae of traumatic brain injury will be briefly reviewed with attention to the implications that this information has for planning psychological evaluation and treatment of the family.

Severity of Injury and Medical Complications

To some extent, the severity of the traumatic brain injury depends on the criteria that are used to measure the injury. Length and depth of coma (Bond, 1990) and number of medical complications that accompany the trauma (Kalisky et al., 1985) are two such criteria. The Glasgow Coma Scale (Jennett & Teasdale, 1981) is a widely used measure of assessing depth of coma. The individual is assessed in terms of his or her response to verbal stimuli, eye opening, and communication. Scores on the scale range from 3 to 14. Very low scores indicate deep coma or limited responsiveness to external stimuli—what the general public commonly associates with coma. Generally, individuals with scores below 8 are classified as deeply comatose and have a greater likelihood of death or poor recovery (Bond, 1990). Higher scores indicate greater levels of arousal. Many individuals with these scores may have been transferred out of acute care medical treatment settings to rehabilitation treatment settings. The Glasgow Coma Scale is widely used in treatment settings and as a variable in research studies of outcome from traumatic brain injury. Eisenberg and Weiner (1987) have discussed some of the limitations of the scale as a measure of posttrauma responsiveness and as a research variable.

Another aspect of the individual's severity of injury is the presence of post-traumatic amnesia, that is the ability to remember things from one day to the next and to be aware of the time and place from day-to-day. Levin, O'Donnel and Grossman (1979) developed the Galveston Orientation and Amnesia Test (GOAT) as a measure of posttraumatic amnesia. Briefly, the test involves a variety of questions about personal information and memory that the individual is asked over a period of days in order to determine if any information is being retained by the individual from one day to the next. An individual may obtain a higher score on the Glasgow scale and still show day-to-day orientation and memory difficulties that are problematic in terms of rehabilitation. Levin et al. (1979) concluded that the GOAT would be a meaningful measure of when the individual had recovered from post-traumatic amnesia. They showed the relationship between the GOAT score and outcome from traumatic brain injury.

Medical complications that accompany the injury are another means of assessing severity of injury (Kalisky et al., 1985). In addition to the actual contusions to the brain, the trauma results in metabolic and chemical changes in the central nervous system. For example, seizures are widely noted after traumatic brain injury (Chamovitz et al., 1985; Jennett, 1990). A greater number and variety of medical complications is suggestive of a more severe injury.

Implications for the Family

The family's emotional reaction to the trauma will be affected by the severity of the survivor's injury. One aspect of this connection is how close the survivor came to death. Families of survivors who suffered particularly severe injuries may have faced the anticipated death of the survivor more intensely than families of less severely injured survivors. For example, they may have had to make decisions about the extent to which life-support equipment should be used with the survivor. Many families have actually been told by emergency medical personnel that the injured family member would not survive. Such experiences have an impact on the depth of the family's distress and their feelings about the survivor's goals in rehabilitation.

A second aspect of the severity of injury that may affect the family is the degree to which long-term changes in the survivor's capabilities can be expected. The relationship between the severity of injury, as measured by some of the variables mentioned above, and the survivor's outcome from rehabilitation is not clear cut (Eisenberg & Weiner, 1987). Nevertheless, it seems fair to say that survivors who have a great number of long-term medical, physical, and psychological complications after injury will be a source of great emotional strain on the family. This strain will affect the family's ability to adjust to the demands of everyday responsibilities.

The rehabilitation professional providing treatment to families can use the information from studies about severity of injury as a way of understanding what the family has faced prior to beginning psychological treatment and in anticipating the family's needs in treatment. In this regard, psychological evaluation of the family should include an assessment of the family's knowledge about the injury in general, the specific problems faced by their family member, and what the family had been told by medical treatment personnel about the severity of the survivor's condition. It should be noted, however, that the relationship between family distress and severity of injury is not a clearly linear one (Brooks et al., 1987). That is, less severe injuries are not necessarily associated with less severe emotional reactions. Therefore, one cannot simply predict the family's distress directly from measures of the severity of injury. The survivor's condition during the course of rehabilitation and the family's functioning must be taken into consideration in order to assess the intensity of the family's emotional reaction.

Physical Sequelae

Severe traumatic brain injuries compromise the survivor's physical capabilities to some degree. Arms may be weakened or paralyzed, fine motor movements such as writing may be slowed or irregular, movements of the mouth for speech or eating may be disturbed. In contemporary American society, physical capabilities are nearly synonymous with independence. Disruption of these capabilities will have an impact on the survivor's independence in mobility, self-care and vocational skills regardless of any other cognitive or emotional difficulties the survivor may have.

Beyond the physical limitations there may be physical disfigurement of the body. The injury itself may result in scars, bruises or fractures. Lengthy periods of immobility during coma and metabolic changes posttrauma may result in calcification of joints drastically limiting mobility and affecting the survivor's posture. Advances in plastic and orthopedic surgery make these changes subject to varying degrees of amelioration. Even if it can be done, the surgery may have to be delayed for weeks or months after the injury in order to stabilize and further evaluate the survivor's condition and responsiveness to such surgery.

Implications for the Family

The family of a survivor with physical deficits must face daily physical evidence of the survivor's incapacity. In general, physical changes that occur posttrauma are not as distressing in the long run to families as the changes in survivor's emotions and behavior (Livingston, 1990). This conclusion, however, is based on observation of the family's adjustment over years postinjury. During this time the survivor's physical status may have stabilized and the family may have achieved some degree of adaptation to the survivor's changed physical condition. In the months immediately after the trauma the family is faced with decisions in rehabilitation treatment that often involve the survivor's physical condition. At this early stage in rehabilitation, physical changes may be a source of significant distress for families. Families may discuss these in the context of discussing their emotional reaction to the trauma.

The outward physical appearance of the brain-injury survivor may have an impact on the family's emotional adjustment that is separate from the survivor's physical mobility. Physical disfigurement is a relative term. Physical scars or limitations that may appear minor to the professional may be distressing to the survivor and family. Moreover, the family of an individual who shows virtually no signs of disfigurement or physical incapacity may still have adjustment problems with respect to this issue. These families may view the survivor as physically intact and expect other aspects of the survivor's functioning to be intact. The concrete evidence of incapacity in the form of physical limitation or disfigurement may, paradoxically, help the family member to acknowledge that an injury has occurred and to adjust their expectations for the survivor accordingly.

Thus, though the practitioner is primarily concerned with the family's reaction to emotional and behavioral changes in the survivor, psychological evaluation of the family should also include an assessment of the family's reactions to the physical condition of the survivor in terms of both physical mobility and physical appearance. The family's values about the physical limitations and physical disfiguration and their expectations for remediation of these problems should be evaluated because they may affect the family's emotional adjustment to the injury. This evaluation is particularly important at the early stages of rehabilitation when the survivor's physical status may be changing rapidly.

Neuropathology and Cognitive Sequelae

The injury to the brain and posttraumatic impairments in the survivor's cognitive skills are hallmarks of a traumatic brain injury (Ewing-Cobbs et al., 1985; Brooks, 1984). A wide range of cognitive impairments among survivors have been noted including difficulties with attention, concentration, memory, reading, writing, arithmetic, reasoning and visual-spatial organization. Because of the importance of these functions for the survivor's ability to manage independently in society and the attention given to such functions in rehabilitation treatment, the rehabilitation professional working with a family of a survivor must be well-versed in the basic neuropathology of traumatic brain injury and the relationship between neuropathology and cognitive sequelae.

The practitioner is not expected to have a depth of knowledge equal to that of an experienced neurologist. Rather, the practitioner should be able to converse knowledgeably with the family about the neurological and cognitive impairments that follow a traumatic brain injury. At times it may be necessary for the practitioner to translate what may appear to be arcane neurological information into practical language for the family. In this way, the practitioner will be able to gain the family's confidence and to establish a treatment relationship with them. Readers wishing more information about neuropathology than is provided in the following section are referred to several resources on the subject (Friedman, 1983; Reitan & Wolfson, 1985).

Generalized Versus Localized Impairment

There are several mechanisms of brain injury in a traumatic incident such as a motor vehicle accident. The primary injury to the brain comes from the impact on the brain matter. For example, the individual in the motor vehicle is moving rapidly and comes to a sudden stop with the impact of the collision. Because of the changes in speed in such situations, the injuries that result are often referred to as acceleration-deceleration injuries. The physical structure of the brain and skull predispose the brain to be injured in certain ways in such situations. A blow to the skull at one point may result in injury to the brain tissue directly below that point on the head. In addition, the brain, surrounded by cerebrospinal fluid within the skull, may be thrown back against the opposite pole of the skull resulting in an injury to the brain at a point far from the site of impact. The bony structure of the skull with protrusions around the temporal and lower frontal lobe areas may result in shearing of the brain matter as it is scraped over these protrusions. Nerve fibers that connect different parts of the brain may be twisted or torn.

There are also secondary injuries that can occur as the result of changes that occur posttrauma. The skull can be thought of as a closed compartment for the brain. Thus, pressure from accumulated cerebrospinal fluid or blood from a ruptured blood vessel may compress specific areas of the brain where this accumulation occurs resulting in further injury to the brain. Chemical and metabolic changes occur posttrauma as the body attempts to make up for loss of fluid or blood, or as the result of injuries to parts of the brain that control the balance of hormones and chemicals. The change in the chemical milieu of the brain's fluids affects the functioning of the brain in the short term and may result in long-lasting impairments.

The result of these various mechanisms of injury is that a traumatic brain injury involves injuries to particular areas of the brain (for example, localized injury) and injuries to the brain as a whole (for example, generalized injury). The combination of both generalized and localized injuries is one aspect of acceleration-deceleration brain trauma that distinguishes it from other types of impairments. For example, localized brain injuries are more prevalent in traumatic brain injuries as the result of penetrating wounds (Grafman & Salazar, 1987) as well as other conditions such as stroke and tumors. On the other hand, conditions such as hypoxia or chemical toxicity affect the brain as a whole resulting in predominantly generalized impairments.

The distinction between generalized and localized injuries is meaningful because each can result in different patterns of cognitive impairments in the survivor. To a certain extent the brain is organized with particular skills or functions being controlled by localized areas. When an area of the brain is injured the functions of that area will be disrupted and the subsequent cognitive changes will be seen in the individual's behavior. For example, language skills are associated with parts of the temporal lobes, usually the left temporal lobe. An injury to the brain in the temporal lobes may result in the individual showing some difficulty communicating with or understanding language.

Localization does not, however, completely explain how the brain works. Complex tasks such as writing, reading or driving a car involve the integrated effort of several areas of the brain. A person's level of alertness and the speed at which the brain works to solve problems are functions that cannot be easily localized. Generalized brain injuries may result in impairments in these types of cognitive functions.

Implications for the Family

Most families of brain-injury survivors, like most of the general population, are unaware of the complexities of brain functioning. The trauma suddenly makes the matter important to them. Families need extensive education about what has happened to their injured family member and why it has happened. This education should be a major part of any psychological treatment.

The families' understanding of concepts of generalized and localized brain impairments may have an effect on how they interpret the injury and on their subsequent emotional reaction to it. Localized impairments may be more readily understood by families. Scars on the scalp or forehead may be evidence of localized injury to the head and the brain area below the skull at that point. The concept of localized organization has had appeal for years as a explanation of brain function (Walsh, 1978, Woodruff & Baisden,

1986). Family members may more readily recognize impairments that clearly affect a specific area of the brain, such as an expressive speech problem or lateralized motor weakness. These problems are relatively circumscribed by nature and can be understood to be related to the site of injury. Research on what aspects of the brain injury families do and do not readily understand would be valuable to the professional planning educational and counseling treatment interventions.

Evidence of generalized injury, such as slowed thinking, may be less readily grasped by the family. The fact that such problems are often seen in response to emotional stress, such as depression, may further complicate the family's understanding of them. Moreover, in the early stages of recovery from a severe traumatic brain injury, the survivor may have such a reduced level of arousal and functioning that specific cognitive impairments are hard to detect. For example, the survivor may be so slow at performing tasks or have such a limited level of arousal that any other specific language or visual–spatial difficulties would not be noticed. It may be difficult for both families and professionals to discern the survivor's actual degree of impairment at the early stages of recovery.

The practitioner should be familiar with the concepts of generalized and localized brain injuries, and the specific brain injury of the survivor in order to assess the family's level of knowledge and their explanations of the survivor's behavior. Education of the family should include some information about the organization and functions of the brain, the mechanism of injury and subsequent cognitive and emotional sequelae. By providing this information directly, the practitioner establishes him or herself as an important educational resource for the family and lays a foundation of trust with the family on which further psychological treatment can be built.

Course of Recovery

Another aspect of traumatic brain injury that distinguishes it from other conditions that impair brain functioning is that the survivor of a traumatic brain injury goes through stages of cognitive recovery. The Rancho los Amigos scale of cognitive recovery (Malkmus et al., 1980; see Figure 1.1) is a commonly used scale that describes these stages in eight cognitive recovery levels. The survivor may progress from very limited levels of response to the environment, in which he or she is totally dependent on others for medical and self-care, up to higher levels of recovery in which the survivor may be able to manage a wide range of independent living activities.

The Rancho scale is widely used and has value as a shorthand for describing some of the characteristics of the survivor. This description is particularly important if a survivor is being transferred between facilities. Being

Table 1.1   The Rancho Los Amigos Levels of Cognitive Functioning

I   No response

Patient appears to be in a deep sleep and is completely unresponsive to any stimuli presented to him.

II   Generalized response

Patient reacts inconsistently and nonpurposefully to stimuli in a nonspecific manner. Responses are limited in nature and are often the same regardless of stimulus presented. Responses may be physiological changes, gross body movements, and vocalization. Responses are likely to be delayed. The earliest response is to deep pain.

III   Localized response

Patient reacts specifically but inconsistently to stimuli. Responses are directly related to the type of stimulus presented as in turning head toward a sound or focusing on an object presented. The patient may withdraw an extremity and vocalize when presented with a painful stimulus. He may follow simple commands in an inconsistent, delayed manner such as closing his eyes, squeezing or extending an extremity. Once external stimuli are removed, he may lie quietly. He may also show a vague awareness of self and body by responding to discomfort by pulling at nasogastric tube or catheter or resisting restraints. He may show a bias toward responding to some persons, especially family and friends, but not to others.

IV   Confused-agitated

Patient is in a heightened state of activity with severely decreased ability to process information. He is detached from the present and responds primarily to his own internal confusion. Behavior is frequently bizarre and nonpurposeful relative to his environment. He may cry out or scream out of proportion to stimuli even after removal, may show aggressive behavior, attempt to remove restraints or tubes or crawl out of bed in a purposeful manner. He does not discriminate among persons or objects and is unable to cooperate directly with treatment efforts. Verbalization is frequently incoherent or inappropriate to the environment. Confabulation may be present; he may be hostile. Gross attention to environment is very brief and selective attention often nonexistent. Being unaware of present events, patient lacks short-term recall and may be reacting to past events. He is unable to perform self-care activities without maximum assistance. If not disabled physically, he may perform automatic motor activities such as sitting, reaching and ambulating as part of his agitated state but not as a purposeful act or on request necessarily.

V   Confused-inappropriate

Patient appears alert and is able to respond to simple commands fairly consistently. However, with increased complexity of commands or lack of any external structure, responses are nonpurposeful, random or, at best, fragmented toward any desired goal. He may show agitated behavior, not on an internal basis as in Level IV, but rather as a result of external stimuli and usually out of proportion to the stimulus. He has gross attention to the environment, is highly distractible, and lacks ability to focus attention to a specific task without frequent redirection. With structure, he may be able to converse on a social-automatic level for short periods of time. Verbalization is often inappropriate; confabulation may be triggered by present events.

Continued

Table 1.1   (Continued)

Memory is severely impaired, with confusion of past and present in reaction to ongoing activity. Patient lacks initiation of functional tasks and often shows inappropriate use of objects without external direction. He may be able to perform previously learned tasks when structured for him but is unable to learn new information. He responds best to self, body, comfort, and often family members. The patient usually can perform self-care activities with assistance and may accomplish feeding with supervision. Management on the unit is often a problem if the patient is physically mobile as he may wander off either randomly or with vague intention of "going home."

VI   Confused-appropriate

Patient shows goal-directed behavior, but is dependent on external input for direction. Response to discomfort is appropriate and he is able to tolerate unpleasant stimuli; e.g., as NG tube, when need is explained. He follows simple directions consistently and shows carryover for tasks he has relearned; e.g., self-care. He is at least supervised with old learning; unable to be maximally assisted for new learning with little or no carryover. Responses may be incorrect due to memory problems but are appropriate to the situation. They may be delayed to immediate and he shows decreased ability to process information with little or no anticipation or prediction of events. Past memories show more depth and detail than recent memory. The patient may show beginning awareness of his situation by realizing he doesn't know an answer. He no longer wanders and is inconsistently oriented to time and place. Selective attention to tasks may be impaired, especially with difficult tasks and in unstructured settings, but is now functional for common daily activities. He may show vague recognition of some staff and has increased awareness of self, family, and basic needs.

VII   Automatic-appropriate

Patient appears appropriate and oriented within hospital and home settings, goes through daily routine automatically but robotlike, with minimal to absent confusion and has shallow recall of what he has been doing. He shows increased awareness of self, body, family, food, people, and interaction in the environment. He has superficial awareness of but lacks insight into his condition, decreased judgment and problem solving, and lacks realistic planning for his future. He shows carryover for new learning at a decreased rate. He requires at least minimal supervision for learning and safety purposes. He is independent in self-care activities and supervised in home and community skills for safety. With structure, he is able to initiate tasks or social and recreational activities in which he now has interest. His judgment remains impaired. Prevocational evaluation and counseling may be indicated.

VIII   Purposeful-appropriate

Patient is alert and oriented, is able to recall and integrate past and recent events, and is aware of and responsive to his culture. He shows carryover for new learning if acceptable to him and his life role, and needs no supervision once activities are learned. Within his physical capabilities, he is independent in home and community skills. Vocational rehabilitation, to determine ability to return as a contributor to

Continued

Table 1.1   (Continued)

society, perhaps in a new capacity, is indicated. He may continue to show decreases relative to premorbid abilities in quality and rate of processing, abstract reasoning, tolerance for stress, and judgment in emergencies or unusual circumstances. His social, emotional, and intellectual capacities may continue to be at a decreased level for him, but functional within society.

Malkmus, D., Hagen, C. & Durham, T. (1979). Levels of cognitive functioning. In *Rehabilitation of the head injured adult: Comprehensive physical management.* Downey, CA: Los Amigos Research and Education Institute, Inc., of Rancho Los Amigos Medical Center.
The Rancho Los Amigos Scale is reprinted with permission of the Rancho Los Amigos Medical Center.

able to describe the survivor in terms of one of the Rancho levels gives the professionals at each facility a means of communicating some understanding of the survivor's capabilities and recovery status.

The Rancho scale is limited, however, in its usefulness. It is an ordinal scale that simply ranks individuals according to a continuum. Differences between levels on the scale are not equivalent. Moreover, the scale describes cognitive deficits of the survivor but does not describe cognitive strengths or areas of intact cognitive functioning (Sachs et al., 1986). This limits the value of the scale for designing treatment interventions. Finally, it is not clear that survivors pass through all stages in the course of their recovery. Some survivors do not progress upward through stages of recovery because of the severity of their injuries. Other survivors may skip some levels of recovery, such as Level IV—agitated stage, a point which is the subject of some professional debate (Corrigan & Mysiw, 1988; Rao et al., 1985). Despite the limitations of the Rancho scale, it is generally agreed that survivors of traumatic head injury undergo a process of recovery, if they are recovering, that can be loosely grouped according to stages.

Implications for the Family

Knowledge of this course of recovery has an impact on the emotional well-being of the family and psychological treatment for the family. Families are understandably anxious about the degree of improvement that the survivor is making in rehabilitation treatment. Scales such as the Rancho scale are appealing because they present information in a brief and concrete way. This information may alleviate some of the families uncertainty about what to expect in the course of recovery. The scale can be a useful educational tool for the rehabilitation professional to put the course of recovery from a brain injury in perspective for the family.

Such scales may, however, increase the family's anxiety. Families and rehabilitation professionals may become preoccupied with the survivor's rating on a scale, and ignore important aspects of the survivor's condition that are not quantified on the scale. For example, a survivor at Level VI on the Rancho scale may make substantial improvements in his or her ability to manage personal care activities, eating and may participate more actively in rehabilitation therapy sessions, yet still not be independent enough to warrant being moved up to Level VII on the scale. Though this survivor stays at the same level of functioning with the respect to the Rancho scale, clearly he or she has made major improvements.

The rehabilitation professional must consider the effect information about the survivor's level of recovery has on the family's emotional state. In psychological treatment the clinician must balance information about the survivor's progress that is obtained from scales and tests with other sources of information such as subjective professional observation. Families will need to be educated about the limitations of the Rancho scale or any other measure that attempts to quantify the survivor's condition. The clinician must also differentiate the family's anxiety that is the result of misinterpretation of information from brain injury recovery scales from anxiety that is the result of the family's uncertainty about the survivor's well-being and future.

Cognitive Sequelae

Changes in the survivor's cognitive status after an injury are among the most frequently studied in the research literature. "Depending on the nature and severity of the head injury almost any type of cognitive disorder may be seen" (Joynt & Shoulson, 1985). Generally, difficulties with attention, concentration, memory, academic skills, visual–spatial skills, motor speed, language, and reasoning have all been observed among brain-injury survivors.

The cognitive difficulties observed in the traumatic brain-injury survivor will differ depending on the survivor's level of recovery. At lower stages of recovery (Rancho levels II, III and IV), the survivor's impaired levels of arousal and attention will be most evident, overshadowing any other cognitive problems that may exist. At higher levels of recovery (Rancho VI, VII, and VIII), the survivor may show more differentiation in cognitive skills and weaknesses. Neuropsychological testing by the psychologist as well as language and sensory-perceptual testing by speech or occupational therapists are valuable methods of assessing the survivor's cognitive skills at these levels of recovery.

Cognitive remediation is a general term for a variety of techniques that are used to stimulate a survivor's cognitive recovery. Cognitive remediation is a reeducation process, helping the survivor to relearn skills that he or she once knew how to perform. Often the survivor will benefit from learning al-

ternative strategies for performing a task. For example, as a result of the
brain injury the survivor may have impaired visual–spatial skills resulting in
difficulty with directionality, finding his or her way, and in using maps. If
the survivor has relatively well preserved language skills, he or she may
learn how to use verbal cues, extensive written directions, or signs in order
to travel from one place to another independently.

Implications for the Family

The cognitive sequelae of the traumatic brain injury cause tremendous
emotional stress and adjustment difficulties for the family. The survivor's
cognitive problems usually involve very basic skills of attention and memory
in addition to other problems. All families must adjust to a family member
whose cognitive capabilities in the long- or short-term are different than
they were in the past. The survivor's cognitive impairments will have a major impact on the family's patterns of activity, division of responsibilities at
home, and communication patterns with the survivor. The specific effects of
the survivor's changed condition on family structure will be discussed in
more detail in Chapter Two. The rehabilitation professional must assess the
family's level of understanding about the relationship between the brain
injury, cognition, and the survivor's behavior in his or her work with the
family. In psychological treatment, education of the family should include
explanations about how the brain injury caused the observed cognitive dys-
function, the nature of the cognitive skills themselves, and the impact of
these problems on the survivor.

The survivor's cognitive difficulties also affect the family because family
members often relate cognitive difficulties with school difficulties. In school
and in brain-injury rehabilitation settings individuals are evaluated in cognitive skills, and taught basic academic and life skills by a variety of professionals. It is common for the survivor and family to refer to the rehabilitation therapy sessions as "classes" and to the therapists as "teachers". This
association may be positive or negative for the survivor and the family depending on their understanding of the cognitive difficulties experienced by
the survivor and the nature of cognitive remediation treatment. The notion
of brain-injury rehabilitation as a reeducation process is a framework for
family members and survivors to understand the purpose of many rehabilitation activities. In addition, however, many of the concerns that family
members experienced when the survivor was in school prior to his or her
brain injury may resurface when the survivor is attempting to recover cognitive skills in a brain-injury rehabilitation program. These concerns may be
particularly acute for families of a survivor who was still attending school at
the time of the injury, and is uncertain about his or her ability to return to

school after rehabilitation. The rehabilitation professional must assess the family's reaction to the survivor's past academic career and to educate the family about cognitive remediation, and its similarities with and differences from basic academic training.

Psychological testing and the other cognitive evaluations that are conducted within a rehabilitation center may be a source of confusion and concern for the family. Here again, family members may associate the testing that is done in the rehabilitation center with testing that has been done in the school setting. Family members' values about standardized testing may affect their emotional reaction to the survivor's performance on such testing. For example, family members may express skepticism about the results of such testing by remarks like, "I don't think my child was ever very good at tests like that." Or, "I don't think anyone would be able to answer some of those questions." Some families may overvalue the test results, as noted above in the discussion about rating scales, and ignore capabilities that the survivor shows in nontesting situations. On the other hand, the results of standardizing testing can be seen as a valuable basis for the family's understanding about the survivor's cognitive problems postinjury. In psychological treatment, families may discuss their emotional reactions to the trauma indirectly in terms of their feelings about the survivor's cognitive capabilities and how these are expressed in testing situations and everyday life. The rehabilitation professional must be able to present to families a balanced impression of the value of standardized testing as a tool for understanding the survivor's cognitive difficulties and in designing treatment. The professional must also be able to recognize the close connection between the family's emotional status and the survivor's cognitive performance in order to make proper psychological treatment interventions.

Emotional/Behavioral Sequelae

Along with cognitive sequelae, the emotional sequelae of brain injury have received much attention from professionals and families. Changes in the emotional/behavioral status of the brain-injury survivor are widely noted by clinicians and researchers (Brooks et al., 1987; Eames, 1988; Eames, Haffey & Cope, 1990; Grant & Alves, 1987; Tate, 1987; Willer et al., 1988; Wood, 1988). These emotional/behavioral sequelae can be grouped into four general categories: those that occur as part of the course of recovery from the brain trauma, those that are attributable to the cognitive sequelae of the brain trauma, those not directly attributable to cognitive sequelae but of organic origin, and those that are the result of the survivor's everyday life experiences. These groups of emotional/behavioral sequelae will be discussed briefly, after which their impact on the families' adjustment to the trauma will be examined.

Sequelae related to course of recovery. Agitated behavior is perhaps the most marked behavioral problem associated with the course of recovery from traumatic brain injury. On the Rancho scale, the agitated stage of recovery (Level IV) occurs after the survivor has progressed from the lower stages of reduced cognitive arousal. Agitated behavior may include hyperactivity, particularly in response to changes in the environment or to overstimulation. Flailing motor movements, cursing, screaming, and ripping clothing may all accompany generalized agitation. These behaviors do not represent emotional reactions to environmental or personal events in the same way that a person who has not had a brain injury might respond to such events. Rather, these agitated behaviors are expressions of the inconsistency with which the survivor is able to control behavior and to modulate the experiences of the world around because of the severely compromised brain functioning. Ideally the survivor passes through the period of agitation and enters a stage of recovery characterized by more purposeful and consistent, though still confused, behavior. This progression is not always so orderly. Survivors may remain in the agitated stage of recovery for varying periods of time, or may not seem to pass through the agitated stage of recovery at all.

Sequelae as a result of post-traumatic cognitive changes. Some behavioral problems, particularly those that occur at stages of recovery after the agitated stage, can be attributable to underlying cognitive impairments (Prigatano, 1987). At these stages of recovery the individual may show impulsive or poorly planned behavior, inappropriate social behavior, repetitive or inflexible behavior. These behaviors are problems for the survivor in terms of his or her ability to participate in the rehabilitation program and in independent living. They do not, however, necessarily imply a change in the individual's emotional state or personality. For example, in a person who has not experienced a brain injury repetitive or inflexible behavior may be the result of an angry mood or a stubborn personality. In the survivor of a brain injury the same behavior may indicate an underlying cognitive difficulty in developing alternative approaches to solving problems, perseveration, or limited awareness of performance feedback.

Sequelae of other organic origin. Some behavioral changes are not clearly attributable to underlying cognitive impairments although they have resulted from the neurophysiological effects of the trauma (see Heilman, Bowers, & Valenstein, 1985). The survivor may show emotions that are inappropriate to or out of proportion with a given situation. Outbursts of rage, inappropriate laughter, excessive crying, lack of affect, physically threatening or aggressive behaviors all interfere with the survivor's ability to become integrated into the rehabilitation treatment program and into the family. Again, these behavioral changes do not necessarily indicate a change in personality or disturbance in mood as they might if they occurred in a person who had not experienced a brain injury. Rather, they occur because the brain-injury survivor is unable to effectively control the expression of emotion.

Denial is a frequently reported emotion/behavioral reaction to the brain injury (Caplan & Schechter, 1987; Deaton, 1985). In the survivor, denial may be the result of cognitive impairments from the brain injury. The survivor may have difficulty recognizing concrete objects or body parts connected to his person. The survivor may also have difficulty recognizing problems that he or she is having, or seeing implications of these problems for adaptation to everyday life (Heilman, Watson, & Valenstein, 1985; Mesulam, 1985).

Denial may also be an emotional reaction to the brain injury. In this regard denial is understood as a "defense mechanism in which (one) avoids becoming aware of some painful aspect of reality. To bolster this effacement of reality, a fantasy is formed in the mind which erases the disagreeable or unwelcome fact" (Moore & Fine, 1968, p. 30). For the brain-injury survivors, the trauma and the feelings that accompany it constitute an extremely "painful aspect of reality." The "fantasy" that survivors may develop takes many forms. They may fantasize that their limitations would not be so severe in another setting (for example, home rather than rehabilitation facility) or with another person (for example, a new therapist) assisting them; they may believe that they are able to do many treatment activities but simply don't want to do them; or that they were never able to do these activities even before their injury. As Deaton (1985) has noted, explanations of denial in survivors as the result of organic changes in the brain or as the result of a psychological method of handling anxiety are not mutually exclusive. "Denial in brain-injured patients is frequently characterized by both organic underpinnings and functional utility in reducing anxiety" (Deaton, 1985, p. 232).

Sexual behavior problems among survivors may result from the injury to the brain (Wood, 1987; Zasler, 1988). All of the survivor's behavior problems have an impact on the survivor's interpersonal relationships and represent problems in the well-modulated expression of emotion. Certain of these problems are more sexual in nature because they involve acts judged to be an expression of sexual feeling in noninjured adults (for example, kissing; petting; masturbation; intercourse) or the intent to establish intimacy beyond what is expected in everyday social contacts between adults. Problems in control of sexuality include a range of behaviors that, though not always inappropriate in and of themselves, are often expressed in inappropriate situations. Examples of such behavior are sexually suggestive comments or gestures, attempts by the survivor to touch others inappropriately, and masturbation.

Sequelae as a result of life changes. Some behavioral and emotional changes that occur in survivors of traumatic brain injury are not the result of the stages of recovery nor neurophysiologically based changes in cognitive or emotional control. Some changes are the expected result of the life experiences that survivors have undergone in the course of their lives. The traumatic brain injury and the subsequent rehabilitation present the survivor with unusual and emotionally intense life experiences. It is expected that the experiences will have a lasting impact on any person's attitudes and emotional state. Anecdotally, survivors often report that the injury and rehabilitation period have aged them emotionally. They have been exposed to life experiences in a short period of time that never occur to many people at all. As a result, after the injury they feel older than their peers. Other self-reports of survivors indicate they experience changes in attitudes about life goals, religion and family.

The nature of these changes is an area worthy of careful documentation. Mood changes such as depression, anxiety, or loss of self-confidence are all expected reactions to the exceptional event of the trauma. Documentation of the attitudes and beliefs of brain-injury survivors would assist professionals and families in understanding and treating the emotional difficulties of the survivor more effectively.

In addition to the experience of the brain trauma and subsequent rehabilitation, the survivor is likely to experience natural events during the course of treatment. During the long course of rehabilitation treatment, births and deaths in the family, changes in living and financial situation, and changes in current events occur. These events can have an effect on the survivor's emotional state as they would on any individual. For example, a survivor's feelings of depression after a brain injury may be an expected reaction to depressing family events, such as family death (Sachs, 1984), rather than to anything directly related to the survivor's brain injury.

Implications for the Family

Emotional and behavioral problems in the survivor have a powerful effect on the family's reaction to the trauma. These problems affect two sensitive areas of family functioning: control and communication. Each family places its own value on behavior control. For example, a survivor may continually curse or pound the walls when frustrated. A family that places a high value on self-control and compliance with social norms will react quite differently to this problem compared to a family that does not place as high a value on self-control. The former family may judge the survivor's behavior problem as "bad." They may experience a sense of shame or anger about it and make great efforts to change the behavior. The family that places less importance on self-control may not perceive the survivor's behavior as problematic.

They may even be disturbed by the professional's suggestion that it is a problem for the survivor.

Each family has a different style of communication. The family's reaction to the behavior problem may be affected by what they believe is communicated by the behavior. For example, noncompliant and aggressive behaviors are often interpreted as expressions of anger. Families that tended to suppress expression of anger may show a different emotional reaction to such behavior than would families that expressed anger more freely. Similarly, families that demonstrate and talk about sexual feelings privately may be shocked or embarrassed by the survivor's inappropriate sexual behaviors. Other families that are more open about sexual expression may interpret behaviors more positively, seeing them as evidence of recovery.

The survivor's expression of denial can interact closely with the family's acknowledgement of the trauma. Family members may have difficulty facing the painful reality of the trauma and may develop the belief that the survivor's condition is not as bad as professionals may think it is, or that the survivor will improve in response to a change in environment. As disruptive as the family's denial may be, the situation is complicated further when the survivor shows denial. The survivor's denial may exacerbate the family's denial or make family members uncertain about the survivor's actual status. Research on the relationship between denial behaviors in families and survivors would be of great benefit to rehabilitation professionals designing psychological treatment interventions.

The family's reaction to the behavior problem is also related to what the behavior problem implies about the survivor's recovery. The behavior problem represents a marked change in the survivor's behavior, one that has wide-ranging effects on the survivor's interpersonal relationships. It may be difficult for the family to deny the impact of the trauma in the face of such overt changes. The prospect of the behavior problem representing a long-standing personality change may cause great uncertainty and anxiety in families. Changes such as broken bones or facial scars are concrete problems for which specific treatment interventions can be provided and a known outcome can be achieved. Behavior changes do not immediately suggest a clear treatment plan nor outcome to families.

Clinicians would benefit from research on the relationship between family values, family communication patterns and family's emotional reactions to the survivor's cognitive and behavioral functioning. The clinician must assess the family's values about schooling, self-control and communication among other subjects as a prelude to psychological treatment. However this assessment must be carefully objective. The goal is to appreciate the family's values, not as right or wrong, but as a means of understanding the family and focussing psychological treatment intervention for the family.

TREATMENT SETTINGS FOR TRAUMATIC BRAIN-INJURY REHABILITATION

The fact that traumatic brain-injury survivors appear to go through stages of recovery has led to the development of specialized treatment facilities to address the needs of the survivors at these different stages (Uomoto & McLean, 1989). NHIF (1990) maintains a directory of brain-injury rehabilitation facilities in the United States and describes the types of programming that each facility offers. In the following section five categories of treatment facilities will be briefly described: acute medical care, acute rehabilitation care, postacute rehabilitation, community living rehabilitation, and long-term care. The implications of this continuum of rehabilitation care for the survivor's family will also be discussed.

Acute Medical Care

After a traumatic brain injury, the survivor is treated at an emergency or acute care medical facility. Treatment is focused on assuring the individual's survival from the injury. Extensive medical and nursing interventions are used to treat the emergent medical problems that occur after the injury and to stabilize the survivor's condition. In order to transfer the survivor to another treatment site, such as an acute rehabilitation facility, he or she must be medically stable. The transfer will often be facilitated if the survivor shows evidence of cognitive arousal and is not dependent on medical equipment, such as respirators, for essential life functions.

Acute Rehabilitation Care

The key treatment issues for the survivor at the acute medical care facility are relatively straightforward when compared to those that arise in an acute rehabilitation program. The focus of an acute rehabilitation program is to maximize the survivor's capacities in physical and cognitive functions while still seeing that the survivor's medical needs are met. In the acute rehabilitation program, the survivor may progress from a stage of relative dependence on professional staff to dramatically more independence. For example, the survivor may repeat key developmental milestones such as walking, talking, eating, and reasoning.

Because the focus of treatment in an acute rehabilitation facility goes beyond the survivor's medical and nursing needs, the treatment program involves an interdisciplinary team of professionals that is larger than the number of professionals who may have treated the survivor at the acute medical care facility. Usually this team includes a physician, nurse, psychologist, speech therapist, physical therapist, occupational therapist, social worker, and recreational therapist. Depending on the survivor, the length of stay at an acute rehabilitation program may be measured in weeks or months.

Postacute Rehabilitation

The postacute or transitional care setting represents an important decision-making point in the survivor's recovery. It is at this stage that decisions are made about the survivor's ability to return to community living. For this reason, the postacute rehabilitation program is customarily designed to challenge the survivor in ways that he or she could not have been challenged at the acute rehabilitation stage (Sachs, 1986). Rather that focussing on recovery of discrete cognitive or physical skills, the postacute environment is designed to address the survivor's ability to live independently, to work independently, to use social support systems in the community, and to adapt emotionally to his or her current capabilities.

Though there is an interdisciplinary team of professionals working with the survivor at the postacute facility similar to the acute rehabilitation facility, the emphasis in postacute care is on nonmedical treatment. Medical involvement may be limited to consulting professionals from the community rather than a staff physician. Rehabilitation therapy activities are usually closely linked to activities that the survivor will perform in the community. Thus, cognitive remediation exercises may be linked to the survivor's work activities or to daily living activities such as money management. Often, postacute facilities include supervised community living arrangements such as described below.

Community Living Rehabilitation

For those survivors who are able to manage a wide range of daily living and working tasks, community living programs have developed. These programs approximate the survivor's return to the community. Such programs are often in apartments or houses in the community. Survivors live in these settings and take responsibility for the upkeep of the residence. They may go out into the community to structured work or leisure activities.

Staff supervision at such programs in less intensive than at the previously mentioned settings. Most of the survivors are not involved in formal rehabilitation therapy activities such as physical or occupational therapy. They may have close involvement with a vocational counselor or a psychologist for supportive therapy. Specially trained aides may supervise and assist the survivors in managing the tasks of home care and community integration.

Long-term Care

Survivors of severe traumatic brain injury may not be able to achieve independent living. A survivor's recovery may slow at any phase in the continuum previously described. Some survivors remain in lengthy coma, whereas others emerge from coma but have significant dependency that does not enable them to leave rehabilitation care facilities.

Long-term care programs provide ongoing medical, nursing, and rehabilitation services to brain-injury survivors at various levels of recovery. Coma management programs provide such services to survivors who are in lengthy coma and have not responded to other rehabilitation services. Other long-term rehabilitation programs may serve survivors whose recovery is very slow or who are not anticipated to recover to the point of managing less restrictive living environments.

Though these programs are usually seen as serving survivors who do not recover well from their injuries, clinical experience indicates that at times survivors may be appropriate for more intensive rehabilitation programs after a period of time in a long-term care program. For example, a survivor may show signs of cognitive arousal even after months in a coma at which point he or she may appropriately be transferred to an acute rehabilitation program. A survivor may have medical or surgical problems that need to be resolved before intensive rehabilitation can be provided. He or she may benefit from long-term care with low intensity rehabilitation therapy while these medical and surgical problems are treated. After he or she is medically stable, such a survivor may be appropriately transferred to an acute or postacute rehabilitation program.

Implications for the Family

The family's emotional adjustment to the survivor's injury will be affected by the care that the survivor receives at the different rehabilitation care facilities. Recognizing the impact that the continuum of care will have on the family will help the professional to design effective psychological treatment for the family.

A fundamental implication of the different sites for rehabilitation treatment is that the family's educational needs will change over the course of rehabilitation. Families of survivors in acute medical care are overwhelmed by the complexity of medical care and equipment needed by the survivor. They may need to make decisions about how much life support to provide to the survivor or about approving delicate medical procedures. Families of survivors at acute and postacute rehabilitation facilities, however, have questions about the purpose of various physical and cognitive therapy activities. These families may be concerned about the effect that the survivor's physical and cognitive limitations will have on his or her ability to resume previous educational, work, and family activities. As a part of psychological treatment for the family, the rehabilitation professional must provide information to the family members to help them understand the treatment that the survivor is receiving.

It is important that the family be involved in selecting the rehabilitation facility for the survivor to the extent that there are some choices available. Unfortunately families often tour and select facilities without being adequately prepared for the task. The emotional distress of families, particularly in the weeks immediately after the trauma, makes them vulnerable to subtle or direct marketing pitches about rehabilitation programs.

The family may also be confused by the differences between rehabilitation facilities and the appropriateness of a given facility for the survivor. For example, families considering a transfer of the survivor from an acute rehabilitation to postacute rehabilitation program are occasionally led to expect the same type of treatment will be provided when, as described above, this is not the case. Thus, in addition to providing educational information about rehabilitation treatment, the professional will also need to provide the family with information about the different types of rehabilitation facilities and help the family to evaluate the information they receive in order to make an informed decision. Questionnaires about selecting a rehabilitation facility may be particularly helpful in this regard (NHIF, 1986).

The family's emotional needs will also vary over the course of rehabilitation. If the survivor improves, he or she will repeat key developmental milestones (for example, eating; walking). Emotional conflicts between parents and child that occurred earlier in life with respect to these milestones may be reenacted. Family members, particularly parents, may see the rehabilitation period as an opportunity to "remold" the survivor (McLaughlin & Schaffer, 1984). For survivors who do not progress well in rehabilitation, family members must adjust to radically different expectations and plans for a changed living situation for the survivor. Psychological treatment for the family will need to be sensitive to the different emotional issues that will arise for the family during the course of rehabilitation. The practitioner will need to respect the family's level of emotional recovery from the trauma in planning psychological treatment intervention at a given treatment facility. The family's level of recovery may be quite independent of the survivor's level of recovery and the location of treatment. For example, simply because a survivor has entered a community living rehabilitation program does not mean that his or her family is equally far along in accepting the survivor's injury.

A related implication of the different treatment sites for the survivor is that the family's involvement in treatment will vary. Families feel the need to be involved in the care of the survivor from the very outset of treatment. This involvement may include attending rehabilitation therapy treatment sessions, speaking to staff members or funding representatives, making recommendations about the course of treatment, and actually performing some of the treatment activities. This involvement may be beneficial to the course of the survivor's treatment and may help the family members feel that they are doing all they can for the survivor. As part of psychological treatment, the practitioner can suggest to the family members the best means by which they can be involved in the treatment of the survivor.

The team of professionals that works with the survivor at the different treatment sites will vary as noted in the brief descriptions above. Family members must interact with this wide range of professionals. The different roles and responsibilities of the professionals may be confusing to the family members. The practitioner can be helpful to the family by clarifying the roles of the team members and facilitating communication between the treatment team and the family thereby assuring that the family receives consistent information from team members.

OUTCOME

The survivor's outcome from a traumatic head injury is of primary importance and perhaps primary uncertainty for professionals and families. It is a complex topic that cannot be covered fairly in a limited summary. Levin, Graffman, and Eisenberg (1987) provide an excellent review of clinical and empirical issues related to outcome from traumatic brain injury.

Two general problems in determining outcome from traumatic brain injury are identifying the characteristics of positive outcome and choosing appropriate measures of outcome. The determination of what constitutes positive outcome is difficult because the survivor's outcome can be judged from many different perspectives. Medically, positive outcome might be described as medical stability or the lack of any recurring or emergent medical problems directly related to the injury. From a neurobehavioral perspective, outcome might be judged in terms of the survivor's ability to demonstrate appropriate behavior and to perform certain cognitive skills. Positive psychosocial outcome might be seen in the survivor's ability to adapt emotionally to his or her limitations, to reintegrate into society, to live with family, or to return to work. In effect, outcome must be judged from multiple perspectives. However, the more complex the model of outcome becomes, the more complex the task of measuring outcome becomes.

The Glasgow Outcome scale (Teasdale & Jennett, 1974) is a commonly cited measure of outcome, grouping outcomes from brain injury into five general categories. Brooks (1984, 1987) discusses how this scale is used to judge outcome and relates it to other aspects of the survivor's condition in order to develop some prognostic model of recovery from traumatic brain injury. The Glasgow outcome scale offers global ratings of recovery that may not be helpful in describing the specific functioning of a survivor (for example, work performance; cognitive skills) at each of the levels of recovery. To this end, medical tests and brain scans, results of neuropsychological tests, and ratings of the survivor's behavior in terms of social adjustment and work activities have all been used as measures of outcome in addition to the Glasgow scale (Levin, Graffman, & Eisenberg, 1987; Bond, 1990).

Implications for the Family

Predictions about the survivor's outcome is the question rehabilitation professionals are most frequently asked to address by family members. Unfortunately, this is the question to which professionals feel most uncertain about giving a specific answer. One implication of the outcome data is the effect it may have on the family's working relationship with the rehabilitation professional. The rehabilitation professional will have to ascertain what information the family has already been told about the survivor's outcome in order to anticipate the family's treatment needs. For example, by the time of their first meeting for psychological treatment in an acute rehabilitation setting the family may have already been informed in the emergency room that their family member would not survive. The fact that the family member did survive and is now in the rehabilitation facility creates a wariness in the family of any further predictions about the survivor's outcome that professionals may give to them.

On the other hand, the family may have been given feedback to suggest overly positive expectations about the outcome of the survivor. When the survivor does not appear to be meeting these expectations at all, or not meeting them as rapidly as had been hoped by the family, the family may enter psychological treatment in a state of confusion and distress about the outcome of the survivor.

The role of multiple perspectives in judging outcome points to the importance of family values and judgments in determining the outcome. As will be described in Chapter Two, each family has certain values and beliefs.

The survivor's ability to return to work, to live independently, to have intact memory skills, or to walk independently are all outcomes on which each family will place a different value. The family's adjustment to the survivor's recovery may be affected by the congruence between those aspects of recovery that the family values and the survivor's actual condition. It would be beneficial to rehabilitation professionals if empirical research could identify the relationship between family values, recovery and emotional adjustment to injury.

The long course of rehabilitation and the lack of much concrete data on which to base predictions of recovery place the family in a state of uncertain anxiety that may span months or years. Without concrete feedback about their expectations for the future, families may develop expectations for the survivor that turn out to be unrealistic. Yet, for the family to give up such expectations is tantamount to giving up hope. Thus, the family must find some way of maintaining hope while still addressing their day-to-day needs and those of the survivor.

This discussion about outcome also implies that the family will approach psychological treatment, indeed rehabilitation treatment in general, with some skepticism about the rehabilitation professionals' ability to predict the outcome of their family member's recovery. The practitioner must assess the family's receptivity to treatment intervention at the outset of treatment. The practitioner must also assess family values in order to understand what expectations family members may have for the survivor and why these expectations are important for the family. In psychological treatment, the practitioner must help the family to maintain hope during the long course of rehabilitation, while still focussing the family on concrete issues that must be addressed in the survivor's recovery.

SUMMARY

The professional providing psychological treatment for families of traumatic brain-injury survivors must be knowledgeable regarding the sequelae of traumatic brain injury, the rehabilitation services offered at brain-injury rehabilitation centers and the continuum of care in which such services are provided. With such knowledge the professional can be a reliable source of information for the family and begin to establish a trustworthy relationship with the family that will be important in psychological treatment. Moreover, having a solid foundation of knowledge about traumatic brain injury and the implications of this information for the family will allow the professional to anticipate some aspects of the family's emotional state and concerns even before the first meeting with them. Thus, without prejudging the family, the professional will be able to enter psychological treatment with the family prepared with a context in which to view the family's reactions to the trauma. In the following chapter, this context will be integrated with information about the functioning of the family system.

2

The Family System and Traumatic Brain Injury

Family members of traumatically brain injured adults are like refugees. Any attempt to assess or treat them must begin with this acknowledgement. The trauma forces the family out of its familiar life and into the foreign, confusing, and often threatening world of rehabilitation care.

The notion of family members as refugees highlights the essentially involuntary nature of their involvement in the rehabilitation process, particularly psychological rehabilitation. The family's involuntary involvement in treatment is the first problem for the rehabilitation professional faced with providing psychological services to the family. Prior to the trauma, most families were functioning well without the need of professional care. Even among those families with preexisting adjustment problems (which as noted in the previous chapter is rather common), it is fair to say that most of them also had not reached the point of seeking professional psychological assistance.

The first task of the rehabilitation professional, and one that will be repeatedly emphasized, is to develop a trusting relationship with the family. Brain-injury rehabilitation will span a long period of time and require the cooperative efforts of the practitioner, the family and the survivor. To accomplish the ambitious goals of brain-injury rehabilitation, the practitioner must be able to gain the family's trust. This can only be accomplished by respecting the family. In speaking about family therapy, Whitaker and Bumberry (1988) make this point nicely by stating, "Your impact (as a therapist) can only come from the personal process you participate in with (families) . . . Real growth (in therapy) is something that the therapist and family do with each other" (p. 38). By recognizing and accepting the family's status as refugees, forced out of a life that they did not wish to leave, the practitioner can make an initial step toward developing a trustworthy relationship with the family that will help the family grow beyond the trauma.

The uncontrollable suddenness of the trauma for the family and of their entry into the rehabilitation care system poses a second problem for the rehabilitation professional. Models of family therapy (Erikson & Hogan, 1976) were developed in response to problems that are generally gradual, not sudden, in onset. For example, the marital couple experiencing conflicts in their relationship, or the parents who cannot control their eight-year-old child, did not have these problems foisted on them instantaneously. Assessment and treatment intervention for such families was designed, at least in part, to examine the evolution of the problem situation and the role of different family members in creating and resolving the problem. For the family of the traumatic brain-injury survivor there is no development of the problem on which to reflect in treatment. The trauma did not evolve, it burst into being.

Despite the uniqueness of their predicament, the family of a brain-injury survivor is first and foremost a family and, after that, the family of a survivor. Development of a treatment plan for such families should begin with an understanding of the general issues that concern the functioning of any family. These issues may then be adapted to the specific problems and needs of the survivor's family. Though family theory and therapy literature has developed in response to problems other than traumatic brain injury, the general understanding of family functioning that such literature has provided is pertinent here. An attempt will be made to integrate some general concepts of family functioning with the special situation faced by a family of a brain-injury survivor.

STRUCTURE OF THE WELL-FUNCTIONING FAMILY

The concept of a well-functioning family is, of course, an ideal. Each family will have variations in their ability to cope with events during the course of life. An assumption basic to the understanding of how a family operates when it is functioning well and when it is not well is that the family has an organized structure. "Family structure is the invisible set of functional demands that organizes the ways in which family members interact" (Minuchin, 1974, p. 51). Minuchin and his associates have elaborated on the structure of the family and how an understanding of it can lead to therapeutic interventions for family problems.

It is useful to look at several characteristics of family structure and how they appear in a well-functioning family as a basis for examining how the family may be stressed by a family member who has a traumatic brain injury. Several characteristics are commonly mentioned in the family therapy literature and will be discussed here (Fleck, 1985; Lidz, 1976; Minuchin, 1974; Whitaker & Bumberry, 1988). These are:

- Cohesion of family members
- Family identity or theme
- Family relationship with the outside world
- Family boundaries and communication patterns

Cohesion of Family Members

The family is a group of individuals. To function effectively, the family must maintain a balance between the needs of the individual family members and the needs of the family as a whole. In this way the family members can feel a "sense of separateness and individuation" (Minuchin, 1974, p. 47) in their identities and actions and a sense of connectedness to other family members or togetherness (Bowen, 1978).

A well-functioning family is able to achieve this balance of separation and togetherness, and to maintain it over time. Family members may pursue their individual tasks and goals while the family as a group is able to meet family needs. An example of this balance can be seen in how a family spends money. Certain expenses benefit the family as a whole (for example, house; car) whereas others meet the needs of specific family members (for example, clothing; entertainment; medical expenses). Over time, the well-functioning family is able to allocate money in a way that is balanced between family and individual needs.

Certain individual needs can only be met, or are best met, by the whole family. An individual's need for affection or for a sense of belonging are usually best met by the family as a whole (Ackerman, 1958, p. 112). In the well-functioning family the individual feels this connection to other family members, and values his or her membership in the family in order to meet the need for affection and belonging. However, this sense of belonging is not too strong as to limit the individual from expressing him or herself as a separate person outside the family by developing outside friendships and activities.

Family Theme and Identity

Underlying the balance between individual and family needs is a consensus of values or beliefs. Minuchin and Fishman (1981, p. 207) have noted, "A family not only has a structure but also a set of cognitive schemas (sic) that legitimate or validate the family organization. The structure and belief structure support and justify each other" (see also Fleck, 1985). The shared sense of what values, beliefs, and behaviors are acceptable and important to them allows the family to set priorities for its actions and to feel confident about its decisions.

For example, how a family balances work and leisure is often an indication of the underlying values that a family places on such behaviors. This may be seen in how frequently the family schedules vacations or in what times of day or week are reserved for work or leisure activities. Regardless of how a family divides time between work and leisure, the fact that there is some shared consensus about it allows the family to work well as a group and to meet the needs of the group and the individual members.

The Relationship with the Outside World

The family is a group of individuals and society is a group of families. The family serves as "an intermediary between the individual and society" (Ackerman, 1958, p. 59). It is through the family that the individual is educated about society and prepared to join society. In order to accomplish this goal each family must, in some manner, interact with society at large.

The well-functioning family is able to interact with the outside world and mediate its culture for the family members. By doing so the family not only balances its own needs with the needs of the individual, but also balances the needs of society with the family's needs. An educational curriculum in grade school is an example of this complex balance. Social norms and regulations designate that certain subject matter will be covered in school classes. Within this framework each family helps the individual to develop his or her own special skills. A family that values mechanical ability may place greater emphasis on these areas when they are covered in school compared to a family that values language skills. The education of an individual is the result of interaction between the individual's skills, interests, and needs; the family's values; training provided to the individual; and societal values.

Because of this interrelationship between the family and society, societal changes may have a significant effect on the family's ability to function effectively (Simon, 1985). As society changes "the family which must always accommodate to society is changing with it" (Minuchin, 1974, p. 47). For example, within the past 20 years greater numbers of women have entered the workforce outside the home. Whether because of economic necessity; greater work opportunities; or the political impact of feminism, this societal change has an effect on the structure of the family. The division of responsibilities within the home has sometimes changed, methods of caring for children within the home and in society at large have shifted from home based to community based arrangements, and the values parents place on educational and vocational achievement for girls are different than they were in previous generations. Societal changes may occur gradually or rapidly. In any case, the well-functioning family is able to accommodate to these changes while still providing for the needs of family members.

Family Boundaries and Communication Patterns

Any well-functioning organization, such as a business, community group or town, has a set of operating procedures to assure that work is done in an efficient and proper manner. Similarly, a family operates as an organization with certain structure and guidelines. Though not often in writing, the family's organizational structure designates how duties are divided among family members, the roles of each family member, and the patterns of communication. Some of these rules will be similar for all families and others will be idiosyncratic for a particular family (Minuchin, 1974).

One of the most readily noted aspects of a family's organizational structure is that it is organized in a hierarchal manner (Napier & Whitaker, 1978) with respect to generations. Certain boundaries exist between the generations in the family, that is, between the adults and children. Some actions and privileges (for example, discipline, sex, or money management) are reserved for adults. Other activities are not so restricted. Even within each generation activities such as child care or money management might be divided between mother and father according to family rules. In a well-functioning family these duties and roles are flexible, able to be modified with the advent of new circumstances, yet clear enough so that each family member is able to know what is expected of him or her.

Communication between family members will show certain patterns depending on the nature of the family's values. Communication may rely more on words or actions, and may be channeled from parents to children in a way that varies from family to family. In a well-functioning family communication is the method of accomplishing tasks, resolving problems, and helping family members to feel connected to each other. The actual pattern of communication is important but more critical is the fact that communication channels are clearly understood by family members and flexible as needed. For example, there may be an understanding in a family that is planning a vacation that the ultimate decision rests with the parents. The well-functioning family will have a pattern of communication that allows everyone in the family to express an opinion that is considered by the parents before they reach their decision.

Developmental Aspects of the Family

The preceding discussion describes the family in a state of dynamic balance between the needs of the individual family members and the family as a whole. The family mediates the society's culture for the individual, and edu-

Table 2.1 Continuum for Characterizing the Well-Functioning Family

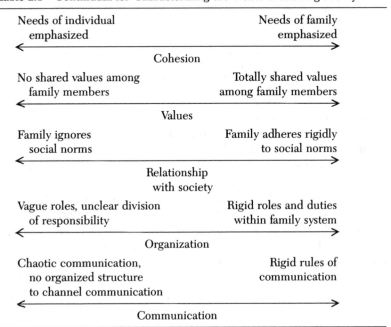

Needs of individual emphasized	Needs of family emphasized
←	→
Cohesion	
No shared values among family members	Totally shared values among family members
←	→
Values	
Family ignores social norms	Family adheres rigidly to social norms
←	→
Relationship with society	
Vague roles, unclear division of responsibility	Rigid roles and duties within family system
←	→
Organization	
Chaotic communication, no organized structure to channel communication	Rigid rules of communication
←	→
Communication	

cates and supports that individual in entering society. Some of these key components of the well-functioning family can be seen along a continuum (Walsh, 1982) that is illustrated in Table 2.1.

In discussing the well-functioning family the element of flexibility has been emphasized. As family members inevitably grow and events in society change, the family faces new problems and goals. The organizational structure of the family must be flexible enough to meet these challenges but not so flexible that it becomes unstable. "The healthy family is one that is dynamic, not static. It is in the process of continual evolution and change" (Whitaker & Bumberry, 1988, p. 198).

The structural approach to the family tends to ignore the developmental aspect of family functioning (Minuchin, 1974). Lidz (1976), for example, discusses family development in the course of his description of the development of the individual. With specific attention to families with disabled family members, Turnbull et al. (1984) discuss how a structural understanding of the family can be broadened by attention to the family life cycle. From marriage through the birth and growth of children to the old age of parents, each stage of development presents the family with tasks and challenges that must be mastered. Simply saying that the family is dynamic and in transition acknowledges the general nature of this development. Closer attention to what tasks, developmental stressors, and transitions the family must face at different points in its development amplifies and deepens one's understanding of the family's functioning (Turnbull et al., 1984).

For example, changes in the way a family operates are experienced after the addition of a new family member whether through birth, adoption or the addition of an older family member to an existing household. Each of these ways of adding a new family member may change communication patterns, division of responsibilities, and relationships with the outside world. The specific changes that occur will depend on the life stage of the family. The birth or adoption of a child to a young couple recently out of high school with no more than two years experience in their work positions will have a very different impact than the birth or adoption of a child to a couple married over 15 years with well-established careers and lifestyle. Organizational patterns of handling life situations are much less rigidly established in the younger couple than in the older couple. Structural characteristics of the family have to be interpreted in light of the family's history and development.

THE IMPACT OF THE TRAUMATIC BRAIN INJURY ON FAMILY STRUCTURE

With this background about family structure and development it may be easier to appreciate how an event such as a traumatic brain injury to a family member can disrupt the functioning of even the most flexible and adaptive family. The description of a family's reaction to the trauma has been described excellently by clinicians (Lezak, 1978, 1986, 1988; Roman, 1974) and by personal experience of family members (Burke, 1984; Warrington, 1981). In the following section, a description of the impact of a traumatic brain injury on the family will be provided that attempts to integrate the information about family structure and development.

Cohesion of Family Members

A traumatic brain injury radically changes the family's balance of individual and family needs. Suddenly the needs of one individual take on greater importance. The needs of other individuals or the needs of the family as a whole may be overshadowed. This creates a strain on the family because everyone feels neglected. For example, parents of survivors often report little time for their noninjured children or for each other. Family projects, vacations or other expenses are put aside during the time of the rehabilitation treatment. The emotional strain of the trauma may leave the family members feeling abandoned and unsupported. The sense of cohesion, or togetherness, that characterized the family before the trauma is lost. In extreme cases, there may be extreme "disorganization of family ties" (Ackerman, 1958, p. 100). Individual family members who see little benefit in affiliating with the family may drift from the family. Many of the emotional problems presented by noninjured children or siblings of survivors may be traced to the disruption of family cohesion. The child or sibling who cannot find satisfaction in relating closely to family members may seek support and satisfaction from other sources such as peer support groups or other groups which may make the child vulnerable to pressures toward antisocial behavior or drug and alcohol use.

Family Identity or Theme

Frank (1963) selects the apt term "demoralization" to describe the condition of an individual in psychological distress. This term captures the sense of stress and the loss of values and beliefs that the individual may feel. The individual may be "conscious of having failed to meet their own expectations or those of others, or of being unable to cope with some pressing problem. (The individual may) feel powerless to change the situation or (him or herself)" (p. 314).

The family under stress from the traumatic brain injury may experience demoralization from the collapse of the family theme. The consensus about values and activities, the sense of purpose that may have characterized the family's life prior to the trauma is shattered. On an emotional level, family members may feel lost, their lives without purpose or meaning. In terms of concrete daily events, the family may be unable to make decisions in order to accomplish day-to-day tasks. Activities or decisions that were once accomplished without pause or regret become cause for conflict between family members. This conflict adds further strain on family members and can reduce family cohesion.

Relationships with the Outside World

The disruption both in the family's cohesiveness and the loss of the family theme affect the family's ability to interact effectively with the outside world. The survivor's needs take precedence over the other needs and over the family's ability to interact with others outside the family circle. Family members' involvement in work, leisure, or social activities are more difficult to maintain while one of the family members is recovering from a traumatic brain injury. Moreover, the suddenness and tragedy of the injury may expose to the family the inherent danger that underlies everyday life. Thus, family members may experience a sense of anxiety regarding the outside world, expressed as distrust or fear, that they did not have prior to the injury. These feelings further impede the family's ability to interact effectively with the outside world.

Organizational Structure and Communication

Underlying the aforementioned changes in the family is a change in the family's organizational structure and communication patterns brought about by the trauma (Turnbull et al., 1984). The orderly division of labor, the hierarchy of roles and patterns of communication are all changed as a result of the trauma. No matter what the size of the family, the trauma represents a loss, temporary or permanent, of a family member. The activities that the injured family member performed and the needs that he or she met for the family as a whole are interrupted.

For example, injury to a parent may result in the loss of a wage earner for the family, a source of emotional support and a decision-maker. Because this change occurs suddenly the family does not have time to adapt to it. Thus, the family may show an organizational structure that is rigid or chaotic in response to the trauma.

At times the organizational structure may be changed in a less apparent way. The injury to a parent may lead that parent to show child-like behavior. This disrupts the hierarchal division between parents and children that is characteristic of most families and creates a very difficult adjustment for the noninjured parent and children. The changed organizational structure may be the cause of disruptive behavior in family members who no longer know what is proper and appropriate behavior within the family system. The flexibility and effective organization that characterized the well-functioning family is lost in the aftermath of the trauma.

Family communication patterns may be affected in several ways by the brain injury. If the survivor is in a residential treatment program or rehabilitation hospital, he or she is not readily able to communicate with family members as could be done when everyone was in closer contact at home. Thus, conversations or personal contacts that occurred during the course of an entire day or week must be compressed into a few hours of visitation, phone calls or brief home visits—a situation that is usually dissatisfying for all family members. Communication will also be affected if the survivor has expressive language difficulties as the result of the brain injury. Thus, it may not be possible for family members to communicate in the same manner as they did before even if they have enough opportunities to do so. Family members may be uncertain about how to express their feelings, thoughts, and activities to the survivor in a way that he or she will understand, or they may misinterpret the survivor.

The preceding overview of family functioning and the disruption that may be caused by the traumatic brain injury to a family member is brief and general. "Families everywhere will have certain essential functions in common while also having some very discrepant ways of handling similar problems" (Lidz, 1976, p. 48). The rehabilitation professional must be sensitive to the individual nature of the family while still mindful of the general effects of the trauma on family structure. Moreover, it is important to distinguish between the trauma itself and its effects on the family. Reiss (1981) makes this point in stating, "stress is something that happens to the family; its origins lie outside the family's boundaries. Crisis and disorganization are processes that happen in the family" (p. 176). Current literature on traumatic brain injury and the family has tended to emphasize the stressful nature of the trauma over the specific crises and disorganization that occur within the structure of the family. Comprehensive assessment and treatment of the family must include an understanding of the external stressors and the internal crisis that has affected the family.

DIFFERENCES AMONG FAMILY MEMBERS

Until this point, families have been described in a general way. Yet family members differ in their relationships with the family member who has experienced a traumatic brain injury. These differences have implications for assessment and treatment. In the following section specific issues that are presented by different family members are discussed.

Parents

Parents of traumatic brain-injury survivors are amply represented in the founders and most active members of the National Head Injury Foundation and other injury prevention groups such as Mothers Against Drunk Driving. The prominence of parents is understandable given that traumatic brain injury largely affects younger individuals who have not yet become independent from their parents. In this aspect of their children's situations lies the essential uniqueness of the parents' experience with traumatic brain injury.

Parents of the survivor must face a second, more prolonged parenthood, very often at a stage in their life when they were anticipating an end to active parenthood. The extended parenthood presents parents with several problems or opportunities that they did not have in their first experience with parenthood. In many respects they have a different child. They must accommodate themselves to the loss of the child they had. The survivor may act differently and have new expectations for him or herself compared to his or her premorbid life. The extent to which parents are able to accept this change and develop new standards for their child and for themselves in relation to the child is closely related to their ability to adjust emotionally to the trauma.

The extended parenthood and the particular course of development in traumatic brain injury recovery elicits a remolding tendency that has been described earlier. Parents may be tempted, consciously or unconsciously, to undo or rectify problems in childrearing now that they feel they have a second opportunity to do so.

Parents also face stressors with respect to their marital relationship and their relationship with their other children. Past conflicts about upbringing or marital communication may be reactivated by the stress of the survivor's injury and recovery. These conflicts must be resolved anew. The effort and time required for brain injury recovery may strain relationships by leaving parents with little time for each other or for their other children, thereby straining the cohesion of the family group.

The preceding comments concern parents who are still the primary care givers for the survivor or are legally responsible for the survivor in some way. Parents of adult children who experience a traumatic brain injury will also experience some of the difficulties that have been described. In some way, however, their difficulties will be different because they have less direct responsibility for the child and, if their other children are grown, may no longer have other parenting responsibilities. Parents of adult survivors may also be distressed because they have less occasion and opportunity for involvement with the survivor compared to the spouse or children of the survivor.

Spouses

Regardless of the length of time that spouses have been married, the nature of their marital relationship is different from the relationship between parent and child. Thus, it is expected that the adjustment problems faced by a spouse of a survivor would differ from the problems faced by parents. Examining the differences in the two relationship provides a more specific idea of the unique problems faced by spouses (see Willer et al., 1989; Ziegler, 1987).

Unlike parents a spouse did not usually know his or her partner as a child. Even for spouses who were childhood acquaintances, their knowledge of each other is different than the appreciation an adult parent has of a child. A spouse, therefore, will adjust differently than parents to the infantile, less controlled behavior often observed in the survivor. There are no precedents on which the spouse can base a reaction to such behavior. Spouses may feel confused by such behavior moreso than parents. Parents have an experience with childhood upbringing to draw upon in reaction to the survivor and may readily revive these experiences in their treatment relationship with the child.

Spouses were not involved in making decisions about rearing each other. Thus, the spouse of a survivor may have difficulty making unilateral decisions about treatment planning. Spouses did not share the tasks and milestones of child development together as do parents and children. As a result, a spouse may appreciate the milestones of progress in rehabilitation differently from parents. Again, the spouse has no precedents for the situation.

In fact, the spouse has numerous precedents not to make unilateral decisions about the survivor's care. Marital relationships, though unique for each couple, tend to involve a greater sense of mutuality, parity, and interdependence between partners than relationships between parents and children. When one of the partners is traumatically injured, the structure of the marital relationship changes. The noninjured spouse often finds him or herself in conflict between the need to make treatment decisions for the survivor and the need to respect the survivor's sense of independence. This conflict may be expressed in problems with communication and compliance in the rehabilitation treatment setting. It will also be reflected in the emotional and sexual relationship between the spouses.

On a more concrete level, spouses also share the responsibilities of children and household, something that parents and children usually do not share. The injury of a spouse leaves the other spouse in the stressful role of a single parent. This role, stressful under any circumstances, is made even more stressful by the uncertainty about the course of recovery for the survivor.

Perhaps the most poignant aspect of the spouse's predicament is the finality of the marital commitment. The marital relationship is a commitment from an emotional, legal, sexual, and often religious point of view. Whereas a parent anticipates an end to the dependency and responsibilities of childrearing, the spouse anticipates a lifetime of interdependence. The traumatic brain injury can alter the type of relationship that was prepared for and agreed to in making the marital commitment. Thus, the spouse often experiences intense feelings of ambivalence about the relationship after the brain injury. This ambivalence may vary as a function of the noninjured spouse's personality and values. The sense of ambivalence about commitment is an undercurrent of conflict in the spouse's experience, and must be evaluated and acknowledged by the psychologist working with the spouse.

Children

In the whirlwind of problems that the survivor of a brain injury presents to the practitioner, young children of the survivor and the survivor's young siblings are often overlooked (Duggan, 1984). To a certain extent this is understandable. Young children are not in a position to make decisions about treatment for the survivor. The child, however, is an integral part of the family and the child's emotional well-being can have a large impact on the well-being of the survivor and other family members. Therefore, it is important that an effort be made within the brain-injury rehabilitation facility to incorporate the child into the treatment program.

Piaget (1952) and others (Flavell, 1977; Ginsberg & Opper, 1979) have written extensively about childhood development and how the child seeks to make sense out of the world. The traumatic brain injury to a family member presents the child with an enormously complex experience. In order to create therapeutic treatment interventions for a child, the rehabilitation professional must have an understanding of the intellectual and emotional capacities of the child. Treatment strategies for the child with a family member who has a brain injury need to be tied closely to this understanding of the child's development. Though it is beyond the scope of this book to describe childhood development is detail, in the present section some aspects of childhood development will be reviewed. The treatment implications that can be derived from this understanding of child development will be discussed in Chapter 5.

Infancy and early childhood.   The infant actively interacts and learns from the world. Even in the first months of life the infant uses its limited sensory and motor skills to make sense out of the world. Until age 2, the child's cognitive capacities are primarily defined by these sensory and motor activities. What the child cannot sense, manipulate or otherwise come into concrete contact with, the child cannot comprehend. Memory capacity is similarly limited to brief intervals of direct contact with an object.

When a traumatic brain injury occurs to a close family member of the child at this developmental level, the experience is largely incomprehensible to the child. The child may have some limited awareness that the family member is not at home. However, should the child visit the family member at a rehabilitation facility, he or she may not necessarily show any awareness of a physical change in the injured person The child's reaction to the survivor or to the rehabilitation environment is likely to be one of curiosity. The person and situation are things to be explored in the same way anything else is explored.

This limitation in the child's ability to comprehend the trauma may shield the child from distressing emotional reactions to it. In fact the child's emotional status may be misjudged by adults. Adults very often project their own feelings onto young children. Thus, it is not unusual to hear adults comment, with sincere conviction, that the child is angry or worried about the survivor. The psychologist must help the family and professional team to differentiate what is the child's genuine experience from the family's experience projected onto the child. Worry is a cognitively complex emotion that involves an understanding and anticipation of the future that the child below age 2 does not have. It may be more accurate to speak of the child's anxiety or fear with respect to changes that occur in the present rather than the child's worry about the future.

Preconceptual child (ages 2–5). The development of language skills changes the child's ability to think about events, and to interact with others. Language allows the child to conceptualize an event or object that is outside of immediate sensory awareness. The reasoning skills of children at this stage are characterized by being concrete and egocentric. The child interprets events very literally in terms of his or her own personal experiences or the meaning of the event for him or her. Though language skills develop rapidly at this stage, the child may still rely on sensory-motor means of expressing emotional states. For example, the depressed child may be apt to act out his depression in the form of withdrawn or aggressive behavior rather than make sad statements.

Children are able to establish wider social attachments at this stage as their experiences carry them out of the family into other social settings. Though they may be less overtly dependent on immediate family, they are more aware of belonging to a family unit. They are also more aware of the role each member has within the family unit in terms of what each family member is able to contribute to the family.

The ability to communicate verbally with the child allows adults to explain in some fashion the events of the injury to the child. It also allows the child to express his or her understanding of the events. Preconceptual children may show difficulty understanding and communicating the concept of severity of injury. The child may compare the traumatic injury with minor injuries he or she had and expect recovery to be rapid. Unfortunately television programming for children at all ages continues to promote and reinforce the idea that an individual recovers almost instantaneously from severe injuries.

The greater understanding of family ties and the ability to think about events before they occur may lead the child to experience an emotional reaction to the absence of the family member who is injured. The child may feel lonely or abandoned by the injured parent. There may be a feeling of abandonment from the other parent who is involved in visiting the injured parent. In the case of an injured sibling, the child may also feel abandoned by the attention parents give to that sibling or even fears that the injury could occur to the child him or herself. The child may feel responsible for the injury, perhaps feeling that it occurred because the child was misbehaving, particularly if the child was in the motor vehicle when the injury occurred. These emotional reactions may be expressed in excessive attachment or clinging to parents, fears of new or potentially threatening situations (for example, cars) or reluctance to enter new social situations.

Operational child (ages 6–12).   There are vast differences between children in the range of ages 6–12. Piaget differentiates between children in the range of ages 5–7 (preoperational) and ages 7–12 (formal operational) in terms of their cognitive skills. For purposes of this review with its attention to treatment interventions in brain-injury rehabilitation these children are grouped together.

Children at this stage are making diverse gains in how they think about the world. The influence of school, peer social relationships, and the child's physical development interact to cause the child to make rapid changes in learning during this age period. The role of social influences on thinking and learning can be seen in the effect of learning by modeling. Children are able to integrate and perform complex behaviors by simply observing others and are able to generalize what they learn in one situation to another. Socially, the child is able to become more aware of the larger societal structure. The role of institutions (for example, government, hospitals, schools) and geopolitical entities (for example, cities, states and countries) is appreciated by the child.

The child also gains the ability to think about one or more dimensions of a problem. Piaget's famous experiments on conservation of properties are the best illustrations of this aspect of thought. Increases in cognitive ability also change the child's view of morality. Whereas the preconceptual child may interpret right and wrong in concrete, absolute terms according to certain rules, the operational child is able to recognize extenuating circumstances in evaluating behavior.

These cognitive changes have an effect on how the operational child understands a traumatic brain injury. The child's increased independent skills may give him or her more resources on which to rely in coping with the trauma. The child may be able to accept support from extended family, friends and parents of friends. School and extracurricular activities may provide outlets for emotional stress and distractions from the problems of the survivor. The child's improved ability to interpret events in the world from a less absolute black and white perspective may help the child to understand more of the details about the situation that caused the trauma. Despite these gains in cognitive skills and independence, the child is acutely aware of his or her dependence on adults and consciously experiences intimacy and separation in interpersonal relationships at an intense level. Thus, the child may be susceptible to serious emotional disturbances in reaction to the trauma.

Teenagers (ages 13–19).   The cognitive status of an adolescent is very close to that of an adult, perhaps differing only in terms of life experiences on which the individual can draw in making life decisions. Adolescents are able to think in complex, highly abstract ways. Their ability to think abstractly is often carried to an extreme in their attachment to idealistic causes and notions, and this ultimately brings them into conflict with the adult world. The adolescents' morality can be highly relativistic. Their ability to consider numerous alternatives and potential outcomes to a situation often leads to difficulties in making decisions. Their cognitive abilities, pubescent changes, and the prospect of future responsibilities as an adult, cause adolescents various emotional changes that have been described and are well-known to their parents.

Adolescents may be preoccupied with the justice and meaning of the brain injury. They may wonder about the meaning of the event, whether it represents some retribution or symbolic message about life. Underlying these concerns may be anger and outrage about the event. The disruption that is caused by the trauma may be taken personally. The injured parent may be blamed. As has been previously described, the trauma causes a change in the family's method of handling daily responsibilities and communication patterns. This change may cause conflicts with the adolescent who sees them as infringements on his or her own independence and control. Conflicts may arise regarding visitation or the amount of help the adolescent must provide around the house.

On the other hand, adolescents identify more closely with their parents' experience than can younger children. The trauma may draw them closer to their parents or siblings. They may show more direct emotional support of the noninjured parent. They may welcome the opportunity to serve as a substitute parent for the younger siblings.

Adolescents are very sensitive about their bodies. They may maintain an outward pride and belief in their invulnerability, while privately feeling insecure about their abilities and appearance. Some of the physical changes that occur after a brain injury to a family member may be emotionally difficult for the adolescent to accept. They may deny that such things could happen to them. This attitude may bring them into conflict with other family members who may seek to be protective or judgmental of the adolescents' behavior.

It is important to take into consideration the natural development of problems that are faced by adolescents in addition to those caused by the injury. Conflicts about control between parents and teens are very common.

Families may need to realize that some of the conflicts that the adolescent is expressing are normal, expected events for which the other family members may have a lowered tolerance under the stress of the trauma. On the other hand, the adolescent must understand that his degree of independence is different now than it would have been without an injury to the family member.

SUMMARY

Knowledge of the basic aspects of family structure and development will provide the rehabilitation professional with a framework for understanding the impact of a traumatic brain injury on the family. Combining this knowledge with an understanding of the survivor's condition after a brain injury allows the professional to develop a deep appreciation of the family's predicament. The professional utilizes this appreciation of the family to establish a personal connection with family members and to design psychological assessment and intervention. In Chapter Three, a format for assessment that incorporates the concepts of family structure and brain injury will be presented.

A mother speaks
by Rona

"It's never the same child . . . after a head injury . . ." one of the doctors said to me several weeks after Ben's accident. I could have killed him. I didn't want to hear it. And, although I am otherwise a reasonable and logical person, I didn't believe it for more than a year. Now, nine years later, I can tell you — it's never the same family after a head injury, either.

Before that day in 1981, we were a typical all-American family. Ben's father had an important career. I, having stayed home until my children were in school all day, had become a "successful" career woman, a Public Relations Director at an area hospital. Ben's brother, age 12, was playing soccer, delivering papers, and goofing his way through junior high school. Ben, age 8, was reading everything in sight and hamming it up in class plays.

The accident happened. The particulars of what happened were gruesome beyond belief. For each family I've met since I have known head injury, the trauma that precipitated the injury was gruesome beyond belief. In one case there may have been a drunk driver, in another a lightning strike in the swimming pool, in another some momentary change in routine which preceded the brain injury and which will haunt the surviving family members for the rest of their lives. I felt that no other grief could supercede what my family felt. And I strongly suspected that one does not recover from a grief of that magnitude.

Then it began. Only I didn't realize for more than a year that it was beginning. In addition to the trauma to Ben's brain, some terrible trauma began to happen to each of us in the family. We were never the same after that trauma. Like Ben, we were left with disabilities and deficits of our own, forced to relearn everything we'd ever known, forced to reshape our lives around an unthinkable reality. Parts of the trauma were shared with others, but much of it wasn't. Friends and neighbors couldn't understand Ben's problems and his rehabilitation. They also could not understand what each of us in Ben's family went through over the next few years. Our own extended family members did not even understand what we were going through. The head injury professionals who we were dealing with certainly did not understand.

Ben was in a coma for about a week. We didn't know if he would ever breathe, see, hear, speak, swallow, walk, or talk again. Then he regained consciousness. In addition to our relief, we faced a new realization. Yes, he could breathe. But could he see? Could he hear? Would any of his other faculties ever work again? Over the next few months, we found that he could see, he could hear, he could read, but again, in addition to our relief, there was horror. What good was hearing or seeing when cognition was faulty? "Please let him see again," we had prayed. We felt guilt over having our prayers answered and being dissatisfied with the answer we were granted.

From the beginning I believed that if I only found the right doctor, therapist, or treatment my son could be Ben again. At the end of the first year of his recovery, however, I began to understand that, no matter what, he would never be the same Ben again. That's when I began to put together the information I had been told in the rehabilitation center with the realization that the world did not operate as I had always assumed it did. Things do not happen in a rational fashion. Our best efforts do not always earn us what we seek.

As any mother would, I was willing to do anything under the sun to restore my child to health. (I had decided that I was willing to accept a dysfunctional limb or two.) I was trying as hard as I could to find the answers to Ben's problems. But as much as I did, the answers weren't to be found. But, as I found more and more dead ends, I began to see that what needed fixing was my view of the world. Ben, although he continues to this day to surprise me with new skills and insights, was not going to be the old Ben ever again. In order to do the things that Ben now needed of me, I was going to have to accept his head injury as a fact.

I would say that this thrashing and kicking as I struggled to accept Ben's injury took four years. This is the period when I felt so hostile toward professionals. I felt like saying to them, "You are asking me to accept what is unacceptable. You have the help my child needs but in order to access that help I have to be willing to accept my child's permanent disability." Actually, I still get around accepting the injury when I can. An occupational therapist told me Ben's uncoordinated hands would never be able to button shirts, so I should sew Velcro down the front of his shirts. I defiantly found any number of shirts that can be worn without buttoning—rugby shirts, sweaters, sweatshirts. The only time Ben wears a shirt that needs to be buttoned is when he goes to a prom or a wedding.

Through this long period of fighting to the death my old view of a world that was fair, I fought many other things. I continued to negotiate with the system to get things Ben needed: therapies, school programs, tieless shoelaces. All the while I was really angry. I didn't want to be a therapist and a case manager and a parent fighting the system. I didn't have time or energy left after taking care of Ben to do all the extra running and research and politicking. Other mothers weren't called upon to scale these impossible cliffs.

But if I didn't get these things for Ben, who would? Probably the pace of things that needed to be done is what kept me sane. The more time there was to think, the worse things seemed.

But I did come out on the other end. Finally one day I gave in and said, "OK, I really loved that other child I had, and I'd still like to have him back, but if I can't have that, then I guess I'll make this child the spunkiest head-injured child on the face of the earth." And I have to admit that although I hated the fighting that I had to do for Ben, I was sometimes quite success-ful at it.

So that's where we are. My life will never be the same as the result of this head injury. My child may never be independent enough to live on his own. All my plans revolve around first making arrangements for Ben. His evening bath routine takes an hour every night. The further we stray from the usual structure of his day, the more problem behavior we encounter. But more profoundly, I have had to become a person other than the one I was nine years ago in order to traverse this course life dealt me. There are many won-derful things that have come about as a result of this change. I have learned an incredible amount about who I am and how I got to be where I am. I have met people whose patience awes me as they care for and teach Ben and others like him. I have felt unbelievable kindnesses that sometimes off-set the hurt the injury caused. And I have a completely altered view of the worth of a person, now that IQ is no longer a measurement that means anything.

It isn't fair of me to speak for the other members of the family except to say that each of us suffered through those painful first days and years in our own (no doubt equally painful) way. Ben's father must have felt even more acutely than I the helplessness at not being able to "provide" recovery for Ben. While I was sleeping in Ben's hospital room each night, totally ab-sorbed in rebirthing this child into wellness, he was discussing technical points with neurologists and rigging mechanical contraptions on wheel-chairs. Our communication dwindled and died. Life revolved around Ben's rehabilitation at my emotional level and his factual level. All other facts of our former lives had ceased. When once or twice we tried to get away nei-ther of us had much energy or interest in a life outside of the hospital room. We are now divorced. The tragedy, and I have found it is not unusual among head injury families, is that each of us faced this life crisis without the sup-port of the one person who was most in a position to understand.

Ben's brother, three years older, although he doesn't openly discuss it, has also had a major life change. When his brother was hurt, he was thrust from the world of a goofier-than-most 12 year old into adult realities almost over-night. He learned, as I did, that everything cannot be fixed, that life is in-credibly fragile and that even adults don't know what to do sometimes. He experienced the notoreity of his family on the front page of the newspaper.

He had friends ask him if his brother was a "vegetable." He suddenly had to reliquish most of our attention while we handled Ben's rehabilitation. He certainly saw the withering of our social life as friends grew weary of our obsession with head injury. His future has changed. In some ways, although I hope not in too burdensome a way, his brother will always be a child for him to watch out for.

Again, these changes have not been without their bright sides. Ben's brother quickly became a charming, helpful, and responsible young man at age 13. His goofiness dwindled and his character rose to the occasion. He caused us few worries—at a time when we would have been admittedly ill equipped to handle them. He learned to ride the bus the twenty minutes to visit his brother on school holidays. He took care of Ben with great humor, and readily absented himself when he'd run out of patience. Because he was so honest, we didn't need to worry that he was being taken advantage of.

One of the fathers in the support group I attend calls it "dashed hopes." Yes, surely our original hopes for Ben have been dashed. Also many of our original hopes for ourselves have been dashed. We have disabilities and deficits—holes in our hearts—where the prior life once was. Now, nine years later, we all have new hopes, possibly even nobler hopes than the first ones. But we are veterans of a battle we wished we never had to fight.

3

Assessment of the Family

Although treatment for the traumatic brain-injury survivor often spans several different treatment settings, the rehabilitation practitioner providing psychological services should not presume that a thorough assessment of the family has been conducted at another stage of treatment. The numerous problems presented by the survivor often distract the professionals from attention to the family's concerns. Even when there is a written family assessment by the psychologist or social worker from another treatment facility, some type of assessment with the family at every facility should be conducted. The family's emotional status may have changed since the time of the last evaluation interview. More important, the assessment is an opportunity for the practitioner to establish a personal contact with the family and to begin to develop a working relationship with them that will facilitate the course of rehabilitation for the survivor.

GOALS OF ASSESSMENT

The practitioner must have a clear understanding of the goals for family assessment in order to proceed with it efficiently and methodically. In this way the assessment procedure will appear organized and purposeful. These impressions will facilitate the trust that can develop between the family and the practitioner.

Assessment is more than a casual interview with the family. Rather, it is an opportunity for the practitioner to observe the family and obtain information from them within a structured setting. It is also an opportunity for the family to observe the practitioner and obtain information from the practitioner. If the practitioner can communicate to the family that the assessment process will be beneficial to all involved in it, a large step will be taken toward eliciting support from the family for a rehabilitation treatment program.

Needs of the Family

Viewing the assessment as a cooperative venture between the practitioner and the family means that the practitioner must recognize the family's needs during the initial meeting with them. One basic need is the need for information. This may include information about procedures within the rehabilitation facility, medical status reports on the survivor, professional opinions about the survivor's course of recovery, and community resources to name a only a few.

Beyond the need for information, the family also needs emotional support. In order to establish a treatment relationship with the family, the practitioner must at the very outset communicate support and trust. This may be accomplished through helping the family to feel important, to feel understood, and to be reassured that the survivor will be cared for in the best possible way. The family may express their need for emotional support in their desire to talk to the practitioner about the survivor's current condition, or the survivor's premorbid personality and accomplishments. Because the practitioner is interested in knowing more about the survivor, the family's desire to talk about this is welcomed.

The practitioner must balance, however, his or her desire to collect information about the survivor with the family's need to ventilate feelings. There will be times when the practitioner must listen to some of the family's descriptions about the survivor in order to demonstrate support and caring for the family even if the particular information provided is not directly useful to the assessment process. For example, family members may describe at length particular memories of the survivor prior to the injury, and may become very emotional in the course of doing so. The details of such memories may or may not be helpful to the practitioner in understanding the survivor and the family. Nevertheless, it is important that the practitioner give the family the opportunity to express these memories as a way of showing support and caring for the family.

A third need of the family during their initial contact with the practitioner is their need for control. The trauma presents the family with a situation that was out of their control. The feeling of loss of control also affects the family's attitudes toward treatment of the survivor. They may express the desire to regain control of their lives and of the survivor's life by becoming involved in treatment. The practitioner must respond to this need during the initial contact with the family with some suggestions on how the family can become involved in the treatment of the survivor.

There are undoubtedly other questions and basic needs that families will present at their initial meeting with the practitioner. In any case, in the initial meeting the practitioner must give something to the family: information, emotional support, direction for involvement in treatment, or some other professional advice. By doing so, the practitioner forms a connection with the family that is the basis for a working relationship. If the practitioner maintains a remote stance in which he or she seeks to collect information (i.e., take things) from the family without giving in return, it will be difficult to engage the family in treatment, much less to gain a thorough assessment about family functioning.

Needs of the Practitioner

Though the practitioner must give things to the family in the initial interview, he or she also has needs that must be met during this time. Most basic among these is the clinical assessment of the family. This assessment should include understanding of the family's functioning with respect to the framework previously described in Chapter Two. A formal outline for obtaining this information in an assessment interview is described later in this chapter.

The practitioner also needs to assess both how the family can be best integrated into the rehabilitation treatment program and a mechanism for communication with the family. Although any number of family members may be interviewed by the practitioner, the practitioner must determine the proper person in the family to receive such communication.

The practitioner will need to obtain information about the survivor's personality and his or her role within the family system. The family is the key source of this information. Although the family is usually very willing to talk about the survivor, the practitioner must be able to balance the family's need to talk about the survivor with his or her clinical need for specific information. In fact, families may have more difficulty providing information about themselves because they feel the focus should be on the survivor as the identified patient. This feeling does not have to interfere with the course of the family assessment. The practitioner may be able to observe the family's emotional status and structure in the ways that the family members speak about the survivor. Some methods of doing this will be described later in this chapter.

ESTABLISHING A TREATMENT RELATIONSHIP

Having a clear understanding of the goals of a family assessment, the practitioner's first step in establishing a treatment relationship with the family is getting them to come in for an assessment interview. By personally asking the family to come in for such an interview, the practitioner communicates to the family members that they are an important part of the treatment. Their input about the survivor is important and the family is viewed as part of the rehabilitation process.

Whom to Meet

In contemporary American society it is less clear which people constitute an individual's family than it was a generation ago. Divorce, second marriages, and nontraditional living arrangements multiply the number of people that might be considered a family. This societal change will affect the practitioner arranging to meet family members of a brain-injury survivor for an initial evaluation. A rule of thumb is to include as family the individuals with whom the survivor was living prior to the brain injury and those individuals who bear some legal responsibility for the survivor. Thus, in the case of an injured child, the parents and siblings would be interviewed. In the case of an injured spouse, the noninjured spouse and children would be interviewed.

There will, of course, be exceptions to this. The survivor of a severe brain injury cannot always be counted on to tell the practitioner who is an important family member. The practitioner must exercise his or her clinical judgment in making distinctions between family and other associates, relatives, and friends of the survivor. The practitioner may need to contact by phone all "prospective" family members before deciding on whom to ask to attend a family interview. It might be more expedient, however, if such information was collected prior to the admission of the survivor to the rehabilitation facility. The family members who took a part in the admission process would likely, though not necessarily, be people who constitute the core family members.

In identifying the core family members who will be seen for the initial psychological interview and regular contact thereafter, the practitioner should keep communication open with other individuals who may provide information about the survivor and the family. These individuals include employment colleagues and supervisors, friends, and extended family members of the survivor. They may not be part of a regular treatment but can provide supplementary information about the survivor that may be helpful during the course of treatment. The practitioner's time constraints will make contacts on a regular basis with such individuals impractical. The information that can be gained from contacts with these people must be weighed against the time needed to obtain the information.

The practitioner also needs to make a decision about including the survivor in the initial meeting with the family. This decision will depend in part on the rehabilitation status of the survivor. Clearly, survivors judged to be at Level IV or lower on the Rancho scale would be inappropriate to include in a family interview. Their medical status may prevent them from leaving their room, and their communication is apt to be so limited as to be more disruptive than helpful to the course of the family interview. For survivors at these lower levels of functioning, the practitioner may want to observe the family with the survivor in the survivor's room or in a rehabilitation therapy activity in addition to the time spent in actual face-to-face meeting with the family.

Survivors at higher levels of functioning may be included in the family interview. The purpose of including them would be to observe how the family as a whole interacts and communicates with each other. Survivors at Levels V and VI may have reduced endurance that prevents them from participating in the entire family interview, whereas those at Levels VII and VIII are apt to have greater endurance and ability to follow the course of the interview. Regardless of the survivor's level of functioning, however, it is important to allow the family members some time alone with the practitioner. There may be issues or questions that the family and practitioner are not ready to discuss in the presence of the survivor.

Because of the ambitious goals for an initial family assessment, and the number of people that might be involved in the assessment interview, it may seem necessary to schedule several meetings with the family as opposed to one long meeting. The practitioner's schedule may make one very long meeting impractical. A general rule would be a 60 to 90 minute interview with the identified core family members. After this, questions could be posed to the family about the need for further assessment meetings. In effect the practitioner might say to the family, "We have covered a lot of information about your family member and all of you as a family today. Do you think it would be helpful for us to meet again to give you the chance to add some things that we did not have time to get to today?"

Where to Meet

The environment for the assessment interview will have an impact on the course of the interview. The family is evaluating the practitioner and the rehabilitation facility, just as the practitioner is evaluating the family. A private office that is free from interruptions will communicate to the family the professional nature of the interview and the importance of the family to the practitioner. Although there will be opportunities for informal contact among the family, survivor and practitioner within the rehabilitation setting, it is recommended that the initial interview be conducted within a private office. Likewise, phone interviews are not preferred methods of conducting family evaluations. The phone contact is more impersonal than face-to-face interview and does not offer the opportunity to observe the family directly.

Interruptions that take the practitioner away from the family, although inevitable, also communicate that the practitioner places less importance on the family's needs than on the needs of others. Rehabilitation professionals occasionally complain about families that cancel appointments or are difficult to schedule for appointments without realizing the impact of similar behavior of their own on patients and families. Therefore, interruptions should be minimized as much as possible. If the practitioner is interrupted, he or she should offer the family the courtesy of a brief general explanation for the interruption.

When to Meet

The family interview is designed to obtain information about the survivor and family that is useful in planning treatment for the survivor. Therefore, it is important that the interview occur soon after the survivor is admitted to the rehabilitation facility. Ideally the interview should be scheduled the day of admission because key family members may already be available and prepared to talk about some of the issues that are important in treatment planning. If this is not possible, it is recommended that the interview take place at least within the first week of the admission. Delaying the interview any longer may cause the practitioner and treatment team to miss the best opportunity to establish contact with the family and obtain information from them.

Structuring the Assessment Interview

The varied needs of the assessment interview require that the clinician be organized yet flexible in his or her approach. Sullivan (1953) has emphasized the clinician's communicating a sense of competence through organization of an interview while still being free to participate in and engage the individual being interviewed. In this regard, the practitioner should seek to balance questions and answers in the interview. An extended stream of questions posed to the family may gather specific information but also minimizes the opportunity for the clinician to establish a personal connection with the family or to observe how they interact with each other. On the other hand, the practitioner who spends the entire meeting with the family answering their questions may communicate that he or she is nothing more than a source of information and has no additional responsibilities or goals in the meeting.

Each family will vary in the extent to which it wishes to provide information to the practitioner. The practitioner may have reviewed some information about the survivor prior to the actual interview. At the outset of the interview, however, it is best if the practitioner minimizes the extent of what he or she may already know about the family situation in order to draw out the family and have them present their point of view free from the practitioner's preconceptions. A suitable opening for the practitioner in the assessment interview might be, "I've learned a little bit about your family member from the medical record and had a chance to stop by his or her room but this meeting is an opportunity for you to tell me in your own words about your family member, about yourselves and about what you have been going through since this trauma occured." Such a statement emphasizes that the practitioner is in control of the situation because the medical record has been consulted and the survivor has been seen, but that the practitioner is open to hearing more in order to learn fully about the survivor and the family.

Beyond this initial statement, the practitioner should maintain a inquiring, nonthreatening approach toward the family. The practitioner should not presume that he or she understands the survivor's work situation, living situation or accident circumstances, nor the family's structure and values. Families need to feel that their injured family member is respected for being unique. The practitioner can communicate that he or she has this respect by seeking information and allowing the family to teach him or her what they know about the injury, the survivor, and how the family as a whole operates.

Note Taking

In order to facilitate the development of a personal relationship with the family it is best if the practitioner minimizes note taking during the interview. In this way, face-to-face contact may be made with the family members and the practitioner can observe facial expressions and gesticulations as well as attend to the words that are stated. In order to document the mass of information that families communicate, the practitioner may take notes immediately after the interview ends. If necessary, the practitioner might explain to the family that he or she does not generally take notes in the interview in order to give the family full attention, but will be writing some things down later. In addition, brief written questionnaires may be given to the family in order to collect demographic information and other background about the survivor and family prior to the assessment interview. These questionnaires save valuable time during the interview and communicate to the families the importance of their input.

One instance where notetaking would be recommended is in helping the family to gain information about the trauma and the rehabilitation care system. When families present a long list of questions to the practitioner reflecting their need for information, it would be disrespectful of the family if the practitioner did not write down the questions. After making the list of questions the practitioner could direct the family to the best people on the rehabilitation team to answer each question. Even if the practitioner is able to communicate nothing more than that he or she can be a reliable means for obtaining information for the family, this is a valuable contribution toward engaging the family in treatment.

Eliciting Participation

The practitioner should seek to engage all members of the family by seeking opinions and comments from each person. Though one or two members of the family may dominate the discussion, the practitioner should give each family member at least one opportunity to speak. Observing the family's reaction to the individual who is speaking is a means of assessing the style in which the family interacts with each other, communication patterns, and roles. In addition, each family member has a different perspective on the survivor and on the family as a whole. These perspectives are useful for the practitioner in planning treatment.

Statements that suggest a cooperative relationship with the family will also facilitate the family's involvement in treatment. Using the collective "we" rather than "I" in speaking to the family may express this cooperative feeling. This may be particularly useful when families pose questions that the practitioner is unable to answer. For example, a family may be uncertain about how to organize family visits with the survivor. A response to such a problem that would communicate cooperation might be, "Let's discuss your concerns and what you see as the needs of your family member so that together we can come up with a plan of action."

Such phrasing should be used discreetly in order that the practitioner not imply that he or she is a companion to the family or uniquely knowledgeable about the survivor. Family members know the survivor better than rehabilitation professionals and in ways that the rehabilitation professional can never know the survivor. The practitioner must allow the family this unique role, and not diminish it by implying that he or she shares the same knowledge of the survivor as does the family.

At the end of the assessment interview the practitioner should give a summary statement of the family's situation and the survivor's role within the family. This statement does not need to be an astounding clinical insight. Rather, it serves to conclude the interview and highlight certain aspects that have made an impression on the practitioner. The summary should be presented in a way that the family is free to accept or reject it. In the summary statement the loss and tragedy that has befallen the family and their degree of coping with it should be acknowledged. The practitioner's comments should span the past events that have happened, the present situation, and project forward to the future goals for the family and the survivor.

PROBLEMS IN ASSESSMENT

The Noncompliant Family

The preceding description has taken for granted that the family of a traumatic brain-injury survivor is willing and able to meet with the practitioner in order to accomplish the goals of the initial assessment interview. This is not always the case. A family's premorbid lifestyle patterns or their stressful response to the injury itself may lead them to be reluctant to participate in any interaction with the practitioner in a rehabilitation setting. The practitioner is thus unable to obtain information about the family and the survivor, nor to elicit the family's support for the treatment program.

If the family is reluctant to come in for an initial interview or their behavior suggests that it is more than simply an inconvenience for them to come in, the practitioner must try to understand why this is happening. Knowing why the family does not wish to come in is important for practical reasons and for the information it may yield about the family's structure and emotional state.

Finding out why the family does not wish to meet the practitioner may be as simple as asking the family members. Families sometimes misunderstand the suggestion of a meeting with a psychologist to imply that their own personal problems will be explored or that they will be blamed in some way for the behavior of the survivor. Putting some of these preconceptions to rest may overcome their reluctance to meet for an evaluation interview. The practitioner may explain that the family's information about the survivor is vital for treatment and that the family has a strong influence on the course of recovery and long-term treatment plans for the survivor. Therefore, a meeting with the practitioner to focus on these issues is valuable.

Even if the family is initially noncompliant, several interventions may help to change the situation. Sometimes educational information mailed to the family or left at the facility for them to review may be a way of making an initial contact. This can be general information about traumatic brain injury, or information about the psychological and rehabilitation services available at the facility. The practitioner can then make a follow-up call to see if the family had received the material.

Families of other survivors at the facility may help to break the ice in order to set up an interview. Particularly if the survivor has a roommate at the rehabilitation facility, the families of the roommates are likely to communicate with each other. Having a model of other families who have seen the practitioner for an initial interview may overcome the hesitancy of a noncompliant family.

If these means prove unsuccessful, the family is usually willing to meet with the physician. The physician might be able to inquire about the family's feelings regarding a meeting with the mental health professional and encourage the family to attend such a meeting.

The policies of a rehabilitation facility for traumatic brain-injury survivors can minimize families' noncompliance with psychological interviews. During their tours of the facility and in promotional literature, facility staff can emphasize the importance of family involvement and the policy of an initial psychological interview. Possibly the psychologist or social worker would be available to meet with the families when they tour the facility in order to make a personal contact with them before their family member enters the facility.

The practitioner's job of eliciting a noncompliant family's participation in treatment has been made much easier by the activity of local and national brain-injury support groups. Outreach efforts by these groups may assist the professional in achieving greater family participation in the rehabilitation process. The value of this cooperation between family support groups and professionals is discussed in more detail in Chapter Six.

Despite all of these efforts, there will be some families who are simply unwilling to become involved in the treatment program. This is informative in and of itself about how the family will operate in response to the injury and how well the survivor will be able to be integrated into the family after rehabilitation care is ended. Clearly with such families there will be major obstacles to family involvement in treatment and family reintegration for the survivor.

The family should not be written off too soon because of an initial lack of interest in participation in psychological treatment. Regular progress summaries and other literature can be left for the family or sent home. This communication leaves the door open to the family's changing their minds and seeking to speak to the practitioner at a later date.

In written communications with families who choose to be uninvolved in evaluation or treatment, the rehabilitation team should seek to point out the consequences of the family's lack of compliance with the treatment program. For example, a family may wish to have the survivor return to live with them yet does not participate in treatment in order to learn how to care for the survivor at home. With such a family the rehabilitation team should clarify for the family the consequences that their noncompliant behavior can have for the survivor. Specifically, the rehabilitation team is forced to choose between allowing the survivor to be discharged to home where the family is unprepared to care properly for the survivor and other discharge sites including those far from the family's home.

The practitioner and other rehabilitation professionals must avoid the temptation to react in a punitive or judgmental manner to the noncompliant family. This may be expressed in veiled angry or guilt-laden messages to the family about their lack of involvement with the survivor. These types of responses widen the gap between family and professionals and intensify the family's noncompliance. Moreover, these types of communications suggest that the professionals are allowing personal feelings to interfere with the establishment of an objective treatment program for the patient.

It would be more productive for the professional to consider his or her own feelings of frustration and anger as clues to the family's feelings. The family's frustration or anger about their inability to do more for the survivor or about the injustice of the trauma may be preventing them from becoming more involved in a treatment program. Professional staff may be able to empathize with these feelings rather than criticize them, thereby establishing a basis for closer ties between the survivor, the family, and the professional. The implications of the professional's feelings about families and survivors are discussed in more detail in Chapter Seven.

The Noncommunicative Family

Some families may be compliant about making appointments with the practitioner but have difficulty expressing their needs or providing information in a way that is helpful to the practitioner. At times the noncommunicative family may be a type of noncompliant family. They appear to expect the professional to do all of the work in the meeting without recognizing that treatment is a joint process between professional and family.

When working with families who are not communicative, the practitioner needs to take a more active role than he or she would with a family that is more communicative. The practitioner's goals should include providing information to families and answering questions. Few families are so noncommunicative as to be unable to ask any questions at all about what is happening in the rehabilitation process with the survivor.

In addition, the practitioner should educate the family about how the treatment program involves family input as well as professional input. The practitioner should not feel it is necessary to carry full responsibility for the interview. A briefer interview of 15 to 30 minutes may be suitable for such families. As they become more comfortable with the process of treatment they may be willing to stay for longer interviews.

Some families are noncommunicative because they are uncertain about how to interact with the practitioner rather than because of some reluctance to comply with the treatment. For such families, educational information in the form of written literature, films, or videos may be a means of communicating essential information to them about their role in treatment. Interactions with families of other survivors and support group activities may also be less threatening means of interacting and learning about how they can help their family member.

With such families the practitioner should be modest and not seek to impress the family with his or her knowledge about brain injury or the family. Rather, he or she should seek to build up the family's feeling of importance and esteem about what they have to offer the psychologist. Statements that communicate how the practitioner needs the assistance of family members to learn certain information, or comments about the uniqueness of the family in being able to provide the information would be appropriate in this regard. At the same time, however, the practitioner must not appear to be too needy of the family's help. The family may perceive this as a derogation of the practitioner's abilities.

AN OUTLINE FOR FAMILY ASSESSMENT

In the following section an outline for assessment of the family of traumatic brain-injury survivors is presented. This outline seeks to incorporate the concepts that have been discussed in this book up to this point. That is, the assessment of the family should be a basis on which the practitioner establishes a working relationship with the family. The practitioner should get information from the family about the survivor, about the family's emotional adjustment at the time of the evaluation interview, and about the family structure.

The idea of a structured evaluation tool for families of traumatic brain-injury survivors is not new. Kay et al. (1988) have developed HI-FI, Head Injury Family Interview. This evaluation tool is exemplary for its comprehensive scope and the systematic way in which Kay and his associates have developed it. The HI-FI evaluation is done over a period of days, and was primarily designed for use in an outpatient setting. The interview is being adapted for use in an inpatient setting. Schwentor and Brown (1989) present a similar, though briefer, format for family assessment. Bishop and Miller (1988) reviewed empirical assessment techniques from the general family treatment literature that may be applied to work with families of brain-injury survivors.

The present outline seeks to incorporate concepts of family structure into the assessment. In this regard, it draws on outlines developed by Ackerman (1958) and Fleck (1985). In addition, the present evaluation model is designed to be used within an inpatient or outpatient care setting in which the practitioner has limited time to meet with the family, perhaps no more than two meetings. By using this outline for a family assessment, the practitioner can obtain information about the family's present emotional state in order to make some initial recommendations on family treatment intervention and recommendations to the other members of the rehabilitation team about how to work best with the family members. The practitioner who finds even this outline too lengthy given his or her time constraints may find portions of the outline useful to inquire about specific aspects of the family's reactions to the trauma. Research that identifies efficient and reliable means of assessing family adjustment to traumatic brain injury would be a major benefit to practicing clinicians. It is hoped that the present outline will stimulate further development of such tools.

The general outline is illustrated in Table 3.1. In the following section, the purpose and general interpretive guidelines for each portion of the outline will be described.

The Trauma

The traumatic brain injury is the incident that resulted in the family being seen by the practitioner. The first purpose of discussing the trauma with the family is to acknowledge their primary reason for being in the practitioner's office and to show interest in the welfare of the survivor. The discussion about the trauma and its effect on the survivor is a personal and sensitive issue for the family. Yet, it is one step removed from focusing directly on the family's adjustment. Thus, it is likely to be the easiest way for the family to begin talking with the practitioner.

The second purpose of this section of the interview is for the practitioner to collect information about the family's impressions and explanations about the trauma, its effects on the survivor and the changes noted in the survivor. This information is needed for treatment planning in order to set appropriate goals for the survivor and the family, and to plan for discharge options.

In this section and throughout the interview, the practitioner also uses the discussion about the trauma to observe the family's expression of affect, their communication patterns, and how they treat each other while discussing a sensitive family issue.

Method

In this section of the interview, the practitioner's open-ended questions usually will be sufficient to stimulate discussion from the family. The practitioner can then ask follow-up questions based on the family's comments. As mentioned earlier, collection of information should be balanced with the

Table 3.1   Assessment Outline for Interview of Family

I.   Identifying information

Introductory comment: The following questionnaire asks some questions about the family and its background. In working with the survivor it is helpful for me to have a perspective on the family's history. That is the reason for these questions.

    1. Composition of family:

        a. Basic data: Names, ages, and sex of family members or other people living in home

        b. What is the relationship between people in the home and the survivor? (particularly important for nonblood relations)

    2. Physical setting:

        a. Briefly describe your home: How many rooms does it have? What is the layout of the rooms?

        b. Briefly describe your neighborhood: How close do you live to your neighbors? How close are you to the center of town, or the areas where you would do your weekly activities of shopping, schooling, working, religious activities?

        c. Has the family moved during the life of the survivor? If so, explain the circumstances of the move.

    3. Spouse and/or parents of survivor:

        Basic data: Date of engagement, date of marriage, educational background, brief work history, medical and mental health history, socioeconomic status, history of any separation of divorce, significant deaths of others during your life.

    4. Children and/or siblings of survivor:

        Basic data: Developmental milestones, educational history, medical and mental health history

    5. Extended family:

        What are the family's contacts with extended family members? Describe the frequency and nature of these contacts.

II.   Trauma

Introductory statement: I have some information about your family member and the injury that he/she had, but I would like to have you tell me in your own words, from your own point of view what happened and how you see it. Sometimes the professionals miss some important aspects about the injury and the survivor in the course of treatment. Here is a chance for you to give me more information.

Answer the following questions:

    1. Attribution of the cause of accident

        a. What was the nature of the accident?

        b. To what do you attribute the accident?

        c. What was the survivor's role in the accident?

        d. Did anyone or anything else contribute to the accident as you see it?

        e. Is this the first serious accident/injury the family member has had? If not, what was the nature of the other accidents? How did the survivor react to those other accidents? How did it affect the family?

    1.   f. Were there other serious accidents/injuries to other family members?

Continued

Table 3.1   (Continued)

How did the family member and family react to those? How does that incident compare to the current one?

   2. Family's level of understanding about the survivor's condition
      a. In your opinion what are the survivor's main problems at this time?
      b. In your opinion what are the reasons for him/ her showing the kind of behavior he/she does at this time?
      c. What are your ultimate goals at this time for the survivor and for the family as a whole?
      d. What are your goals for the survivor over the next three months?
      e. What are your goals for yourselves as a family over the next three months?
   3. Family's level of emotional control at this time
      a. How would you as family members explain your feelings at this time about the survivor's injury and his/her condition? How have you expressed these feelings?
      b. How do family members know how the others are feeling about the survivor?
      c. What, if anything, has been a help to you in coping with these feelings? How do you pull yourselves out of feeling ____ and resume some of your daily activities?
   4. Willingness to be engaged in treatment
      a. Have you ever had occasion to consult a psychologist, psychiatrist, or counselor in the past as a family or for one family member? If so, what was your experience and what was the outcome of this contact?
      b. How do you feel about seeing a psychologist now for this family meeting?
      c. Who have you consulted with thus far regarding your feelings about the survivor and his/her rehabilitation and recovery? What were you told? Did you feel that consultation was helpful to you?
   III.   **Characteristic family functioning: what the family is like over time rather than in reaction to the trauma**
Introductory statement: In the next group of questions I want to focus on how the family gets along on an everyday basis, rather than in reaction to the trauma that you have been experiencing. So, try to think about your customary ways of interacting during the past 6–12 months, before the trauma, when answering these questions.
   1. Describe a typical weekday's and weekend's activities for the family.
   2. What kinds of activities are you likely to do together as a family?
   3. How much time do family members spent together as a group?
   4. How often do family members eat together?
   5. How do you know how to get in touch with each other during the course of a day?
   6. What kinds of activities do family members do individually? How do you let each other know when you are doing something alone without the family?

Continued

Table 3.1   (Continued)

7. How do family members know when someone in the family is well or not well?

8. How do you settle conflicts between family members? Give an example.

9. How do family members express anger? joy?

10. How do you show affection to family members?

11. How are duties around the household organized and divided among family members? Give example.

12. How are decisions made in the household? Give example.

13. How does the family decide to spend money?

14. How much time do family members spend on educational activities compared to other activities?

15. How do you react when one of the family members is ill? What do other family members do? Does anything change?

16. Do you belong to a church, synagogue, or other religious institution? How often do you attend?

IV.   **Characteristic family relationships with society:**

Introductory comments: In addition to how the family relates to each other, I want to ask some questions about how you relates to others outside the family. Again, answer these questions with respect to your usual contacts with people outside the family rather than your contacts since the trauma.

1. Who does the family keep in contact with on a weekly or monthly basis (e.g. extended family, friends, work and school contacts, neighbors)? What is the nature of these contacts?

2. What role do extended family (e.g. parents, grandparents, cousins, aunts, uncles) have in your everyday life? Do they help you with any specific activities?

3. To what community activities or organizations does the family belong?

4. Has your involvement in community activities changed over the past year?

5. Are there any people in the community (government, community leaders) that the family turns to for help in day-to-day matters? How have your felt about the help you received in this way.

V.   **Characteristic functioning of family subsystems**

Introductory comments: Until now we have looked at the family as a whole and how you are reacting to the trauma and have related to each other over time. In the next section of the interview, I want to focus on different groups of people within the family. Sometimes the family as a whole may appear to be well or distressed and yet individual members within the family are reacting differently. Each of you can affect the survivor's well-being, so it is important to understand how each person within the family is doing.

A. The survivor

1. What did the survivor (use first name of survivor or refer to relationship, e.g., your father) contribute to the family in terms of his/her practical activities? In terms of his emotional contribution to the family?

2. What things did the survivor do that distinguished him/her from other family members?

Continued

Table 3.1   (Continued)

3. What things do you most admire about the survivor now and in the past?

4. What things about the survivor would you have liked to have changed, or see him/her improve, or did not like about him/her?

5. Who in the family did the survivor most resemble in terms of his/her personality?

B. Other subsystems: Ask each of these questions to the different subgroups of the family members: parents, siblings, spouse, children:

1. How has your relationship with the survivor changed since the injury?

2. What do you miss most about the survivor at this time?

3. How has your relationship with other family members changed since the survivor's injury?

4. Before the injury, with whom in the family would you prefer to spend time?

5. Before the injury, with whom in the family would you feel most comfortable talking about something special or about a problem?

6. Before the injury, to whom in the family did you have the most difficulty relating? The least difficulty?

Rating scale to be completed by the practitioner at the end of the interview

A. Attributions about the accident (rate on 1–5 scale with 1 = not at all, and 5 = entirely)?

To what extent does the family attribute the injury to:

    a. The survivor's actions?   ____

    b. The actions of others?   ____

    c. Chance?   ____

    d. External force (include religious force)   ____

B. Family's understanding about the injury (rate on 1–5 scale with 1 = little to no understanding, and 5 = high degree of understanding, very realistic appraisal of survivor's condition). ____

C. Family's level of emotional control (1 = extreme destabilizing emotional distress, 5 = extreme emotional detachment, overcontrol). ____

D. Family's willingness to be engaged in treatment (1 = very willing to participate, 5 = suspicious and reluctant to participate). ____

E. Family's level of cohesion (1 = needs of individual emphasized, low cohesion; 5 = needs of family emphasized, high cohesion). ____

F. Family's level of communication (1 = chaotic, 5 = rigid). ____

G. Family values (1 = no shared values, 5 = totally shared values among family members). ____

H. Family relations with society (1 = family ignores societal norms, 5 = family adheres rigidly to societal norms). ____

I. Family organization (1 = vague roles, 5 = rigid roles). ____

opportunity for the family to ventilate their feelings. The practitioner should be careful about presuming to know exactly what the family is saying in discussing such emotionally laden topics. The practitioner's questions to the family, therefore, should be designed to obtain more information or to confirm the practitioner's understanding about what the family is saying.

Interpretation

Information gained from this section of the evaluation interview should be used to answer several questions.

To what factors does the family attribute the trauma?   The family's explanation of the trauma, why it happened and, possibly, how it might have been prevented will be an indication of how they experience the distress of the trauma. The practitioner should attempt to understand the family's explanation of the trauma in terms of the contribution that the survivor, external circumstances beyond the family's control, aspects of the family's own behavior, or behavior of other individuals in the survivor's life each had to the trauma. The degree of control that the family feels it had over the injury and the degree to which they blame themselves or the survivor for the injury will suggest how they will react emotionally to the injury and how to focus psychological treatment.

What is the family's level of knowledge about traumatic brain injury?   The family's explanations of what they have been told by other professionals and nonprofessionals, their descriptions of the difficulties that the survivor is facing and their explanations of what happened in general and in specific after the trauma are indications of their degree of knowledge about traumatic brain injury. Difficulty in giving explanations or gross misinterpretations of information from other professionals suggest deficits in knowledge that would be helped by educational approaches to psychological treatment.

How does the family express emotions?   The family's discussion of the sensitive topic of the trauma and the survivor's current condition are an indication of the way that the family expresses affect. There are, obviously, many variations in how a family may do this. Some general dimensions along which to judge this aspect of family functioning include: the degree to which emotions are expressed verbally or nonverbally, how different family members tend to express emotions, the degree to which expression of emotion is focused on one topic (i.e. the trauma) or spreads to other aspects of the family's functioning. Knowing how the family expresses emotions will be useful for the practitioner in psychological treatment and for the members of the rehabilitation team in their communications with the family.

How willing is the family to be engaged in psychological treatment?   The family's behavior during this initial part of the evaluation will provide an indication of how they react to psychological treatment. Families that respond readily to the practitioner's questions, elaborate on their answers in response to follow-up questions, maintain eye contact with the practitioner, and appear to be attentive to the practitioner's comments would seem to be readily engaged in further treatment. In comparison, the family that responds briefly to the interview questions or appears difficult to involve in any further discussion would appear less likely to become involved in psychological treatment.

Identifying Information

Some background information is usually collected at the time of the survivor's admission to a rehabilitation facility. This information is important to the practitioner not just for administrative purposes but in terms of what it says about the family's structure and coping skills.

The general purpose of the identifying information is to obtain more data about the family in order to make normative judgments about their coping strengths and weaknesses. Obviously it is inaccurate to make judgments based purely on such information without observing the family and interacting with them. Nevertheless, information about the family's history can be useful as a predictor of the family's adjustment in the future. Although the traumatic brain injury is a unique, unprecedented event for the family, their reaction to it may be determined in part by their past experiences with stressors and their style of handling them.

The identifying information section of the evaluation also provides information about the financial and social resources of the family. This information is important in predicting the family's ability to assist in long-term care for the survivor when he or she is discharged from rehabilitation facilities.

Method

Generally, it is best to collect much of this information in a written format prior to the evaluation interview. Obtaining such information orally is time-consuming and generally dissatisfying for the family and the practitioner. It may interfere with the establishment of a more personal relationship between the practitioner and the family. Even completing a lengthy written form may put off the family from their involvement in psychological treatment. Some information can be obtained prior to admission or in the admissions packet, thereby removing this aspect of data collection from the direct psychological treatment contact.

However the information is collected, the practitioner should be familiar with it prior to the interview with the family. By sounding familiar with the family's background, the practitioner will communicate that he or she is interested in the family and well-informed about some aspects of the family's functioning. Some time in the evaluation interview can be spent asking for clarification of the information. This clarification process must be done cautiously because family members may be wary of providing more detailed information about past family stressors in the presence of some family members, or may be wary of taking the focus of the interview off of the survivor and on to their more personal affairs. The practitioner can minimize this reaction by focusing his or her questions on matters that will provide a better understanding of the survivor. For example, parents of a survivor may feel uncomfortable discussing their feelings about a period of separation in their marriage. They may more readily discuss how the survivor reacted to the separation.

Interpretation

General information about the family's background yields some hypotheses about their involvement in treatment, the possible discharge options, and their emotional and financial resources. Interpretation of such information would be greatly facilitated by further research studies that identify relationships between family characteristics and the survivor's outcome from traumatic brain-injury rehabilitation treatment.

The degree of stability of the family in terms of changes that the family has undergone in its structure is also important in planning treatment. The family's reaction to their past stressors may be a clue to their reactions to the present stressor of the brain injury.

The Family as a Group

This section of the interview focuses more directly on the family structure. Because the focus is on the family directly, and not the survivor, it is a delicate one for the practitioner to manage. The importance of knowing something about the family structure in order to plan treatment for the family has been described in Chapter Two. In this section of the evaluation, the practitioner seeks to characterize the family according to the variables that were described in Chapter Two.

Method

A loosely structured question-and-answer format is one part of the evaluation method for eliciting information about family structure. The practitioner must go beyond the actual content of what is discussed by the family to attend to their process of discussion. Nonverbal cues in the form of body language and seating within the office are often clues to the family's current patterns of interaction.

By observing the interactions that different family members have with him or her, the practitioner is able to develop hypotheses about the family's structure. Through this method the practitioner is able to determine the family's receptivity to psychological interpretation. This information is helpful in planning the level of treatment intervention as will be described in Chapter Five.

Interpretation

The practitioner must determine the characteristics of the family according to the structural dimensions that have been discussed earlier: cohesion, communication, values and organization. In addition to describing these characteristics, the practitioner must be able to identify areas of relative strength and weakness in the family structure. These areas will be helpful in planning structural treatment interventions in psychological treatment sessions.

The Family and Community

The goal of this section of the evaluation interview is to assess the family's attitudes toward the outside world. This includes the community in which the family lives and works, as well as other social groups outside the family. The rehabilitation facility constitutes one of these other social groups. The family's attitudes about the outside world may have implications for their feelings about the rehabilitation environment and this will have an effect on treatment.

Method

Usually open discussion around the questions listed in Table 3.1 will be sufficient for the practitioner to get information about this matter.

Interpretation

The family's responses to the questions about this subject are evaluated in terms of the nature and frequency of their interactions with the outside world. In addition, how the family speaks about their interactions with the extrafamilial groups is an indicator of their feelings about these groups. The results of this section of the evaluation can be used to make a determination about how to structure contacts between the rehabilitation team and the family, and how much to involve the family in discharge planning by having them contact community resources for the survivor.

Family Subsystems

This section is separated from the section on family structure but its focus is similar. The focus on the family as a group should include focus on the subsystems of the family. By identifying the strengths and weaknesses of each subsystem of the family, the psychologist will be able to judge where the need for treatment intervention is greatest.

Method

The practitioner can ask open-ended questions in order to get some information about these smaller units of the family. The structure of the interview is very similar to that of the earlier section on family structure. The practitioner may want to divide up the family for this part of the evaluation in order to see the parents or the children separately and assess their functioning apart from the family as a whole. Most families will not have a problem doing this, especially if the practitioner is able to present it as a regular part of the evaluation. One way to ease the family into this part of the evaluation is to have made a comment about it at the outset of the evaluation. Then at this stage in the evaluation the practitioner might say something like, "As I mentioned to you, at this point, I'd like to give each of you some additional time to talk about things that you might not have had time to discuss when the family was all together. So now I'd like to ask the children to leave for a few minutes so I can speak to you, Mr. and Mrs. ____ alone."

Interpretation

Interpretation of this aspect of the family should focus on identifying the strengths and weaknesses of each subgroup in the family and any need for psychological treatment among these subgroups.

CATEGORIZING FAMILIES

The practitioner's ability to appreciate the family's unique predicament and how family members, individually and together, have been able to cope with the survivor's injury is a critical part of assessment and the establishment of a working relationship with the family. Notwithstanding this appreciation of the family's individuality, clinical experience indicates that there are similarities between the reactions of different groups of families to the survivor's injury. Barrer (1988) has differentiated types of families in terms of their involvement in rehabilitation treatment and their supportiveness of staff treatment. By categorizing families as high or low on these factors, Barrer de-

Table 3.2   Matrix of Different Family Types

	High Cohesion		Low Cohesion	
	Low denial	High denial	Low denial	High denial
Positive relationship with professional	Command performance family	Overprotective family	Dependent family	Neglectful family
Negative relationship with professional	Bad-match family	Defiant family	Uninvolved family	Isolated family

scribed four types of families, their behavior, and the treatment that can be utilized with them.

As part of a comprehensive assessment process, the practitioner should seek to understand the family in comparison to family types as well as evaluate them as a unique family. Barrer's factors—involvement in treatment and support of staff—can be understood in terms of the general literature on family functioning that was reviewed briefly in Chapter Two. Family involvement in treatment can be seen as a function of family cohesiveness. The family that feels a strong sense of togetherness and attachment to the survivor is likely to be more involved in the survivor's treatment program than a family with a weaker sense of togetherness.

The family's relationship with the rehabilitation staff is one aspect of the family's relationship with the outside world. The family's supportiveness of the staff is a reflection of the degree to which they experience a positive working relationship with the professionals. They are able to establish and maintain relationships with the outside world rather than isolate themselves from such relationships.

In addition to these factors, a third factor is added here that encompasses an important aspect of the family's communication patterns and beliefs: acknowledgement or denial of the implications of the survivor's injury. As noted in Chapter One, denial is a common emotional reaction among survivors and families. Family members vary widely in their acknowledgment of the implications of the trauma and this variation has a major effect on the course of psychological treatment for them.

With these three factors in mind a matrix of eight family types is developed that is illustrated in Table 3.2. These types will be briefly described.

Command Performance Family

Families that demonstrate a high degree of family cohesion, capacity to acknowledge the implications of the injury and an openness to establishing a positive working relationship with the professional are obviously an ideal group of people with whom to work. These families, although not free of adjustment problems, appear to be able to manage the vicissitudes of rehabilitation recovery and are able to use the professional's time well in order to make treatment plans and decisions. These families are apt to impress the professional with their level of adaptation to the trauma. Sbordone et al. (1984) have used the apt term "command performance family" to acknowledge the effort and accomplishment that is involved in balancing all of the demands of the posttrauma situation.

The strengths of such a family can belie weaknesses. The impressive adaptation of the family may mask conflicts about the family's willingness to admit weakness or dependency, or their ability to handle a situation where they do not meet others' expectations of them. In assessing such families, the practitioner needs to be aware of such potential conflicts and look beyond the family's seemingly high level of adaptation without diminishing the accomplishment. That is, the fact that the family is able to show such positive adaptation should not be undermined, but at the same time the practitioner should consider the stresses that the family may be experiencing that are not evident from their outward behavior.

Furthermore, the practitioner may be subject to countertransference or feelings of dependency on the family or a desire to self-disclose the practitioner's own problems because the family seems to manage their own problems so well. Families need to pace themselves through the long rehabilitation course (Barrer, 1988). The practitioner assessing the family needs to be aware of what degree of responsibility the family can manage in the course of the survivor's rehabilitation. The command performance family may be given greater responsibility and tasks in rehabilitation treatment than they are actually able to manage if the practitioner does not recognize the fragility of their seemingly effective level of coping with the trauma.

The Overinvolved Family

The family characterized by overinvolvement differs from the command performance family primarily in their degree of acceptance about the impact of the trauma. They are able to work well with the professional team and remain involved in treatment, but their denial of the severity or permanence of the trauma may lead them to become overly focused on a specific problem area, or overly concerned about seeing evidence of treatment progress. In order to bolster their belief that the survivor's injuries are not severe or permanent, family members may seek to engage the survivor, at all possible times, in cognitive and physical activities and not allow time for passive or leisure visiting activities with the survivor. Difficulties in balancing home life and time at the rehabilitation facility are also noted in these families.

The overinvolved family may be mistaken for the command performance family at the assessment and early stages of rehabilitation. The practitioner making his assessment may intensify the overinvolvement of the family by assuming such families are able to manage large amounts of responsibility in the treatment process and giving them this responsibility. The result of this treatment decision is to make it more difficult for the family to set limits on their time with the survivor and to manage their other life responsibilities such as work or care for other family members. Thus, in the assessment process the practitioner needs to inquire carefully about the family's understanding about the trauma and their expectations for the survivor. The overinvolved family, as well as other families that have a high level of denial, will show difficulties in verbalizing the possibility that the survivor will experience long-term problems from the trauma and discussing the implications of these problems.

Bad Match Family

The bad match family differs from the command performance family only in their working relationship with the staff. The term bad match is used to describe this type of family to represent the complexity and uncertainty about what makes up a good working relationship between family and professional staff. Not all families and professionals can be expected to develop a productive working relationship no matter how well-qualified the professionals are and how desirous and able the families are to be involved in treatment.

An example of such a bad match is the case of cultural or ethnic differences between the professionals and family members. The black, Hispanic, or Oriental family may have their injured family member placed at a rehabilitation facility far from home with a primarily white professional staff. Because of the scarcity of advanced brain-trauma rehabilitation facilities, the low numbers of minority rehabilitation facilities, the low numbers of minority rehabilitation professionals and the fact that brain trauma knows no geographic, racial, or ethnic boundaries, this situation is common. The differences between the family and the professionals may result in communication problems that are disruptive to the development of a working relationship between the family and professional staff.

Obstacles to the effective working relationship need not be ethnic in origin. A clash of personalities between family members and professionals can result in severe disruptions to the course of treatment regardless of anyone's ethnic background.

There may be other characteristics of the family that prevent the establishment of a working relationship with professionals. It may be difficult to predict from an assessment interview which families will have trouble developing a positive relationship with the treatment team. Considering the cultural background of families will help the practitioner be sensitive to each family's need. Sometimes, the practitioner may be able to contact professionals from other rehabilitation facilities where the survivor and family have been treated and inquire of these professionals about the family's relationship with professional staff.

At times, the most effective treatment intervention for a bad match may be a change in staff or facility rather than an attempt to change family structure. If such changes are not possible, the practitioner must avoid blaming the family or seeing them as the defiant or uninvolved family (see below). On the other hand, there may be actual difficulties within the family that are causing them to have problems relating to professional staff. These deserve the attention of psychological treatment rather than wasting time considering transferring the survivor to another treatment site or changing treatment personnel.

The Defiant Family

Working with the defiant family is one of the most difficult tasks for brain-injury rehabilitation professionals. These families have a high level of cohesion that leads them to spend much time in the rehabilitation facility with the survivor. Yet, their relationships with the outside world tend to be antagonistic and their capacity to acknowledge the implications of the injury is low. As a result, they become involved in frequent conflicts with rehabilitation staff.

The defiant family's poor relationship with the staff leads them to challenge professionals on many different aspects of treatment planning and to maintain a skeptical, carping attitude. This may engender counterdefiance in staff which exacerbates the sense of conflict.

The family's difficulty in acknowledgment of the trauma makes them resistant to comments or conclusions from staff that suggest any bad news about the survivor's treatment outcome. These families may project their anger and fear about the trauma outcome onto staff. Thus, the rehabilitation staff are seen as unsupportive or themselves denying the reality of the survivor's improvement in treatment.

A key conflict underlying the defiant family's behavior is trust. They feel betrayed and angry about the trauma. Their trust in others and the world as a whole is disrupted, leaving them with an inability to feel secure about the future. As a result, they maintain an angry, vigilant attitude toward others.

This attitude is often exacerbated by the rehabilitation treatment environment that is confusing and out of their control. The fact that a certain degree of uncertainty and ambiguity is inherent in the present state of knowledge about traumatic brain-injury treatment only intensifies the feelings of these families.

The above-mentioned characteristics of the defiant family make them quite recognizable to the practitioner in the assessment interview. Indeed, if the practitioner notes that he or she is experiencing angry or counterdefiant feelings during contacts with the family these feelings may be a valuable diagnostic clue to the emotional state of the family itself. Identification of the defiant family during the assessment can help rehabilitation staff to plan treatment accordingly and to prepare themselves for inevitable conflicts. This preparation may also minimize the chance that staff will respond to such families in a counterdefiant manner.

The Dependent Family

Families with low cohesion are apt to be less involved in the rehabilitation treatment process in terms of frequency of visitation or participation in therapy activities. They may also be more difficult to involve in psychological treatment because their emotional bond to the survivor and the impact of the trauma on them is less than it is for more cohesive families.

Despite this low level of cohesion, the dependent family maintains a basically positive attitude toward the outside world. Thus, they are able to establish a positive relationship with the rehabilitation professionals. They express acknowledgment of the problems created by the trauma but because of their low level of cohesiveness they have difficulty taking action. They tend to let professionals make the decisions. They may be observed to agree with whatever the professional says by deferring to the professional's experience.

Underlying the passive dependent behavior of such a family may be a number of emotional conflicts. Family members may have a feeling of having failed, even though the trauma was a situation not in their control to avoid. They may experience self-doubt about making decisions because they perceive their previous decisions as failures. The expertise of the professionals and the complexity of the rehabilitation facility are overwhelming to them and may exacerbate their feelings of self-doubt.

The dependent family may, at first, be mistaken for a command performance family. Both show a willingness to be engaged in a working relationship with professionals and an acknowledgment of the survivor's injury. It is only after the practitioner sees the dependent family's limited ability to make decisions or to follow-up on treatment recommendations that the characteristic dependent behavior is observed. Therefore, the practitioner may find it helpful to give all families some tasks to work on early in treatment. Observing the family's reactions to such tasks may be a useful diagnostic tool for the practitioner to identify the type of family he or she is treating.

The Neglectful Family

The neglectful family differs from the dependent family in their level of acceptance of the trauma. They can be recognized by their tendency to give lip service to the professional without the true appreciation of the implications of treatment. They do not demonstrate a strong desire to become involved in the rehabilitation treatment program for the survivor.

This behavior has the effect of angering professionals. Professionals may feel unappreciated, as though their rehabilitation efforts are for naught. Thus, the term "neglectful" may be used by staff to describe such families, implying that the families ought to be more involved or that their lack of involvement and understanding of treatment is in some way intentional. The tendency for professionals to take personally the behavior of families with a low degree of cohesion or high degree of denial of problems is a common one that must be overcome if rehabilitation is to be effective.

The neglectful family's low level of involvement with the survivor may represent a long-standing family trait of low cohesion, or it may be an acute reaction to the trauma. The family may not feel comfortable or able to be close to the survivor at a particular point in time because the emotional stress is too much for them to manage. In either case, challenging such behavior or becoming angry with the family may only intensify it.

The practitioner's assessment of the neglectful family, as well as other families, should attempt to identify to what extent the limited involvement of the family at a given point in time represents a long-standing family trait or one of recent origin. Knowing this information may assist staff in understanding the emotional state of the family, setting realistic goals for treatment with the family and minimizing untoward emotional reactions toward the family's behavior.

The Uninvolved Family

Though all low-cohesion families appear to be uninvolved, the term "uninvolved" is used with this particular type of family. They present a combination of low cohesion and a poor working relationship with the staff despite a general acceptance of the trauma.

Like the bad-match family, the uninvolved family may have a poor working relationships with professionals because of unspecified cultural or personality factors. A change in staff or treatment facility may ameliorate this problem. Unlike the bad-match family, however, the uninvolved family may remain uninvolved regardless of the professional staff working with them. The practitioner must distinguish between the effects on the working relationship of personality factors (matching) between professionals and families, and the effects of low cohesion. For the uninvolved family, treatment to address the low cohesiveness of the family members should come before attempts to change treatment facilities or personnel in order to improve the family's involvement in the survivor's treatment program.

The Isolated Family

The isolated family is so named because they are isolated from each other by low cohesion, isolated from professional staff by weak relationships with the outside world and isolated from their own feelings by their denial of the trauma. These families present as distraught, overwhelmed and unfocused. The enormity of the trauma has taxed all of their resources and left them uncertain about how to make sense out of the situation or where to begin to take action.

The bewilderment of such families and their tendency to be isolated may lead them to be overlooked in the course of treatment. The practitioner should not mistake their lack of involvement for a lack of need. Indeed, the practitioner provides a critical service for such families by seeking to establish a connection with them to lead them out of their isolation.

The discussion of categorization of families in terms of their adaptation to the trauma is admittedly somewhat artificial. Factors such as cohesion, relationships with the outside world, and acceptance are not clear-cut characteristics nor do they vary on a simple high/low basis. Moreover, each family may show characteristics of different types of families during the course of the survivor's rehabilitation. Despite these variations, it is felt that certain patterns of family behavior do exist. It is hoped that the current attempt to characterize families with respect to specific aspects of family functioning will stimulate discussion and research into the characteristics of families after brain injury to a family member. Such work would be of great benefit to the assessment and treatment of families. For the rehabilitation practitioner, an understanding of the family type, what causes the type to develop the way it does, and how the family's characteristics can affect the course of treatment constitute an important part of the psychological assessment of the family.

SUMMARY

Rather than a cut-and-dried process, the psychological assessment of the family should be a comprehensive process of engaging family members in discussion with the practitioner and in involvement in the rehabilitation treatment process. The practitioner seeks to understand the family members as individuals and as a dynamic group. This understanding is accomplished through observation of the family in the psychological interview, in their reactions to the survivor and their interactions with the rehabilitation treatment team. The multifaceted assessment of the family sets the stage for the family's involvement in psychological treatment. The framework for this treatment process will be described in the next chapter.

4

Psychological Treatment Techniques

In the evaluation of the family, the practitioner establishes the foundation of a working relationship with the family and sets goals for treatment. During psychological treatment the practitioner and family seek to achieve these goals and in the course of doing so further develop their working relationship. Before discussing goals and subsequent psychological treatment, some of the practical arrangements of providing psychological treatment will be reviewed. These practical issues are important because they provide a context for the family and for the practitioner that helps to focus their efforts in treatment.

PRACTICAL ARRANGEMENTS

Whom to Meet

The enormous burdens of the brain-injury rehabilitation process and other life obligations lead family members to distribute family duties among the people available. Depending on the family and the survivor, a wide range of individuals may come in to visit or to observe rehabilitation treatment with the survivor. Because psychological treatment is one of many treatments provided to the brain-injury survivor and family, it is likely that the practitioner will have some difficulty assuring that family treatment is provided to the same group of people in each family from one session to the next. For this reason some modifications have to be made in the customary expectation that a set group of family members will participate in family psychological treatment.

In order to maintain consistency in treatment the practitioner should designate one person as the central figure in treatment for each family. This person would be required to attend each psychological meeting and to communicate information to other family members. For example, one of two parents could be designated with this role in the case of an injured child. In the case of an injured spouse, usually the other spouse would be designated with this role. Beyond this contact person, a core group of people should be designated as the individuals involved in treatment with the contact person. These might include the other parent and siblings of an injured child or the children and older parents of an injured spouse. Treatment should thus include the primary person and any other members of the core group who are able to come to the meeting. Individuals who are not members of the core group should be excluded from psychological treatment meetings. These family members may be invited to participate in treatment in other ways rather than psychological treatment sessions. For example, families often report that they would prefer to be with the survivor in physical or occupational therapy rather than come in for a psychological appointment. Other family members not involved in psychological treatment might be able to attend these physical therapy or occupational therapy appointments with the survivor while the central family members meet with the practitioner.

To facilitate communication, some type of treatment summary and family log can be completed at the end of each session. This may be as simple as a list of items that have been discussed during the session. The key family member keeps a copy of the summary in a log book, and a copy of the summary is kept by the practitioner. The log will facilitate communication and consistency between treatment sessions. It allows family members who were present during the session to review what was discussed on their own time. It also allows family members who were not present to keep up-to-date on psychological treatment. Treatment logs are particularly useful when psychological treatment has an emphasis on education or on resolving practical problems. In these cases the concrete nature of the treatment discussion lends itself nicely to summaries in a treatment log.

The practitioner and key family member will need to be mindful of confidentiality in keeping such a record of treatment. This is particularly the case when psychological treatment focuses on emotional support and resolving emotional conflicts. To avoid potential problems it is recommended that the practitioner review the idea of keeping a log of treatment at the outset of treatment. Family members and the practitioner can agree on how to phrase the content of what was discussed in treatment in a general way that does not violate confidentiality.

Despite this written record of treatment, the disadvantage of having one contact person for family treatment is that it allows some degree of distortion to enter the treatment process. The practitioner should keep in mind that the contact person may give a spin to the information that was discussed in the treatment session. Written summaries of treatment can minimize but not remove the effect of this problem.

When to Meet

Individual and family psychotherapy treatments are customarily held on a weekly basis. In a rehabilitation setting, the treatment may vary depending on the immediacy of problems that are being addressed, and the availability of the family members. Yet some minimum treatment frequency should be established to keep open lines of communication. Weekly meetings are a good minimum treatment for an acute rehabilitation setting. Any less frequent treatment may lead the practitioner to lose contact with the family and cause the family to seek out other professionals to help with emotional and psychological concerns. More frequent treatment may be desirable to handle specific, emergent problems. Such a schedule does, however, place an additional burden on the family to come in to the rehabilitation facility when they are already extremely burdened.

At the postacute, long-term care and community reentry stages of rehabilitation, psychological treatment may be, but not necessarily should be, less than weekly. The frequency of treatment at these stages will depend on the specific needs of the family. In general, survivors at these stages are making less dramatic changes in their rehabilitation status. The lengths of stay at these facilities are longer. Thus, less frequent treatment may be advised. On the other hand, families at these stages in rehabilitation may have just begun to accept the long-term realities of the brain trauma and may require more intensive psychological treatment than they did at the acute rehabilitation facility.

Although rehabilitation settings differ in their goals and format of treatment it is important that some system of regular communication between the practitioner and the family be in place. To resolve the matter of frequency of treatment it is recommended that the practitioner raise the issue with the rehabilitation team. Other team members may be aware of issues that the family wishes to discuss or other reasons for setting a particular frequency of visits. The issue should also be raised with the family in terms of what they can realistically manage to do and what their goals are for treatment. Even if the family is unable, unwilling, or not felt to be in need of weekly face-to-face psychology sessions, they might be contacted by phone on a weekly basis by the practitioner. These phone contacts may be brief and limited to asking the family if they have any questions, similar to the educational format of treatment described later in this chapter. If a face-to-face treatment session is felt to be needed based on this conversation the practitioner can schedule it at that point.

Regardless of the actual frequency of treatment sessions, a set appointment time for treatment is desirable. The family and practitioner should determine the date and time. This will help the practitioner and family plan their schedules and make the meetings appear more purposeful and focused. It is not always possible for the practitioner to make a committment to a regular appointment given the nature of admissions and crises that occur in a rehabilitation setting. The set appointment time with the family should be, however, a goal for the practitioner.

Cancelled appointments are inevitable and because rehabilitation psychology treatment services are often covered by insurance policies the families may not face a financial charge as the result of missed or cancelled appointments. Yet, a cancellation policy should be expressed to the family as though they were responsible for the missed appointments. Asking for 24–48 hours notice for a change in appointment allows the practitioner enough time to fill an appointment slot and communicates to the family the value the practitioner places on his or her time with the family. Cancellation policies and therapy schedules should also be reviewed with the rehabilitation treatment team. Although there are cases in which a family may be detained by other important medical or program planning appointments, all staff should agree to encourage the family's adherence to the schedule of appointments and minimize changes to the schedule that might suggest the schedule itself is unimportant.

The practitioner should remain flexible to allow for crisis meetings with the family, those called on the request of the family or on the request of other staff members. In addition, informal contacts with the family that occur when paths are crossed in the rehabilitation facility should not be avoided. For example, if the practitioner unexpectedly meets the family in the cafeteria it is appropriate to stop and chat briefly with them. The rigid psychotherapy policy of few contacts between the therapist and patient between scheduled appointments has no place in a brain-injury rehabilitation setting. The informal meetings with the family solidify the contact that the family might feel with the practitioner and deepen their sense of familiarity with the practitioner. It also demonstrates that the practitioner is an integral part of the rehabilitation facility and in contact with other rehabilitation team members as part of his or her role. The practitioner can increase the probability of such informal meetings by spending a certain portion of the work week in the evenings, when families are more likely to visit, or by doing documentation at the nurses' station rather than in a private office. In this way the practitioner is more visible to families when they visit with survivors.

The practitioner should also be aware that some families may take advantage of such informal meetings. Overinvolved families may seek frequent contacts with the practitioner outside of scheduled appointments. These contacts may lead the practitioner to become resentful or be tempted to avoid running into such families. Other families may feel that a formal meeting with the practitioner is not necessary because they just spoke in the cafeteria or hallway. The practitioner can avoid such misunderstandings by setting proper limits on informal contacts and reminding family members to bring up some of the information discussed informally in the scheduled appointment session.

In addition to informal meetings in which no particular treatment issues are discussed, the practitioner should be available to families in a crisis. These contacts will also deepen the relationship between families and the practitioner. These crisis appointments must be scheduled with care, particularly if they are not requested by the family. Occasionally, other members of the rehabilitation treatment team may observe a problem and request psychological intervention. The practitioner will need to decide whether such a problem warrants an additional meeting or whether it can be handled through regularly scheduled meetings. To request an additional meeting with the family when they may not perceive a need for one may disrupt the trust they have developed in the practitioner and suggest that he or she and other members of the rehabilitation team are plotting treatment without the family's knowledge or involvement.

Where to Meet

Despite the value of informal meetings, the best location for the family's regular psychological treatment sessions is the practitioner's office. It may be difficult to draw families away from the survivor's bedside or from the nursing unit in an acute rehabilitation setting, or from other rehabilitation therapy activities in any rehabilitation setting. Time with the survivor is precious for the families and the practitioner's appointment may be seen as an intrusion. The family and practitioner may be tempted to try to accomplish two things at once by meeting at the survivor's bedside, in a lounge area near the bedside or in a rehabilitation therapy area (for example, the physical therapy gymnasium area). These locations are fine for informal or brief crisis meetings described above but they are not suitable for regular psychological appointments.

The location for psychological therapy should communicate the importance and confidential nature of treatment. Thus, a private office, free from distractions and with minimal chance of interruption is best. If the practitioner's office is not available for some reason, then another private office should be found. Another advantage of regularly scheduled appointments with the family is that office space, a premium in rehabilitation settings, can be reserved in advance. When a regular appointment location has been used the practitioner and family may find that the principles of classical conditioning will favorably affect both of them. That is, the milieu of the office will come to be associated with the therapeutic work that is done in that location thereby facilitating the work itself.

TREATMENT GOALS AND CLINICAL
INTERVENTION

Behavior therapy theories of psychological treatment (Lazarus, 1972; Mahoney, 1974; Rimm & Masters, 1974) have focused on the importance of objective and quantifiable goals for psychological treatment. The fact that
continued reimbursement for traumatic brain-injury treatment is often
linked to achievement of goals makes the statement of such goals a particularly important part of the rehabilitation process. In order to span the
length of recovery for a traumatic brain-injury survivor, goals should be
stated for both the short- and long-term, and be open to reevaluation
(Symington, 1984). A rule of thumb in setting short-term goals is to focus on
a period of 1 to 3 months. This period of time corresponds to seasons of the
year and may be readily grasped by the family (for example, getting through
the winter). Long term goals can be conceptualized in a framework that is
longer than three months.

The actual nature of the goals and subsequent psychological treatment
will vary depending on the family's receptivity to the treatment intervention. It is felt that all families of traumatic brain-injury survivors can be
involved in psychological treatment if the treatment goals can be presented
in a manner that is understandable and meaningful to the family, and if
the subsequent treatment intervention is gauged to the family's level of
emotional adjustment. "The particular approach with a given family will
depend on several factors, including the constellation of the family system,
its adaptability and flexibility in accommodating to the impact of the brain
injury on family functioning, and the physical and emotional resources of
its members" (Rosenthal & Young, 1988, p. 45). Very often treatment is
disrupted at an early stage because goals and treatment interventions inappropriate to the family's level of functioning were set up by the professional.

In describing goals and psychological treatment, four levels are described. These are arranged in order of increasing intimacy and confrontation to the family. Psychological intervention with the families of survivors
will encompass elements of all levels of intervention. The practitioner must
gauge the treatment intervention to the family's needs at that time. For purposes of description, however, each level of goals and intervention will be
considered separately.

FOUR LEVELS OF PSYCHOLOGICAL INTERVENTION

Education

The least intimate but perhaps most important focus for psychological intervention for families is education. In effect, the goals of psychological treatment are to answer the family's questions about rehabilitation and to inform them about the course of recovery in a way that is meaningful and understandable to them. Psychological treatment is an educational process.

This type of intervention is relevant for families at all phases of the brain-injury rehabilitation process. Minuchin (1974), writing about family therapy in general, cites the importance of education as part of treatment. Clinicians and researchers in the field of traumatic brain-injury rehabilitation uniformly recommend family education as a basis for treatment intervention (Greif & Matarazzo, 1982; Kozloff, 1987; Lezak, 1986; Prigatano et al., 1986; Rosenthal et al., 1990). Families have a multitude of questions about the course of rehabilitation, yet the physician or other team members are often too busy to take time to answer them. Gouvier et al. (1988) have noted that family members have many misconceptions about the effects of brain injury even if these are not articulated to the professional staff in their questions. Often families have already received information from friends and associates before they even have had contact with professionals (Felker, 1988). The lack of accurate information about the traumatic brain injury and its effect on the survivor can interfere with the family members' ability "to view the patient more objectively" (Lezak, 1986, p. 245). "Families who cling to incorrect beliefs (about the survivor) are not likely to create an environment that is consistent with promoting optimal recovery" (Gouvier et al, 1988, p. 341). Moreover, the family may feel alienated from the rehabilitation process if they are unable to have their questions answered.

Regular meetings with the practitioner that are specifically designed to review key questions and to discuss the implications of them may be a means of fulfilling this need for families. In this way the family's continued involvement in the treatment process can be strengthened. By showing a willingness to listen to the family's questions and an ability to answer the questions, the practitioner demonstrates his or her concern about the survivor and the family, thereby strengthening the working relationship with the family.

The actual structure for psychology meetings with an educational format need not be any more complicated than reviewing those questions that families have and providing answers for them. The use of educational materials such as written handouts or recommendations for books and video resources can be incorporated into the treatment session. The NHIF maintains an extensive list of such resources available via mail order.

> Case example: A 30-year-old man, in a post acute rehabilitation program, was physically unimpaired but showed confusion, expressive and receptive language difficulties and impaired memory. His parents were seen by the psychologist for an initial meeting. In the course of this meeting, it became clear that basic concepts about their son's injury had not been explained to them at the acute medical nor acute rehabilitation settings. Although they recognized that he had sustained a serious injury and required rehabilitation, they were baffled by his behavior and by the different treatments provided within the rehabilitation setting. The psychologist decided to spend the first several meetings simply answering the parents' questions about their son's behavior. This included understanding concepts such as coma and its relationship to the injury, and the nature of the cognitive difficulties he was experiencing and how they were related to the brain injuries.

It is helpful for the practitioner to have a general outline of the key points he or she wishes to cover during the course of such an educational meeting. For example, when the survivor is at an early stage of recovery, the practitioner may want to bring up the topics of cognitive arousal and agitation if the family has not asked any specific questions about them. In this way, the professional is anticipating issues that may arise and this may allow families the freedom to ask in more detail about these topics. The ability to cite or provide other educational materials in the course of such sessions is not only helpful to the family but lends greater credibility to the practitioner's experience. This is important as a basis for developing trust with the family.

Educational contacts between the practitioner and family can be formalized into a group educational format. Some rehabilitation facilities have provided such educational programs in the form of 4 to 8 week groups with a different topic presented each week. These groups are moderated by a mental health professional and other rehabilitation staff, and may be integrated with support groups that are discussed in Chapter Six. Such educational groups provide the shared experience with other families that may be supportive to each family member, and the groups stimulate a wider range of discussion. Such groups should not, however, be seen as a substitute for regular meetings with the practitioner. The goal of psychological intervention with families at the early stages of rehabilitation is to establish trust between the family, the practitioner, and the rehabilitation facility. This trust will be critical for the difficult decisions of rehabilitation treatment in the future. This is best done in individual meetings.

For a family especially reluctant to participate in psychological treatment, the educational approach to treatment is apt to be less threatening than more traditional verbal psychotherapy. If the family is still uncertain about their involvement in psychological treatment of this type, the educational approach can be presented by having the practitioner claim that the meetings are useful to clarify questions he or she may have about the family. The practitioner might say to the family, "Even if you don't have any pressing questions at the time of our regular meeting, it would be useful for us to meet because I may have some questions myself or questions raised by other team members that they did not have a chance to ask you before."

Treatment intervention to meet educational goals is different than psychotherapy treatment. Treatment sessions may be limited to 20 to 30 minutes weekly. No attempt is made to confront the family by investigating underlying emotional conflicts. Beyond answering the family's questions, the goals are to continue the family's meetings with the psychologist on a regular basis, to keep open lines of communication and to prepare the family for issues that the practitioner anticipates will be of concern to the family during the course of rehabilitation. In this way, family participation in treatment is solidified; a means is established for handling crises that may occur in the family or between the family and the treatment team.

The disadvantage of such a framework for psychological treatment is that it is dependent on the amount of educational information that the family needs at a given time and which rehabilitation professional should properly provide the information. For example, families may be better able to have their questions about physical therapy directly answered by the physical therapist, rather than waiting for a meeting with the psychologist. In fact, it is sensible to have the physical therapist answer such questions as long as the focus remains on the question at hand. When the discussion goes beyond the question to issues of an emotional nature, however, the physical therapist or other rehabilitation therapist may be unwilling or unprepared to handle the problem. Thus it is essential that team members agree on a means of handling the family's questions. There should be encouragement among all team members to have the family meet regularly with the practitioner for these purposes.

Case example: The physical therapist asked the psychologist to discuss with the family the slow progress that their family member was making in physical therapy. The family had continually asked the physical therapist if the survivor would ever walk stairs independently. The physical therapist did not feel that walking stairs independently was a realistic goal. In discussing the matter with the psychologist the physical therapist revealed uneasiness about telling the family such negative information, fearing the family would get angry or upset with the therapist. The psychologist explained to the physical therapist, however, that she was not comfortable giving the family information about the survivor's physical functioning. It was agreed that both the psychologist and physical therapist would meet with the family and discuss the survivor's goals for walking. As expected the family became upset with this news. But using their expertise together the physical therapist and psychologist felt that they were able to give the family a consistent message while still showing support and understanding to them.

Another potential disadvantage of the educational format for psychological intervention is that the practitioner will feel that he or she must be able to answer all of the family's questions. At times, the practitioner may appropriately refer the family to other members of the rehabilitation team in order to answer a particular question, or promise to contact the team member him or herself and report back to the family with an answer. However, many aspects of brain-injury rehabilitation and recovery are uncertain and there will be no clear answer. Telling the family honestly "I don't know," and expressing the desire to assist them in finding an answer to their questions will facilitate their trust in the practitioner. Having shared with the family his or her own uncertainty about a given question, the practitioner may be able to use the opportunity to discuss with the family "the unavoidable uncertainty" of some aspects of brain-injury treatment and the effect of the uncertainty on the family (NIHR, 1984, p. 3).

Resolving Practical Problems

The traumatic brain-injury survivor's hospitalization presents the family with practical adjustment problems in daily living. Often these practical problems have emotional implications for the family. For example, concerns about visitation policy while the survivor is hospitalized, concerns about schooling, finances, or discharge planning are problems that require a concrete solution yet have emotional underpinnings. Some families may feel that the resolution of these concrete, practical problems has a more direct impact on the survivor's recovery than resolution of underlying emotional concerns. A family's personality style may lead them to resolve emotional problems indirectly by working through concrete problems. The psychology treatment session with the family can provide a nonthreatening environment in which to review the problem, decide on a plan of action, and if necessary discuss the emotional ramifications of the decision.

The precedents for such a focus for psychological treatment have been described by D'Zurilla (1988). "A problem is . . . a life situation that demands a response for effective functioning, but for which no effective response is immediately available to the individual (or group)" (D'Zurilla,

1988, p. 87). He describes a method for assessing the problem, generating alternative responses, and implementing a course of action as part of the psychological treatment process. The importance of taking into consideration emotional factors and the importance of a "positive therapeutic relationship" (p. 117) are also cited as components of the problem-solving approach. With specific regard to professional treatment of families with a disabled family member, Goolsby (1976) notes that "a forum, where ideas can be tested and feedback given on probable consequences of a specific course, can be of real help (to the family)" (p. 333).

In treatment sessions, the practitioner can avoid offering opinions or making decisions about the question at hand by clarifying at the outset of treatment his or her limitations in offering information and by adopting a moderator or facilitator role rather than an expert role. Using the format developed by D'Zurilla (1988) the practitioner should approach the problem through several steps: defining the problem, generating alternative courses of action, making decisions about the alternatives, implementing a plan of action and reevaluating the situation to see if the problem has been properly solved (p. 92).

The practitioner encourages the family members to define the problem by describing it in specific terms. The practitioner then serves as a moderator to help the family brainstorm different methods of solving the problem. The advantages and disadvantages of various courses of action with respect to a problem are discussed by family members. Rather than attempting to resolve the problem for the family, the practitioner encourages the family to develop a method of handling the problem that is comfortable for them. Comments from the practitioner are seen as suggestions not prescriptions. The practitioner may also assist with implementation of the selected course of action, particularly if it involves other members of the treatment team or aspects of the rehabilitation facility's functioning. During the course of the regular meetings with the family, the family and the practitioner can reevaluate the problem and determine if any modifications in the selected course of action need to be made.

Awareness of the feeling expressed by family members in a discussion can be used by the practitioner to help families recognize the emotional impact of the problem on them. In this way, the transition to discussion of emotions can be made without overtly confronting the family about these issues. For example, parents that were discussing decisions about who would visit the survivor were, with the practitioner's facilitation, able to also discuss some of their feelings about their control over the survivor. Their wish to remold the survivor after the injury was one aspect of their wish to monitor his social relationships by controlling visitors.

In pursuing the problem-solving approach to treatment, it is important that some method of documentation be developed by the practitioner. This documentation should indicate the alternatives considered and the plan of action selected. Some clinicians have emphasized the value of placing the information in the form of a contract (DeNour & Bauman, 1980, p. 27). The contract provides a focus for discussions in psychological treatment sessions and a record of the work accomplished in order to minimize misunderstandings and misinterpretations.

The advantages of setting this focus for treatment is that there is a means of resolving such problems in a formalized manner, one that combines the family's view of the problem with the input from the professional team via the practitioner. The practitioner and family work together in a productive manner, one that does not necessarily require the family to be overly emotionally intimate with the practitioner. "Therapy is biased towards the pragmatic and the practical" (Jennett & Teasdale, 1981, p. 268) rather than emotional problems. This can give the family a sense of purpose and motivation for treatment and a clear way of determining if treatment has been beneficial. The beneficial effects of problem-solving skills in family members has been associated with increased compliance with treatment (Evans et al., 1987, p. 515) and with their behavior toward the survivor (Braswell & Kendall, 1988).

> Case example: The family of a 15-year-old boy, at Level V on the Rancho scale, discussed with the psychologist whether his girlfriend should visit. Although the psychologist recognized that this problem represented strong emotional concerns about parental control and disapproval of the survivor's past relationship with the girlfriend, treatment focused on discussing the matter of visitation from a more practical standpoint. The family was focused on the potential advantages and disadvantages that such a visitation would have for the survivor. These advantages included the possibility of increased socialization, cognitive and emotional stimulation, Disadvantages that were cited included the depression, frustration or other emotional disruption that would be caused by the visit. The psychologist met separately with the girlfriend to discuss her feelings about visiting.

This example shows that the family was able to discuss an emotional issue in a more comfortable way by focusing on the practical aspects of the problem. The practitioner chose to mediate between the girlfriend and the family rather than incorporating the girlfriend into the family meetings. Because the girlfriend was not formally a member of the family and, in fact, the family had reservations about any involvement with her, it did not seem appropriate to allow family sessions with the practitioner to be diluted by the addition of an outsider. The focus of discussion on what would be best for the survivor himself rather than on the family's direct feelings about the matter was also a way of presenting the issue in a manner that would be less threatening to the family. The decision about visitation in this case was intentionally omitted to emphasize that the manner in which the practitioner presents and discussed problems with the family is more important in terms of the relationship between the practitioner and family than the actual decisions that are made.

The disadvantage of the problem-solving treatment focus is that it is again dependent on having practical problems to discuss. Some goals such as discharge planning or academic and vocational planning are ongoing problems that require regular discussion. Even with these problems, there may be periods of time when nothing further needs to be discussed. This is especially possible given the long period of time which brain-injury rehabilitation treatment may span. At such times, the family's commitment to psychological treatment may waver.

Another disadvantage to such a treatment focus is that the importance of a psychologist or a mental health professional is not readily apparent to the family. The problem-solving approach to treatment, like the educational format described earlier, presents a different role for the psychologist than the family (or the psychologist) may expect. The impact of the psychologist may be diluted by the family's contacts with other rehabilitation team professionals. For example, decisions regarding medication usage or surgery may appear to the family to be issues to discuss with the physician rather than the mental health professional. Furthermore, if the emotional aspects that underlie the practical problems are not addressed, the mental health professional may inadvertently communicate to the family that such emotional matters are not important.

Finally, the practitioner who designs treatment with a focus on practical problems may be asked to offer comments on matters beyond his or her area of expertise. For example, the practitioner may be asked to comment on legal or medical issues in the course of discussing a given problem. It is a fine line between facilitating a discussion on a subject and offering information or judgments that, though well-supported, may be outside of the practitioner's realm of training and expertise.

In order to overcome these potential disadvantages of a problem-solving approach to treatment, there must be a clear understanding among rehabilitation team members about how to handle key decisions or problems that the survivor and family are facing. This understanding means an agreement among team members that certain practical problems will be addressed by the practitioner in his or her meetings with the family and not dealt with in other rehabilitation therapy sessions. Such an agreement can be accomplished through general discussion among all team members.

After it has been determined that the practitioner will handle discussion of certain practical problems, other team members may give their input on the matter to the practitioner via regular team meetings or through informal meetings with the practitioner. When the matter comes up in meetings between the family and other team members, the practitioner will need to give the rehabilitation staff ways of redirecting the family in a clear but not antagonistic manner. For example, the rehabilitation therapist might be instructed by the practitioner to say, "I know that this question is an important one for you, but I think that the psychologist would be best able to help with it. If I take time out of my physical therapy session to talk to you about it, it will result in less physical therapy treatment for the survivor and that will not be helpful to him/her."

Ventilation and Support

The uncertainty and change imposed on a family by the traumatic brain injury may leave them with little time themselves to grieve for the losses they are experiencing and to express the powerful emotions they feel. The practitioner can provide a nonthreatening, supportive environment for this emotional expression to occur. Thus, an appropriate goal and direction for treatment with the family members may be simply to give them the opportunity to become aware of their feelings, and to express them without having to discuss or reflect on them.

This treatment focus is more consistent with what many people expect from a psychological treatment session than the other treatment foci mentioned previously. The value of ventilating emotions in psychotherapy has been amply described by many practitioners in the field (Rogers, 1951; Bugenthal, 1987; Yalom, 1985). The mental health practitioner is an objective, yet involved, professional who attempts to facilitate the family's ability to handle the emotional aspects of their predicament. The psychological treatment session becomes a haven from the activity of the rest of the rehabilitation therapy program. The practitioner allows the family to express feelings without judging the feelings. The practitioner seeks to support the family by validating their experiences as a normal reaction to a traumatic event and supporting their coping skills as family members. "The nurturance, healing, and support a family offers its members are vital for the individual family members and for maintenance of the family system. The therapist must be aware of the importance of these functions and know how to encourage them" (Minuchin, 1974, p. 156).

It is especially important to present an atmosphere that is nonevaluative and affirmative of the family's right to their feelings. Rehabilitation treatment for the brain-injury survivor, and life in general, is focused on continuous evaluation and reevaluation of one's standing with respect to another person or to norms. The survivor is assessed and reassessed in terms of his or her progress in therapy. Likewise, families question whether their feelings are appropriate or inappropriate for their situation. In the psychology session, evaluation is suspended. All feelings are permitted to be expressed and are supported as a means of working through the emotional sequelae of the trauma (cf., Lezak, 1978).

> Case example: The spouse of an injured woman discussed with the psychologist his feelings of wishing to reject and run away from his wife. He had never been unfaithful to his wife although their relationship was marked by periods of stress during which they were briefly separated. He experienced intense feelings of guilt at having these thoughts and questioned whether he was ever committed to the marriage in the first place. These feelings were punctuated by numerous vivid memories about his past relationship with his wife. The psychology sessions were focused on letting him express these feelings without any attempt to speculate or introspect about the cause of such feelings. The psychologist attempted to confirm that such feelings were commonly experienced by individuals in this predicament and did not indicate that anything about this man's commitment to marriage or to his wife at the present time was flawed.

This case also indicates an area of adjustment difficulty for many family members: the tendency to judge present behavior by past, pretrauma standards. In this case, the man judged his marriage by the criterion of not having any second thoughts about his commitment to her. Were he to have been seen for psychological treatment prior to the accident with the presenting problem of thoughts about leaving or rejecting his wife, certainly one hypothesis to be investigated in treatment was his level of commitment to his wife and his feelings about the relationship. Under the stress of the trauma, however, such thoughts are not necessarily indicative of underlying problems in the relationship. The practitioner must be able to differentiate the acute emotional reaction to the trauma from any long-standing emotional reactions. In working with the family, the practitioner must be able to educate the family member about the influence that both acute and longstanding difficulties have on the individual's present behavior and to refrain from automatically judging present behavior by past standards. The trauma is a unique situation that should be judged by unique standards, many of which the family member may not have yet formulated.

The principle of suspended evaluation during a psychology treatment session is difficult to enact. The practitioner must be mindful of the influence his or her values have on his ability to provide support. The practitioner may struggle with his or her temptation to evaluate families' feelings as appropriate or inappropriate. The fact that the family member is feeling comfortable enough to express the feeling should be supported regardless of the nature of the feeling and the practitioner's own reaction to it. "The therapist should be a healer: a human being concerned with engaging other human beings, therapeutically, around areas and issues that cause them pain, while always retaining great respect for their values, areas of strength, and aesthetic preferences" (Minuchin & Fishman, 1981, p. 1). In the case mentioned above, one challenge for the psychologist was not allowing his feelings about marriage and commitment to interfere with the family members' expression of such feelings and subsequent discussion of them.

The practitioner must recognize that ventilation and support of emotions may be ends in themselves for some families. Many of the powerful feelings of grief, anger, and sadness experienced by the families are normal reactions to a traumatic situation. These reactions do not necessarily indicate underlying pathology. Treatment that becomes focused on a deeper analysis of the sources of symbolic meanings of a family's emotional reactions may force some families into a level of intimacy greater than they wish to tolerate. If they withdraw from treatment for this reason, they will be deprived of the important opportunity to ventilate feelings and to validate them as normal reactions.

Moreover, the practitioner must be sensitive to how embarrassing or humiliating some families may find these emotional reactions to be, regardless of how normal they may be. The practitioner should reinforce the family members for having the courage to express such distressing feelings by acknowledging how difficult it might be to do so. At times, families may seek to avoid contact with the practitioner in order to avoid further embarrassment or they may come to associate the therapy session with the distressing emotions that are expressed in the sessions. As one family member has said, "I feel that every time I see you, I'm going to talk about something that makes me cry." To avoid this situation, the practitioner should forewarn family members that it is a common occurrence in psychological treatment for individuals to want to withdraw from treatment after having expressed sensitive or emotionally intense feelings. If the practitioner notices that a family appears to be avoiding treatment after an emotionally tumultuous session, he or she should bring this to the family's attention and help the family to overcome any tendencies to withdraw from treatment that they may be experiencing.

The issue of crying in treatment deserves several comments. The practitioner should not equate crying with emotional expressiveness nor vice versa. The trauma causes a wide range of feelings in family members. Some of these may cause the family to cry in sadness, anger, frustration, or shame. The fact that the family members are tearful does not necessarily mean that the session has been a valuable one for them. The practitioner must be able to help the family members recognize the connection between their inner feelings and the outward expression of it, which may be crying.

Similarly, the absence of crying in a treatment session does not mean that the family has not used the time well for emotional expression. There are many other behavioral expressions of inner feelings besides crying. In a psychological treatment session these may include: yelling, ruminating, arguing, moving about the room or silence, to name a few. The family members' decision to cry or not cry about something may reflect their degree of comfort with the practitioner or be a characteristic way of handling distressing emotions. Well-meaning, but untrained, counselors may attempt to elicit crying from a client because the counselor believes that to do so would be the equivalent of healthy emotional expression. The result of such a treatment intervention is the exact opposite; the client feels controlled and manipulated rather than supported by the counselor. Bowen (1978) has recognized this point with families in stating, "an attempt to get the family to express feelings at the moment of change . . . does not necessarily increase the level of emotional integration" (p. 325).

The practitioner must have a refined clinical sense of how much emotional expressiveness the family can tolerate, and when intervention should be made to facilitate further expressiveness or to allow the family to regain self-control. A family member that has been expressing grief or sadness throughout the treatment session may need a period of five or ten minutes before the end of a session in order to regain composure. It would be appropriate for the practitioner to allow time for this rather than cutting the person off at the rigid time limit regardless of their emotional state at the time. This can be done with an informal statement such as, "We will need to stop our session in a few minutes. Take these few minutes now for yourself to compose yourself before we stop."

Although some families may come to associate the psychology session with the expression of emotions, emotional expression is not and should not be limited to psychological treatment sessions. Other rehabilitation team members need to know how to handle the family should the family become distressed during these other rehabilitation treatment sessions. The practitioner will need to develop a system by which rehabilitation professionals such as physical, occupational, and speech therapists and nurses handle such situations. This system should include methods by which the rehabilitation therapists can let the family members express these feelings without involving the therapist in actual counseling. Such involvement would detract from the rehabilitation therapy session or cause the therapists to become embroiled in an emotional situation with the family that is beyond their training to handle. One method of handling this need among other team members is for the practitioner to provide ongoing educational presentations to the rehabilitation staff on basic listening skills.

Resolving Emotional Conflicts and Structural Intervention

At times, education, practical problem-solving, and support are not sufficient psychological interventions for the family. The trauma and the events that follow it may cause emotional conflicts to surface that impede a family's ability to make decisions in treatment and to participate in treatment. In these circumstances, it is appropriate to set resolution of these conflicts as the goal and focus of psychological treatment.

The resolution of such emotional conflicts may be vital to the course of rehabilitation treatment. The psychologist may feel best prepared to help the family in this area. However, the family must be able to tolerate such a focus of treatment before it is begun. The family may be uncomfortable with a focus on their own conflicts and may see this as depriving the survivor of attention and needed treatment intervention. They may feel blamed or exposed by the attention given to their own problems.

> Case example: A forty-year-old woman had been married to her husband for ten years when he suffered a head injury and required lengthy hospitalization in acute and residential treatment programs. One of his continuing problems, resulting from his injury, was temper outbursts with physically threatening behavior toward her during their time together. She stated that their relationship had been a positive one prior to the injury and that this behavior was not characteristic of him. She attempted to remain involved in treatment by visiting him frequently and taking him out of the residence to home and family but she became increasingly alienated from him. In addition ,this woman had been offered a new job and was uncertain about accepting the additional responsibility although she was pleased by the opportunity. She vacillated about accepting this position. She recognized that it was difficult for her to make a decision to take a new job because the job responsibilities might take her further away from her husband, yet in a way she was seeking something that would take her away from her husband. The psychologist identified two aspects of the woman's difficulty that needed to be examined in psychology treatment sessions: her concern about her overall commitment to her husband, and her willingness to set her own needs ahead of or at an equal level to the needs of her husband. Psychology treatment sessions were divided between individual meetings with the woman to discuss her emotional conflicts about making decisions for herself, and meetings with both spouses to discuss their relationship and the impact of the husband's behavior on it.

The above case example illustrates emotional difficulties that were almost certainly the result of the trauma. This conclusion was based on the fact that the relationship between the spouses was not reported to be problematic prior to the head injury, the husband's change in behavior was the result of the injury, and the wife did not report evidence of her indecisiveness prior to the injury. As mentioned in the previous section on supportive treatment, the practitioner must be able to differentiate between the contribution of preexisting and trauma-related emotional stressors in developing an effective treatment plan.

Often this differentiation is made easier by evidence of preexisting problems. There may have been previous psychological treatment sought out by families for problems that are now resurfacing after the injury. In these cases, it is helpful for the practitioner to obtain information about past treatment that has been provided. If the treatment provider is in the geographic area of the rehabilitation facility, it may be helpful to incorporate this person into treatment planning with the family's permission. If this is not possible, the practitioner should be aware of other community resources for helping families with particular conflicts that may be outside his or her area of expertise. The treatment team should be flexible enough to incorporate external people into treatment planning for the benefit of the family and the survivor.

> Case example: A 16-year-old girl had parents who had been divorced several years before her injury. After the injury, conflicts between the parents arose again regarding the extent to which each parent would be involved in treatment with the girl. Conflicts also arose regarding financial issues, home visitation, and discharge. Although the girl had been living with her mother and other siblings, the father now wanted more involvement in the treatment. The psychologist felt that the parents' conflict was interfering with treatment planning and that attention needed to be given to the parents' relationship before other issues could be resolved for the girl. Though the emotional issues involved were complex, the father seemed to be experiencing some degree of guilt about his previous lack of involvement with his daughter and sought to undo this guilt through his current involvement. The mother was angry about loss of control over the daughter and potential loss of control to her ex-husband. Psychological treatment intervention focused on discussion of the parents' relationship and how they viewed their relationship in the context of their daughter's injury. The goal of this treatment was to increase their awareness of the emotional factors affecting their behavior and to increase the communication between the parents about their daughter's behavior in order to help them make effective decisions in treatment.

How emotional problems are resolved depends on the nature of the problem and its relationship to the trauma. Methods of psychological intervention for handling emotional distress are nearly innumerable. In the present book, the importance of understanding family structure in order to plan and implement psychological treatment has been emphasized. In the general family therapy literature, specific techniques of treatment intervention have been developed to apply this theoretical knowledge of the family's structure to the treatment situation (Haley, 1976; Minuchin, 1974; Minuchin & Fishman, 1981; Sherman & Fredman, 1976; Whitaker & Bumberry, 1988). These structural interventions may be adapted to the treatment of families of the brain-injury survivor. These may be particularly useful in treating emotional problems that arise as the result of the trauma. Several interventions will be described and illustrated.

The rationale of structural interventions in psychological treatment is that the family has a certain structure that has developed in response to the personalities of the individuals in the family, and to the environment in which the family functions. It follows, therefore, that changes in the environment may cause a change in structure of the family. In brief, "family therapy postulates that transactional patterns depend on and contain the way people experience reality. Therefore, to change the way family members look at reality requires the development of new ways of interacting in the family" (Minuchin & Fishman, 1981).

A psychological treatment session is a unique environment in which to make such changes. Ideally, the psychological treatment session occurs in a private and supportive setting in which the practitioner works as a concerned but objective professional. With his or her knowledge of the family structure and the problems that the family is seeking to resolve, the psychologist affects the structure of the family within a treatment session by his or her behavior. "Changes in a family structure contribute to changes in the behavior and the inner psychic processes of the members of that system" (Minuchin, 1974, p. 9). The therapist becomes a member of that structure in the course of working with the family. The changes that occur in the treatment session may provide the family with insights or opportunities to develop alternative ways of handling their presenting problems. Several structural treatment interventions are described below. These are only several of the many techniques of structural family intervention that are employed by practitioners in the field (Sherman & Fredman, 1986). The techniques that follow were selected to illustrate the way in which understanding of family structure can be applied to psychological treatment interventions for families of survivors.

Supporting Generational Boundaries

Although parents and children are part of the same family, they do not have the same responsibilities and privileges, nor is communication evenly distributed across family members. The concept of generational boundaries refers to the differences in responsibilities, roles, and communication patterns between members of different generations (for example, parents and children) within a family. This has been described in Chapter Two. It is characteristic of most families, as previously described, for there to be some boundaries between generations. The practitioner needs to be aware of the family hierarchy and respect it (Haley, 1976).

A dramatic change in the family, such as caused by a traumatic brain injury to a family member, can alter the family structure in such a way as to affect the boundaries between generations. This is particularly the case with an injury to a parent of young children. The injured parent is likely to show immature or dependent behaviors as the result of the brain injury. At the same time, the noninjured spouse may rely on children to carry on some of the tasks that the injured parent previously performed. Children may, deliberately or indirectly, become involved in the care of the injured parent. Communication patterns between all members of the family change. In the case of a severely injured parent who does not return home to live with the family, the spouse and children may manage for a lifetime in this new family structure. If the injured parent does return to live with the family, however, conflicts may arise between the survivor's expectations and the new family structure.

Case example: A 35-year-old father of three children was injured in a work-related accident. He was involved in acute rehabilitation treatment for 6 months and postacute, residential treatment for 8 months. During the postacute treatment he was permitted to spend weekends at home with his family. He had also improved from a physical and cognitive standpoint to a point at which he was able to participate in most aspects of family life. His wife reported to the psychologist, however, that he had great difficulty with his children in the area of discipline. The children (ages 7, 10, and 13) did not listen to the father when he asked them to do something; particularly the oldest child who had taken on some responsibility for managing the behavior of the younger children. Prior to the injury, the children were not reported to be usually disobedient and their father took most of the responsibility for discipline. Since he had been away in treatment programs, his wife had taken over the leadership of the household and the children tended to listen to her orders sooner than those of their father. A further complication of this matter was that that man had decreased frustration tolerance since the time of his injury. Although his cognitive functioning had improved he had particular difficulty understanding and communicating subtleties in contacts with others. His wife and the psychologist recognized that this was another reason for his difficulties in relating to his children on home visits. Treatment intervention for this situation involved meeting with the entire family and structuring the session so that father and mother were the primary discussants about what activities would be done on weekends and how problems with the children would be handled. The children were given the opportunity to speak at certain times during the session, but at other times the parents were asked to agree on how to handle the children's interruptions. Through this focus the psychologist was able to observe how the father related to the children and how the father and mother related in their handling of the children. This information allowed the psychologist to make observations and suggestions to the parents about their behavior and to reestablish the father's role as a parent.

The technique of supporting generational boundaries can be helpful in this situation. The practitioner seeks to reestablish the boundaries between parents and children in such a way as to allow parents to have a relationship together, to allow the survivor to relate to his or her children as a parent, and to allow parents to make decisions about childcare together.

Reestablishing generational boundaries can be initiated by several concrete interventions. Within the treatment session the practitioner should attempt to separate the parents and children. Although it is beneficial to have family meetings with the entire family in question, the time may be divided. Within each weekly meeting or from one week to the next the practitioner can alternate meeting with the parents separately and then the full family.

When meeting with the parents separately, they should be encouraged to make decisions about family matters together without the need to discuss the interventions with children or outside individuals. When the entire family is together, the practitioner takes the role of supporting the parents' decisions and their roles as family leaders. Children are asked not to interrupt the parents when they are speaking and to abide by any rules that the parents set.

These interventions alone will not change the family structure. The reactions that they elicit from family members may be particularly meaningful. The difficulty that the noninjured parent may have in making joint decisions with the survivor may be more evident when it occurs within a psychological treatment session. The problem may then be discussed as it is occurring, in a concrete way that will help the noninjured parent to recognize the effect of the spouse's injury on him or her. The reactions of the children to the limits set on them by the practitioner in reinforcing generational boundaries in the treatment session may help the family to see how their behavior as individual family members affects the behavior of the family as whole. The insights derived from these discussions and the opportunity to practice a new way of relating to each other may help the family to change.

Allying with a Subsystem

The previous technique of reinforcing generational boundaries attempts to make a structural change in the family in order to resolve a problem. Within the family there are several subsystems, perhaps the most obvious of these being the subsystems of parents and of children. Communication in the family may be disrupted if the balance of power between these subsystems is not equitable. In order to redress this balance, the psychologist may ally with one of the subsystems during a treatment session. In doing so, the practitioner lends support and power to the subsystem and forces the others in the family to consider that subsystem's point of view in family decisions.

This technique may be most relevant to family work that involves the way in which parents relate to a child who is a brain-injury survivor. Parents may not effectively incorporate the survivor into the family communication and decision making. The survivor may be unable to communicate as well as in the past due to sequelae of the injury. As a result, the survivor's needs are neglected by the family, affecting the survivor's mood and behavior.

The rehabilitation psychologist is often in an ideal position to make an alliance with the survivor in family meetings. Having worked with the survivor and been involved in treatment team review meetings about the survivor's progress, the psychologist may know the survivor's needs and frustrations. The parents, even if they are involved closely with the care of the survivor, may have difficulty accepting the survivor's points of view in a situation.

Case example: Parents of a 23-year-old survivor now living at home brought their son to see the psychologist because they felt that he had difficulty relating to them and to others. He was described as being very quiet and withdrawn at home, but suddenly he would have outbursts without apparent provocation. During these outbursts he would be angry and insulting to his parents, and shove furniture about in the house. The family was interviewed as a whole and the son was seen separately. In the meeting with the family as a whole, the psychologist observed that the parents, particularly the mother, did almost all of the talking. When asked a question by the psychologist during the family meeting the son spoke in brief phrases and did not maintain eye contact. In the individual interview, he was observed to speak more but tended to be slow in his verbalizations and to become distracted by tangential or circumstantial details in making his points. The psychologist felt that some of the problems that the son had in relating to his parents were the combination of his cognitive difficulties in expressing himself and possible difficulties with behavior control as the result of his injury, and his parents' unwillingness to modify their level of conversation with him. By not changing their level of communication with him the parents in effect were denying the changes that had occurred in their son. The psychologist structured treatment sessions by allying with the son in conversations with the parents. This involved encouraging the son to speak in full sentences, allowing him to complete his thoughts, and amplifying or inquiring about tangential ambiguities in his expressions. The psychologist attempted to balance this by encouraging the son to speak in more concrete terms so that his parents would be better able to understand his points.

The practitioner allies with the survivor, or any other subsystem of family members, by listening carefully to what the survivor has to say and allowing the survivor the opportunity to be heard by others (Sherman & Fredman, 1988). By doing so the practitioner gives credibility, confidence and support to what the survivor is saying. The practitioner may seek to clarify or amplify what the survivor is saying by pointing out to the other family members the effect of their behavior on the survivor and offering suggestions on ways in which they are able to better manage the survivor in order to meet their needs. The practitioner's comments are designed to point out to the family their interdependence and how the behavior of one family member affects that of other family members.

Alliances with the survivor or other subsystems are not permanent in the psychological treatment session. The practitioner does not want to lose the objectivity that he or she hopes to communicate to family members. Nor does the practitioner want to overcentralize his or her role with the family, but rather to allow the family's own patterns of handling the problem to be expressed (Minuchin, 1974, p. 140). Moreover, the intervention has to take place within a well-established relationship with the family. Otherwise, the parents may feel betrayed or mistrustful of the practitioner's alliances.

Reframing

Paradoxical techniques are an integral part of many family therapy treatments (Papp, 1981). It is beyond the scope of this book to review them in detail. One of these techniques that is most relevant to the work with families of brain-injury survivors is reframing. In reframing the practitioner attempts to make a behavior or a situation more acceptable to the family by reinterpreting it in a different light. By viewing the behavior or situation differently, the family may then change its behavior in response to this changed impression.

The field of brain-injury rehabilitation is filled with examples of opportunities for reframing. Many times reframing is part of the educational process that is so important to family treatment. The family may, with their limited knowledge of the situation or behavior, interpret a behavior in one way. With more information, the family may see the behavior in a different light.

Depression after traumatic brain injury is one common example. Depressed behaviors such as sad mood, listlessness, and sleep disturbance may begin to be noted in the survivor during the course of recovery. Assuming there is no underlying neurological problem causing these behaviors the family may be distressed to see depression in the family member. By reframing, the practitioner can point out that depression is actually a positive sign because it indicates that the survivor is improving to the point that he or she is aware of difficulties and remembering what he or she could do before the injury. Therefore, rather than a reason for concern, the depression is a reason for satisfaction. This knowledge may lead the family to react differently to the survivor when he or she shows depressed behavior.

Another frequently occurring problem that may be ameliorated by reframing is anger as it is expressed in behavioral outbursts by the survivor. Family members may view any behavioral outbursts or expressions of anger by the survivor as a negative event. In fact, many times such behavioral outbursts are a source of distress for families as will be discussed in Chapter

Five. Yet, at times, such outbursts may be a sign of progress for the survivor, indicating improvements in expressive communication, awareness of frustration or obstacles in the environment or an appropriate reaction to the limitations of the trauma.

Case example: A 25-year-old woman who was over two years postinjury had a history of behavioral outbursts provoked by becoming frustrated with a rehabilitation task. She was able to be redirected from these outbursts because she had such limited attention and memory skills that she did not ruminate about her problem and quickly forgot what caused her to get upset. Her parents were closely involved in her treatment. During the course of her care, she was observed to have longer outbursts that were not as easily ended by redirecting. In addition, she began to make statements expressing her disappointment in herself and anger about her limitations. She continued to have severe attention and memory problems but was observed to be able to remember more things from day to day. Her parents were angry with the staff about their daughter's increase in behavioral problems. They challenged the staff to develop a behavior management program for her or to change therapists to minimize the frustration that their daughter felt. The staff felt that the increase in outbursts was a sign of progress, that she was becoming more aware of her problems, and was able to remember the problems over time. The psychologist made this point to the family in the course of explaining why other interventions designed to decrease the outbursts may not be beneficial. Rather, some group counseling with the woman was begun to give her another outlet for expressing her feelings.

Another common area for reframing concerns dependence and independence. The family may be very involved in the care of the survivor and feel that they are making their best efforts to help the person become more independent. By being so involved, however, they may inadvertently be causing the survivor to become more dependent. He or she may come to expect family help rather than do things independently. Interpreting the family's helping in this way may cause them to change their behavior. The practitioner can offer concrete suggestions about how the family can offer help in a way that fosters, rather than undermines, the independence of the survivor.

A paradoxical technique that does not involve reframing is having the practitioner make predictions about the survivor's or family's behavior. For example, the practitioner may predict that the noncompliant behavior of a given family member will continue after treatment is terminated or when the family member returns home. If the prediction is proved false, the noncompliant behavior of the family member will have been resolved. If the prediction comes true, the practitioner may have gained greater respect from the family for his or her clinical acumen. This may give the practitioner greater leverage with the family in attempting to make changes in the problem behavior in the future.

Prescriptive Techniques

The practitioner may make specific suggestions to the family for changes in their behavior outside of the treatment session. Minuchin and Fishman (1981) refer to this general group of interventions as enactment. The goals of these changes would also be to modify family structure in such a way that maladaptive behaviors or emotional reactions to situation would be changed. The reactions that families have to these changes could be discussed during the treatment sessions with the psychologist.

One type of prescriptive treatment intervention is the establishment of family meetings or councils. In such meetings family members gather at a designated time to discuss issues of concern. The goal of such meetings is to encourage family communication and to establish a time in which other needs are put aside in favor of facilitating communication and togetherness for the whole family. For families of brain-injury survivors, often there is little time for such discussions that might have occurred regularly around the dinner table prior to the injury. Moreover, family members may feel isolated from each other as a result of the hectic pace of keeping up with responsibilities. Finally, the meeting is a way of handling problems at one time, rather than letting such problems be disruptive to the family during the week at several different times. One such family set a 24-hour rule, in which any major problems among family members would be discussed by the family within 24 hours. This rule allowed the family the flexibility to not discuss every issue immediately when it arose, something that may not be beneficial if emotions are running high at the time. But it assured that time would be taken to handle the matter within a given period of time.

Prescribed vacations may also be a way of helping families to cope. These are structural interventions because they are prescribed to specific family members who may need to improve their bond or to separate from other family members. For example, the child who has been involved too closely in the care for his father after the father's brain injury, may experience behavioral or mood disturbances because of his resentment of this role. Prescribing a vacation away from the family for this person is not only helpful for the person as a break, but also forces other family members to see how they would handle the responsibilities in other ways and to structure their lives accordingly.

Summary of Treatment Levels

The distinction between four different levels of treatment goals and interventions are not intended to be rigid. It is likely and desirable that the psychologist will select goals for treatment from each level and that the treatment intervention will change over the course of time. Whatever treatment goals are selected it is important that this selection be based on the assessment of the family's needs and their ability to participate in treatment. Equally important is the need to coordinate psychological treatment goals with other rehabilitation team professionals. The consistency across team members can help to solidify the family's involvement in treatment and prevent future disruption or sabotage of treatment that may occur wittingly or unwittingly.

TECHNICAL DECISIONS IN PSYCHOLOGICAL TREATMENT

The clear statement of goals, the development of guidelines for the structure of psychological treatment meetings, and the ability to be flexible in treatment across the different levels of treatment intervention will establish a sound basis for psychological treatment. During the course of treatment, the practitioner will be faced with several decisions that, although common problems in all types of psychological treatment, require a different response in work with the families of traumatic brain-injury survivors. In the following section these situations will be discussed and some methods for managing them will be offered.

Giving Information and Advice

Psychodynamic approaches to psychotherapy (Langs, 1973; Blanck & Blanck, 1974) emphasize the importance of the therapist's maintaining an objective stance with respect to the patients' presenting problems. Simply giving advice, taking sides in a discussion or offering the therapist's own opinions are discouraged unless these interventions are made in the context of an analysis of the patient's motivations for needing such information and the effect that providing such information will have on the working relationship between the psychotherapist and the patient.

In the realm of family theory and treatment, Haley (1976) has cogently discussed the impact that information provided by the therapist can have on the relationships that develop within treatment. "Information and coalition are synonymous. The act of giving and withholding information across a boundary is an act of forming and dissolving coalitions ... The therapist's position in a hierarchy is largely determined by his control of information" (pp. 217–218). Thus, the decision to provide or not provide information within a treatment session has many implications for the therapist's ability to form bonds with the family members and to accomplish structural treatment interventions.

The role of the psychologist as a source of information and need for education of families has already been discussed. In the milieu of traumatic brain-injury treatment the psychologist will be faced with an intense pressure to go one step beyond providing information and be asked to offer advice to the family. The psychologist will find that all other disciplines providing services to the survivor (for example, medicine, rehab therapies) readily offer opinions within their areas of expertise to the survivor and family. For example, the physical and occupational therapist routinely advise families on suitable home modifications and special equipment needs. Physicians routinely offer their advice on medical matters to families and patients. However, as a result of the traditions of psychotherapy the psychologist is usually ill-prepared to handle requests from families for personal advice.

The practitioner who offers personal opinions about a matter takes several risks. The family's understanding about the opinion, or any other information for that matter, may be difficult to judge. The practitioner's therapeutic efficiency will be undercut unless he or she makes an effort to ensure that the family clearly understands the information that has been communicated. The practitioner should recognize that some people feel it is more polite to feign understanding of a comment from another person rather than to ask for clarification (Minuchin & Fishman, 1981).

Even if the family appears to correctly understand the practitioner's opinion, they may use the information to discredit the practitioner when the advice proves ineffectual. Conversely, the advice may be used as justification for actions beyond what the practitioner may have intended. Families commonly report how the opinions of neurologists or neurosurgeons who saw the survivor at the emergency room have been disproved by the survivor's recovery. They may be similarly suspicious of any other professional advice offered to them about their family member even though their uncertainty may lead them to request such information.

Case example: The siblings of a 55-year-old divorced man discussed with the psychologist the man's long history of difficulties with money management that predated his head injury. This included incurring numerous debts. As he recovered, the family members were uncertain how much control to give him over his money. They asked the psychologist for general recommendations about how much information they should give him about his current financial state including settlement from his accident. They also had specific questions about how much independence the man should have in making decisions about finances. They asked the psychologist how much money the man ought to spend on holiday gifts and on gifts to his children, who lived on their own.

The psychologist attempted to focus the family on discussing their reasons for and against sharing such information with the man. The family members, however, repeatedly asked the psychologist for his opinion and advice.

A strategy for handling requests for advice from families is to provide advice or an opinion but to make efforts to minimize the possible misinterpretation of the opinion. First the practitioner must communicate to the family that all of their questions are important and deserve an answer. This is accomplished by the practitioner's overall behavior of empathy and interest in the family and their predicament, and by the practitioner's manner of structuring psychological treatment to encourage questions and open discussion.

The practitioner should explore with the family their reasons for seeking out an opinion. Although the apparent reason is for information in order to answer a question, there may be covert reasons for a family's desire to obtain outside opinions. It may reflect the family's own uncertainties about their judgment, their reluctance to take control of a situation, or to take responsibility for the outcome of the decision, their feelings about authority or some other reason unique to the family's structure and personality. The discussion of such reasons may lead the family and practitioner to greater insight about their reactions to the trauma.

When the practitioner has an understanding of the overt and covert reasons why an opinion is desired, he or she should clarify the limits of his or her expertise with the family and refer the family to an appropriate professional if necessary for more complete information. The practitioner should provide the family with written notes, booklets or other evidence of the information and opinion given. The family treatment log described earlier is appropriate for this purpose. This documentation may minimize future questions or misunderstandings about the information and avoid the practitioner's becoming involved in a future contradiction of his or her past words should the question come up again.

The practitioner should offer his or her advice in the most specific and concrete manner possible. General statements or predictions about a variety of situations are apt to be misinterpreted and erroneous. Specific opinions about a particular situation or set of conditions are more easily grasped and minimize the potential for misunderstanding.

In offering the advice, the practitioner should also make clear that the ultimate decision and responsibility for a matter rests with the family. Thus, in the example above, although the practitioner might offer advice about how the survivor should manage his money, the family and the survivor are ultimately responsible for the consequences of any given decision about money-making. In this regard, the practitioner must not overvalue his or her expertise and ability to solve problems for the family. By overvaluing his or her abilities, the practitioner can create a situation in which the family will become overly dependent on the practitioner's opinions about any matter.

Though the technique of offering advice should certainly be handled on an individual basis, in the brain-injury rehabilitation environment it is felt that advice-giving can be appropriate. As Yalom (1985) has noted in his observations of advice giving within group therapy situations, though direct advice is not usually beneficial, "indirectly, however, advice giving serves a purpose; the process, rather than the content of the advice, may be beneficial since it implies and conveys mutual interest and caring" (p. 12).

Case example: The wife of a severely impaired man had become pregnant before her husband was injured. As the due date for the pregnancy drew closer, she was uncertain about whether her husband should be present at the labor. He was dependent on nursing care and in a wheelchair. On one hand, she wanted to share the joy of the birth with him. On the other hand, she was uncertain whether the experience would upset him more than please him because of his changed condition. She discussed at length the advantages and disadvantages of each decision. She asked the psychologist his opinion and the psychologist felt that it would not be advisable to have the husband present at the delivery but that the ultimate decision was hers and she should make preparations for having him present in case that was her decision. In fact, she chose to have her husband present. The delivery went smoothly and her husband and she felt that they had shared an important experience together, one which drew them closer after months of rehabilitation treatment had kept them apart. The woman continued to be in contact with the psychologist after the birth and was able to use psychological treatment sessions in order to discuss other issues that were important for her and her husband. The psychologist felt that his experience in discussing the matter with this woman and honestly sharing opinions had also deepened the trust between them and enabled them to continue to work effectively on other issues.

Balancing Confrontation and Support

Support is essential at all levels of psychological treatment. By creating an emotionally supportive atmosphere the practitioner facilitates the development of a trustworthy relationship with the family. This allows the practitioner and family to discuss emotionally sensitive issues in therapy sessions in a way that does not threaten or intimidate the family.

Support is not a passive process. Rather than unconditionally accepting and encouraging all aspects of family functioning, the practitioner actively demonstrates caring for the family's abilities and seeks to reinforce those aspects of the family's functioning that appear adaptive and beneficial to the rehabilitation process. "(A) crucial component to the whole issue of caring is to be respectful of the resources and capabilities of our clients . . . While families may approach us in the midst of a crisis, they are by no means help-less. By virtue of their interconnectedness they have tremendous resources to tap" (Whitaker & Bumberry, 1988, p. 174).

The search for understanding is part of support. Families of brain trauma survivors have undergone a tragedy. All feelings that they experience are worthy of the practitioner's attention and care. In any family, some aspect of their functioning can be found that is admirable or worthy of support. For example, even the most angry family can be appreciated for their devotion to the survivor and the most withdrawn family for their ability to carry on with their own affairs in the face of tragedy. The practitioner's search for un-derstanding about how the family has reacted to the trauma will communi-cate that their feelings are important and will not be demeaned.

Beyond the search for understanding, the practitioner's support is selec-tive. Aspects of the family's functioning that are facilitative of positive treat-ment outcome are reinforced. These might include abilities to express feel-ings openly, to balance life at home and with the survivor, to maintain hope for the future and to make decisions. Research that identifies specific family traits judged to be helpful to recovery will provide practitioners with direc-tions for more clearly focused support in treatment sessions. In sum, the framework for support involves an ability to understand all aspects of the family's reaction to their trauma while selectively encouraging them to make active decisions in daily care.

Support in psychological treatment is easiest when the family voluntarily brings up issues for discussion that are relevant to the rehabilitation proc-ess. Yet, the family cannot always be counted on to do this. The practitioner may need to raise certain issues to the family before the family has thought of them. This confrontation must be done in a way that engages the family to help make a decision about the issue at hand and does not create a feel-ing that the practitioner's support is being withdrawn.

Confrontation is in fact part of the support that the practitioner provides to a family in a treatment session. The practitioner's decision to confront the family with an issue conveys a degree of involvement and conviction that most individuals in psychological treatment seek from the professional (Bugenthal, 1987). Seen in this way, confrontation is a way of supporting and facilitating the family's ability to resolve their presenting problems in psychological treatment. "In order to be truly caring you must also develop the capacity to be confrontative. You need to be willing to challenge people to face issues they'd prefer to not acknowledge. When I push a family or family member to take a position, I'm conveying I do care" (Whitaker & Bumberry, 1988, p. 173).

Challenging, or confronting families about a given treatment issue be-comes easier when the practitioner has supported independent thinking and decision making in the family as part of treatment. Ideally, the family will be able to examine a given issue on their own in the supportive presence of the practitioner. If not the practitioner should confront the family by encouraging them to address the advantages or disadvantages of a particular course of action. The practitioner further confronts by expanding on particular advantages or disadvantages as a way of enhancing the family's awareness of the decision they must make. The confrontation might include comments about other clinical situations where families have faced similar decisions.

> Case example: Parents of a 20-year-old man who was at Level VI for several months at an acute rehabilitation setting had apparently decided to take him home after his discharge. The rehabilitation team discussed the advantages and disadvantages of such a plan and concluded that the care needs of the survivor were greater than what the family could manage. There was ample financial support for extended rehabilitation care. In the psychology treatment session, the psychologist asked the family to discuss the pros and cons of taking the survivor home as opposed to placing him in an extended care facility. The disadvantages of home placement were discussed over the short term of the first month after discharge and over the extended long term of several years postinjury. This was done in order to paint a more vivid picture of the responsibilities family members would face. The intrusion of the survivor on the family members' daily lives, the exhaustion and frustration that the psychologist had observed in other families were also brought up to this family.

Mentioning other individuals or families who have been involved with similar circumstances is a confrontative technique that needs to be used sparingly. It provides the family with information and gives the impression that the practitioner is familiar with the particular presenting problem. On the other hand, it encourages comparisons between families and implies that the family's own situation is not unique.

The practitioner may also have to confront the family with an issue that has not been directly discussed with the family. The psychologist often is the individual selected by the treatment team to confront the family about a given treatment issue that the whole team feels is important. The other rehabilitation therapists on the team may feel uncomfortable bringing up a sensitive emotional issue with the family for fear of being unable to handle the family's reaction. A rehabilitation therapist may also wish to preserve his or her positive working relationship with the family and fear that confronting the family will make the family angry with him or her as a person and professional.

In this situation the psychologist must first clarify his or her role within the rehabilitation team and the team's feeling of the need for the psychologist to intervene in the matter at hand. There will be occasions when it is appropriate for the psychologist to confront the family rather than anyone else on the team. These would be in cases where the matter is emotionally sensitive and might logically lead to discussion of an emotional nature. Although the psychologist may not have been discussing the matter directly with the family, if the psychologist has been meeting regularly to discuss other emotional issues, it would not be intrusive for a new matter to be brought up in the discussion.

At other times, the psychologist is called upon to confront the family in matters that are not within the psychologist's realm of work with the family. In such cases, the psychologist's role should be as consultant to a particular rehabilitation team member. The psychologist should work with this team member, advising him or her about how to bring up this matter with the family and discuss it productively. At times, it may be most effective if the entire rehabilitation team meets with the family. This may be reassuring to the individual team members and allows the psychologist to facilitate discussion and remain supportive of the family rather than confront the family on an issue about which the psychologist may be poorly informed.

Case example: A physical therapist asked the psychologist to discuss with family members of a survivor the fact that the survivor was unlikely to ever be independent from a wheelchair. As a result of his assessment and work with the survivor the physical therapist felt that the survivor had severe physical limitations. The family had argued with the therapist and felt that the therapist was not trying hard enough to improve the survivor's physical mobility. The family wanted the therapist to do more walking exercises with the survivor. The therapist felt that the psychologist might be better able to make the point about physical mobility to the family. The psychologist, on the other hand, felt that the physical therapist was the appropriate person to discuss the matter. The psychologist had little knowledge of physical rehabilitation and the family knew this. It was unlikely that the psychologist could give the family meaningful information. The psychologist gave the physical therapist some guidance on how to discuss the matter with the family in a way that would minimize emotional arguments in the treatment area. In her treatment sessions with the family, the psychologist tried to supplement the physical therapist's work by discussing the general topic of denial with the family and how the family's reaction to the survivor's physical condition might be one example of the family's denial. It was also agreed the entire rehabilitation team would meet with the family to discuss the survivor's progress.

However the support and confrontation is presented to the family, it is hoped that the family will be able to reach a decision about a given treatment issue that facilitates the rehabilitation process. It is possible, however, that the family will select a course of action that is counter to what the practitioner and rehabilitation team would like. This should not be an occasion for disruption of psychological treatment. It is in these situations that the practitioner's ability to be available and to maintain an objective stance with the family will be most severely tested. A strongly established working relationship between the family and practitioner will be able to survive such times in rehabilitation care.

Interpreting Family Functioning

The previous section focused on confrontation as it is used to give families feedback about practical problems that they may face in the course of the survivor's rehabilitation process. Another aspect of confrontation is the interpretation of the family's feelings or other aspects of family functioning that may not appear to be directly pertinent to the rehabilitation of the survivor. These aspects of family functioning include the family's behavior, family structure and motivations for their behavior.

Confrontations about these aspects of the family are delicate because they address more personal parts of the family's functioning. The family may perceive these issues as threatening or alienating because they focus on the functioning of the family as a whole or family members rather than on the survivor. The family of the brain-injury survivor did not voluntarily seek out psychological treatment but rather found themselves placed in a psychological treatment situation as a result of the injury. The family members are not looking to the psychological treatment as means of increased growth or personal awareness as much as they are seeking ways of managing practical problems with the survivor and coping with a family crisis. For this reason, the practitioner needs to respect the family's essential ambivalence about psychological treatment when offering interpretations and confrontations about all aspects of family behavior, particularly those that focus more on the family than on the survivor.

General guidelines for offering interpretation include keeping in mind the timing and specificity of the interpretation. A strategy for making such interpretive confrontations is to link them to decisions that the family must make. Even when the practitioner's interpretive comments seem accurate and timely, they are unlikely to be effective unless the family is in a receptive mood. For example, when a family appears to be facing a decision point and is experiencing conflict about the decision, interpretation of their behavior is appropriate in the psychological treatment session. At other times, interpretation should be used sparingly, if at all. As Sullivan (1940, p. 187) has warned, "the supply of interpretations, like that of advice greatly exceeds the need for them." The following examples illustrate some of the ways in which interpretation of family functioning can be used.

Case example: As the survivor's discharge from an acute rehabilitation setting approached, family members were faced with the need to make home modifications to accommodate the survivor who was still physically limited. In therapy sessions, family members hesitated to agree on modifications and appeared to be haggling over specific details of them. The psychologist interpreted the family's behavior as an attempt to deny the concrete impact of the trauma by avoiding making a permanent change in the home environment. Psychology treatment sessions focused on discussion of this issue in order to facilitate a decision.

Case example: A woman, married to a survivor, experienced extreme uncertainty about a decision to live alone and to transfer her spouse to a longer term supervised care center rather than take him home with her. The psychologist interpreted this uncertainty as a reflection of her ambivalence about the need for independence versus dependence on her spouse. Treatment sessions focused on understanding the issues of dependency and independence in the context of her particular life experiences and present predicament. The goal of psychological treatment was to help the woman make decisions with which she could be content.

Case example: Parents of a 12-year-old survivor discussed their ability to visit and become involved in treatment. They were constrained by various obligations to work and to other children. In the course of this discussion, the father referred to numerous work obligations that over the years had left him little time for his wife and children. The psychologist felt that the father's overinvolvement in work activities may have been a way of expressing his distance from his wife and children and expressing his ambivalence about his marriage relationship as a whole. At the time of the discussions with the psychologist, a satisfactory visitation and treatment involvement policy had been agreed on by both parents. Therefore the psychologist did not choose to interpret the possible underlying motivations for the father's behavior in the course of treatment.

In the first two case examples, the family members were in conflict about a decision to be made. Understanding the underlying motives for this conflict helped to focus treatment and to help them reach a decision. In the third example, the family was not near a decision about treatment. Although an interpretation about their behavior might have been accurate, it was not necessary to the course of treatment at that time and would not have led to meaningful change in their behavior. The contemplated interpretation in the third example might be kept in mind for a future occasion in which the family was near a decision in treatment. In such a situation, the practitioner might make reference to the previous discussions in light of the future decision. Thus, though the interpretation was not made at a particular time that the information was brought up, it can be used in the future.

In addition to the timing of the interpretation, the practitioner should consider the confidence and specificity with which he or she offers interpretations to the family. Even when an interpretation appears needed, the interpretive comment can be presented in ways that are more or less confident and specific.

Families at early stages of treatment may receive less confidently stated, and less specific interpretations best. These appear less threatening and do not place the family in a position of having to accept or reject the practitioner's remarks. At a later stage in treatment, the practitioner may need to be more specific and confident in his or her interpretive remarks. At this stage, the practitioner and family will, hopefully, have developed a firm working relationship that will allow them to be frank in stating their points of agreement and disagreement.

The nature of the family's response to interpretations of different types is another area of research that would benefit clinical practice. In any case, the practitioner needs to be flexible and keep in mind a wide range of methods of presenting information to families so that it is acceptable and useful to them.

Finally, in interpreting the family's behavior, the practitioner needs to provide the family with alternative behaviors. To undermine the family's coping strategies without providing a reasonable substitute is a destructive rather than constructive intervention. For example, a family member may be reluctant to take a survivor out of a rehabilitation facility for dinner or shopping because of embarrassment about the survivor's behavior. In addition to any interpretive discussion about the relationship between the feeling of embarrassment and the family's feelings about the survivor's condition it would be helpful to provide the family with alternative methods of handling the survivor in the community. One way of doing this is to have the family join the rehabilitation staff for a group outing and observe how the staff handles the survivor. The staff could then assist the family in learning behavioral management strategies that they could use on their own.

Self-disclosure

The practitioner who is able to engage the family in regular treatment sessions for the period of rehabilitation care will find that a very close relationship develops with the family. This relationship is the result of the frequency of contacts between practitioner and family, the intensity of emotions expressed in the treatment sessions, and the wide range of information, advice and interpretations that the practitioner offers to the family.

In the context of this relationship with the family, the practitioner will be faced with the dilemma of using self-disclosure in treatment. Traditional psychotherapy training and techniques, and family treatment techniques tend to discourage its use. According to the traditional model, the practitioner maintains a professional distance from the patients or families in order to proceed with treatment goals in an objective manner. Sharing personal information with the family or patient may disrupt the practitioner's ability to maintain this objective stance. "When clinicians are unwilling to draw a boundary between themselves and their clients and insist on sharing all, they not only risk failure but even risk doing harm" (Haley, 1976, p. 213).

There is great value in this tenet of traditional psychological treatment for brain-injury rehabilitation psychology. Work with survivors of traumatic brain injury and their families is emotionally absorbing. Any rehabilitation professional may become so absorbed by the needs of the family as to lose objectivity. As will be discussed in Chapter Eight, the professional needs to be mindful of the effect of his or her own values and emotions on the course of treatment with these people.

Despite these injunctions against self-disclosure, the approach to psychological intervention that has been emphasized here is different from traditional psychotherapy. The role of the psychologist in brain-injury treatment is broader than the role of the psychotherapist. Therefore, different rules for handling self-disclosure are felt to apply.

Families of head injured adults face huge uncertainties for which they seek out professional advice. The answers do not always lie in the families themselves, ready to be uncovered by psychotherapy treatment. Families also feel tremendous alienation from the medical and rehabilitation environment. They need the assurance of a personal bond with the professional to overcome that alienation. For these reasons, it may be appropriate for the therapist to use self-disclosure in psychological treatment. Self-disclosure, used sparingly, can be appropriate and effective when it leads to achievement of therapeutic goals. For example, it may be used to help families recognize or accept an aspect of their own behavior in order to resolve an emotional conflict, or to emphasize a particular point in therapy.

Case example: Parents of a survivor who had recovered well from her injury and was involved in community reintegration activities were felt by the psychologist to be overprotective of their daughter. They had a difficulty seeing the extent of their own behavior and tended to justify their caution by saying that they did not want their daughter to move too quickly in work or independent living activities only to have a failure or disappointment. The psychologist felt that the parents' behavior was interfering with the progress their daughter could make on her own. The psychologist shared with the parents that their behavior reminded her of her own overprotectiveness toward her children. Even her knowledge as a psychologist was not enough to prevent her from being worried and cautious when her children tried a new activity. Though this information did not have an immediate impact on the parents of the survivor, in the subsequent sessions with the psychologist they were able to admit more readily to their own overprotectiveness and some of the fears for their daughter that underlie it.

There are potential pitfalls to such an approach. The practitioner's self-disclosure can be viewed as an attempt to trivialize the family's experience. Most rehabilitation professionals have not experienced traumatic brain injury in their own families. The family may not see a connection between the practitioner's own experience and theirs. Self-disclosure can also be seen as an attempt at self-aggrandizement by the practitioner. The practitioner may suggest by his or her comments that he has resolved the problem where the family has not. Finally, self-disclosure can be used against the practitioner by having the family bring up details about it in future discussions.

To avoid these pitfalls, the practitioner must thoroughly examine his or her motives for self-disclosure before using it. Often consultation with a colleague or formal supervision will facilitate this process. In general if self-disclosure is to be used, it should be specific to the particular family and to the therapeutic treatment. Thus, as in the above example, it would be appropriate for the practitioner to share with the family his or her feelings about some of his or her past experiences more so than the details of the actual experiences themselves. Bugenthal (1987) speaking about individual therapy states this point clearly, "Disclosure of process and responses—feelings and thoughts about the work and the way it is going—is usually more suitable (and more what patients validly seek) than is disclosure of details of one's personal, extratherapy life" (pp. 143–144).

SUMMARY

The model of psychological treatment that has been presented in this chapter is broader than psychotherapy treatment. The practitioner's role includes providing the support, interpretation and confrontation that make up what is considered psychotherapy treatment. However, the practitioner is also an educator and consultant to the family and part of a rehabilitation team that needs assistance in handling psychological treatment issues. This unique role requires modifications to the traditional tenets of psychotherapy treatment. In the following chapter, this model of psychological treatment will be applied to some of the common problems that families of brain-injury survivors present.

A sister speaks
by Susan

My brother was very intelligent, attractive, and a good athlete. He had a bright wit. He had some hang-ups, but generally fit the description of an All American male. I remember that he filled out my financial-aid papers for college and located our older brother's first job. He received academic and athletic scholarships at the US Coast Guard Academy.

I was a typical, proud, older sister. Inwardly, I wished to be like my brother and tried to keep up with his verbal wit. These traits have diminished. My feelings of adoration for my younger brother have faded. When he was eighteen years old he was the victim of a severe head injury in an accident. That event changed both of us.

I was nineteen when my brother was injured. In the days and weeks after my brother's accident, I was lost in a flurry of learning head injury lingo, visiting my brother, and questioning why this happened. As he progressed I began practicing physical therapy exercises with him and taking him out shopping to achieve independent living. Independent living is a phrase I hate at this time. I've come to feel that most severe head injury survivors never become fully independent.

At this juncture in my life my brother is difficult to describe. He is still intelligent and keeps an interesting conversation afloat but sometimes he forgets what he said and repeats himself. He also tends to personalize the conversation, focusing on himself instead of the broader topic. If I point this out to him he will usually retreat from the conversation. He still enjoys clowning around and being witty, but he's lost his punch. He seems corny rather than ingenious. He keeps up an active exercise routine, but will never play football, lacrosse, or jog like he did before his injury. He has an unsteady gait that inhibits him from being a fine athlete again.

There are also some newly acquired traits. He becomes easily depressed and excessively focused on religion. When these traits are present he sounds like a broken record repeating a Bible verse over and over. Or he'll say, "If God is love, how can there be evil?" Then, after a thinking process, he deduces that God is nonexistent or equal to the Devil. This hurts me deeply because we both affirmed God's importance in our lives.

I no longer wish to be like my brother. Instead, I hurt for him. I see how lonely and misplaced he's become. Subconsciously, I do not look forward to

121

seeing him at the holidays like my other siblings. He doesn't ignite the same anticipation or exude the same excitement as they do. He doesn't have a wife or job responsibilities that relate to my lifestyle. He doesn't share little tips or scoops like he used to about car buys, gardening, dining out, recycling, videos, or investing.

It is more work being with my brother than it was before his injury. This has been the hardest change. My other relationships are a mutual exchange, but this is no longer the case with my brother. I keep a watch out for him like a parent with a disabled or delinquent child. I am happy and supportive when he is doing well; and angry and withdrawn when he's depressed and excessively religious.

I love my brother. I know "the accident" caused most of the changes. It is not his fault so I do not mind the extra work that is required when I am with him. I love him and he's my brother. In our relationship we are close like a spectator in a stadium is to the game. But, we used to be players together on the field.

5

Special Treatment Issues

TREATMENT FOR PARENTS, SPOUSES, AND CHILDREN

Until this point, families have been discussed in a general way. Obviously this is a simplification. Each member of the family has a unique relationship with the survivor and has his or her own patterns of emotional adjustment. The rehabilitation professional will need to consider the individuality of family members in designing psychological treatment interventions for them. Some of the individual differences between family members were discussed in Chapter Two. In the following section, the implications of these differences for psychological treatment will be discussed.

Parents of Survivors

Psychological treatment for parents should be designed to have both parents involved in regular meetings with the psychologist. This arrangement enhances communication, avoids misinterpretations, and helps the practitioner to see the full picture of the presenting problems. Psychological treatment can fill an important educational need by providing referrals to appropriate parties to help parents resolve matters such as the survivor's return to school, parental guardianship, and power of attorney. General advice about the importance of pacing oneself, making time for each other and for other children can be offered to parents. This should be done with the qualification that it is still a normal reaction to the trauma that these activities will be neglected however important it is to spend time together or with other children.

Because parents feel a conflict between their various reponsibilities, treatment should begin by designating one parent as the primary contact for the professional staff. Often this is the parent who is most available in terms of his or her daily schedule to be contacted by staff. This designation should not be seen as an excuse for the other parent's involvement in treatment to lapse or for that parent to feel less important. The outset of treatment should also include a discussion of the amount of participation to which parents feel they can commit, and their feelings about discharge planning. By discussing these issues at the beginning of treatment, the psychologist communicates to the parents that they need to consider how they will balance their time commitments for themselves, for the injured child, and for other family members. It also encourages them to think ahead, to consider the extent of their commitment to the child after discharge.

In planning for the parents' involvement in psychological treatment the practitioner must also consider the relationship between the child and the parents as it existed prior to the brain injury. The parents' characteristic methods of interacting with the child are a starting point for developing a plan for their involvement in treatment. It may be unrealistic to expect that the parent who has had little involvement with his or her child prior to the injury to become suddenly more involved after the injury. Such changes in behavior of family members do occur in the context of the trauma, but the best predictor of how the parent will behave in the future is the parent's behavior in the past.

In brain-injury rehabilitation facilities, usually one psychologist will work with both the survivor and the family. As a result of this arrangement the psychologist can end up in the difficult position of supporting the parents while representing the needs of the survivor to the parents. It is helpful to have the survivor and parents participate in the treatment together when issues that affect the survivor and the parents are discussed. This plan is usually most effective when the survivor is at a higher level of functioning (Rancho Level VII and VIII) and is able to engage in some degree of meaningful verbal discussion over a period of time. By having the survivor present in treatment the practitioner can be more objective in his or her own work. Rather than serving as a communication link between survivor and parent, the practitioner can mediate the discussions and allow each side to present its feelings to the other. Observation of the parent-child interaction may give the practitioner some additional issues to discuss in treatment.

It may even be helpful to include the lower functioning survivor (Levels V and VI) in some discussions with the parents. Observation of the interaction between the parents and survivor is illustrative of the parents' communication patterns and emotional reactions to the survivor. Communication problems or misinterpretation of feelings between parent and survivor may give the practitioner directions for education and clinical intervention. Positive interactions between parents and survivor can be reinforced by the practitioner's comments.

By working with both families and the survivor the practitioner must also be careful to respect confidentiality guidelines. If the parents are guardians of a minor child or have obtained power of attorney, the practitioner may be obligated to share the progress of the survivor's psychological treatment with the parents. Parents may ask the practitioner directly about the progress of their child. The practitioner must use clinical judgment in respecting the parents' need and right to know information about the survivor while not disrupting the relationship with the survivor. Legal counsel may help the practitioner to clarify his or her role in these situations.

Most often, however, parents are respectful of the survivor's psychological treatment and will be content to know that regular meetings are taking place. The practitioner can take a hierarchal approach to the problem of what to tell the parents about treatment with the survivor, beginning with general information and providing more specific information as it is requested. This is illustrated in the following example.

- General statement about meetings: "I had the chance to see Joe yesterday and we talked for about 30 minutes."
- General statement about the topic: "I had a chance to see Joe yesterday and we talked about his adjustment to the hospital and about his therapy."
- More elaborated statement: "Joe talked about his difficulties in adjusting to the hospital and his exercises in occupational therapy for his hand."
- Specific statement about treatment: "Joe discussed feeling upset with you. He feels that he is in the hospital because you want him to be. He does not want to be here himself. He feels angry with you about this."

How much information parents desire to hear and how much they will respect the privacy of their child's psychological treatment may indicate their degree of involvement with or separation from the child and their feelings of trust in the practitioner and their issues of control. These issues may be grounds for future discussions between parents and practitioner.

Parents of adult children, that is children who were living apart and independent of parents prior to the brain injury, pose different problems in psychological treatment. Most often, these parents are not guardians of the survivor and do not have power of attorney. Yet they are interested in the care provided to their child and are involved in treatment. The practitioner needs to balance these parents' involvement with the involvement of the spouse and of the children of the survivor.

Case example: A 41-year-old survivor was divorced from his wife and had lived alone prior to his injury. His parents, in their 70's, were actively involved in his treatment. The survivor planned to return home to live with his parents after discharge from the postacute treatment facility. The parents were both physically well and the survivor had made extensive recovery from his injury to the point where he was judged to be Level VIII on the Rancho scale. The psychologist included the parents in regular treatment sessions and discussions with the survivor.

Case example: Parents of a married man with two young children were in frequent contact with the man prior to the injury. They appeared to have had a close relationship with him and his wife as well as with the children. They visited frequently and participated in treatment activities. The psychologist, however, set limits on their involvement in counseling sessions, preferring to communicate and plan treatment directly with the man's spouse.

As mentioned earlier, at the outset of treatment the practitioner should clarify with the family who will be the primary contact person for the practitioner. This decision should be based on the legal responsibility of family members for the survivor, the survivor's wishes and the involvement of the family members in the survivor's discharge plans. In the first example above, the parents were judged to be appropriate contact people because of their involvement in the survivor's discharge plan, his divorced status prior to the injury, and his willingness to include them in treatment. In the second example the parents, though positively involved in treatment, were not judged to be the primary contact people because the survivor was still married and planned to return to live with his spouse after discharge from the rehabilitation facility.

One means of involving all parents of adult children in treatment is in terms of gathering background information about the survivor and in some ancillary treatment activities. Parents may be able to provide detailed information about the survivor's schooling or early medical history that is important in treatment planning. Parental involvement in a day or evening visit away from the treatment facility may relieve the spouse of some burdens. Their efforts may be especially appreciated by the spouse in helping to care for the children of the survivor.

Parents of any age child may, in the course of treatment, present some problems in their marital relationship outside of their relationship with the child. These may be brought on by the stress of the trauma. As such the practitioner should seek to intervene in order to alleviate the problem. At times, however, the discussion of this relationship problem may lead to discussion of pre-existing problems in the relationship.

Case example: Parents of an injured child revealed during the course of sessions with the psychologist that they had been separated for several months. This occured about five years prior to the trauma. Though they had resolved the problem, they now experienced feelings that were similar to those they experienced at the time of the separation. They were concerned that they might seek to separate again and feared that this would have a negative impact on their child's recovery.

This is a delicate treatment situation. The psychologist cannot ignore the problem because it does affect the course of treatment, but attention to the problem may require more time and expertise than the psychologist is required to give. In such a situation, it is recommended that the practitioner discuss the problem only with respect to its effect on the survivor and his or her treatment. The parents should be encouraged to discuss the problem as a whole with another professional who is in the general community or a consultant to the facility who does not work with the survivor. This referral allows the practitioner within the rehabilitation facility working with the survivor and family to maintain his or her focus of treatment on rehabilitation issues with respect to the trauma.

Spouses

Differences between the roles of the spouse and the parents with respect to the brain-injury survivor have been described in Chapter Two. There are also differences between each spouse in his or her interpretation of the marital commitment. The practitioner must begin treatment intervention with the spouse of a survivor by discussing with the spouse his or her feelings and values about the marital relationship and his or her relationship with other family members, particularly parents of the survivor. This understanding serves as a basis for formulating treatment interventions.

The spouse usually feels isolated by the trauma. The partner who shared joys and responsibilities is not available the way he or she was before the injury. The injury may revive conflicts between the spouse and in-laws that intensify the isolation. Therefore, psychological treatment with a spouse should seek to establish a sense of connection and trust.

One way to accomplish this connection is to provide the spouse with information about common reactions to brain injury. This information may legitimize the spouse's reactions and show that the practitioner is seeking to appreciate the spouse's unique situation, rather than challenge it. It is also recommended that the practitioner designate the spouse as the primary recipient of treatment information and for making treatment decisions about his or her spouse if the spouse is cognitively or otherwise unable to make decisions independently. This role may help the spouse set limits on the extended family. The practitioner should not avoid contact with the extended family as noted in the previous section. They provide useful information about the survivor and can be a means of support. The guidelines of their involvement should be clarified and communicated to them by the spouse with the practitioner supporting the spouse.

Conflicts between the spouse and extended family may require a meeting between all parties and the practitioner. It may be necessary to appeal to family members to suppress, temporarily, their differences in the interest of the survivor's treatment. Conflicts in the family can have a deleterious effect on the survivor's recovery although clear documentation of this effect is not seen in research literature. A problem solving approach to treatment may be beneficial in this situation. In this approach the family members develop a contract among themselves that describes the extent of their activities with the survivor. Issues such as visitation, participation in treatment, and home visits can be clarified in the contract and violations of the contract can be discussed in family meetings. The practitioner facilitates resolution of the conflict but tries to avoid making the rules of the resolution.

Psychological treatment sessions with the spouse alone often focus on the changed relationship with the spouse. Spouses understandably express grief, anger, and loneliness about their changed life. The opportunity to express these feelings in a supportive setting without challenge is a relief to the spouse. A spouse may also be uneasy with the amount of control he or she has in the relationship. The problem of taking responsibility and making unilateral decisions needs to be discussed in psychological treatment.

> Case example: The husband of an injured woman took a large degree of control over decisions for his spouse. This was greeted with pleasure from the professional staff at first because it alleviated the staff's responsibilities. As treatment progressed, the staff began to recognize that the husband was not allowing his wife much opportunity for making decisions even about things such as clothing she wore, expenditure of money within the hospital setting and correspondence.

> Case example: The wife of an injured man was faced with taking responsibility for a wide range of financial obligations that included her husband's business as well as other investments. Having not had responsibility for this in the past, she was uncomfortable and uncertain about how do this effectively. Extended family were available to assist her but she was reluctant to involve them in internal family affairs for fear that they would become overinvolved. Her children were not old enough to assist her in managing the situation. Certain financial decisions appeared important to be made in a timely way yet she was reluctant to make them.

In the first example, the spouse had difficulty accepting the role of professional staff in the decision making process and the limits of his ability to control the outcome of his wife's treatment. He had become accustomed to making decisions without consulting his spouse about certain things. Psychological treatment for this man focused on helping him to recognize how his feelings of control were related to the loss of control he had experienced as a result of his wife's trauma.

In the second example, the spouse was experiencing emotional conflict over the amount of power she wielded over her husband's well-being. Having always been accustomed to deferring to his wishes in the past, she became anxious at the prospect of unilateral decisions. Psychological treatment focused on discussing her changed relationship under the circumstances of the trauma and how her feelings about this change caused her to avoid making decisions.

These examples were chosen because they depict traditional sexual roles and how they may interact with treatment planning. The practitioner must be mindful of the roles that characterize each spouse as individuals in their marriage prior to the trauma. These roles represent underlying personal values and experiences that will affect the course of treatment. Though the practitioner may hold values that are different from those of the family members, an attempt to force these values onto them will threaten them and alienate them from treatment.

Participation in psychological treatment should include joint meetings with the spouse and survivor. As noted, survivors judged at Levels VII and VIII on the Rancho scale are best able to participate in such meetings constructively. The goal of such meetings may be to resolve a particular problem, such as sexuality which will be mentioned later in this chapter, or to improve communication.

> Case example: The wife of a survivor was reluctant to have joint meetings with her spouse and the psychologist. Though she was considering a divorce, she did not want to get into a lengthy discussion about it in a psychological treatment session. The psychologist confronted her on this behavior, pointing out that it might represent difficulties in communication with her husband, fear that she would hurt her husband's feelings, or ambivalence about the divorce decision. In individual meetings with the survivor husband, the psychologist found that the husband maintained the unrealistic expectation that his wife's desires for divorce were not serious. Ultimately, the psychologist was able to get both partners together in a treatment session to discuss the issue and delineate each partner's feelings about the relationship. This enabled the husband to make alternative living arrangements with the help of the rehabilitation staff, and the wife to continue with divorce proceedings under a lessened emotional burden.

As discussed in Chapter Two, communication patterns are often drastically changed after severe traumatic brain injury. The noninjured spouse may be hesitant to share feelings with the survivor for fear of hurting feelings, guilt about having negative thoughts, or fear of disrupting treatment. The survivor may have difficulty communicating feelings for various cognitive or emotional reasons secondary to the brain injury. Increased communication between partners may often ease emotional distress and allow for a resolution of treatment decisions.

Joint meetings are also educational in that the communication between partners provides each with feedback about the impact of one partner's behavior on the other. The practitioner may be able to expand on what is communicated between partners and provide additional information that is useful to the partners. For example, Williams and Freer (1986) discuss the value of education to spouses about the consequences of aphasia, a problem that has a marked effect on interpersonal communication, and the positive effect this education had on the marital relationship.

Children

The discussion of the impact of the survivor's injury on child relatives was discussed in Chapter Two. In that chapter, children's reactions were examined with respect to the child's level of cognitive and emotional development. In planning psychological treatment intervention with child relatives of survivors it is also helpful to take a developmental perspective.

Infancy (0–2 Years)

Treatment interventions for the child at this age are best directed at the child's caregiver rather than the child. Though the child's emotional status may not be affected by the trauma per se, the effects of the trauma on other family members can be disruptive to the young child. The family should be helped to maintain some consistency in the routine for the child's benefit. The support of extended family and friends may need to be substituted for that of parents.

The child should not be excluded from the treatment setting. The presence of a child can be beneficial to the survivor's mood. It allows the survivor to maintain a contact with the child, especially important in the case of an injured parent. The child's presence may lighten the mood of other family members. Moreover, exposing the child to the treatment setting at an early age may facilitate the child's ability to make sense of the survivor's experience and to participate in treatment activities when the child is older. Research on effective methods of child involvement in brain-injury rehabilitation care would greatly assist professionals who must work with families on this issue.

Preconceptual Child (2–6 Years)

Treatment for the preconceptual child must take into account the child's changing language and reasoning skills and the child's tendency to express oneself in a preconceptual manner. Creative play therapy may be the treatment of choice for children judged to be experiencing an untoward emotional reaction to the trauma. Such modalities are an expressive outlet for the child. They also provide the professional with some ideas about how the child conceptualizes the trauma. This information may be helpful in counseling the parents.

Story books about hospitalization experiences and the trauma may be useful to the children at this age. Illustrations provide concrete images to facilitate their understanding. Adults or professionals should seek to help the child differentiate the trauma from the other everyday injuries the child may encounter. Unfortunately there are few story books focusing on brain injury and this is a valuable direction for future development of resource materials.

The child should be allowed to visit the injured family member in the hospital setting, especially if it is a parent. Children at this age have an active imagination, which is one reason for their varied fears. Seeing a family member firsthand is likely to be less fearful than what the child can imagine from what he or she is told or overhears. The visit to the facility should be made interesting rather than depressing. The child can be shown different types of therapy and medical equipment, and different types of jobs that people do within the facility in addition to seeing the family member.

It is not unusual to see a regression in the progress made in some developmental areas by children at this stage. The practitioner can be helpful to the family by educating them about this possibility and how to set appropriate expectations for the child at this stage.

Operational Child (7–12 Years)

Because the children at this age may vary widely in their cognitive and emotional skills, treatment must include a diversity of modalities. The family should be told to expect more overt expression of emotion from these children than from younger children. As noted in Chapter Two, the child may become angry at the injured parent for not being available, or redirect this anger at the noninjured parent. On the other hand, the child may be overprotective of the noninjured parent. Fears of motor vehicles or generalized fears to other situations may be noted in these children.

The prominence of school in the child's life allows the practitioner to use a wide range of educational information in therapeutic work. Most likely, verbal psychotherapy will need to be supplemented by nonverbal expressive activities for preconceptual children. These may be done on an individual or group basis. However treatment is designed, it should allow the child to express his or her feelings and to have these feelings be recognized as appropriate reactions to the trauma (see Kushner, 1981).

The operational child may be better able to differentiate the experience of the trauma from his or her own injury experience. Though the child may express fears of injury, attachment to, and protectiveness of parents, they are able to be reasoned with in order to work through the intensity of their behavior. The focus of treatment should be on helping to bolster coping strategies and defenses that such children have: helping them to realize that their emotional reactions are understandable, that their fearfulness is a reaction to the trauma, and that the trauma is an exceptional event.

Visitation continues to be important for the children in this age group. They may be interested in and able to participate in parts of therapy with the injured individual at this stage. This is beneficial in helping to establish a connection between the child and the injured family member. Participation should not, however, be required. Contacts with other close family members as a means of balancing the loss of attachment to the injured individual is also of continued importance.

Teenagers (13–19 Years)

As mentioned in Chapter Two, some teens respond readily to the opportunity to be supportive of the injured or noninjured family members after the trauma. Teenagers desire to be treated as adults. After the trauma, the teen may see the opportunity to assist the survivor in rehabilitation activities, or to assist parents at home with child care responsibilities as a chance to demonstrate his/her independent capabilities. Thus, in psychological treatment the teenager should be given the opportunity to contribute to the care of the survivor or to the family as a whole.

The teenager's ability to identify more closely with the parents' experiences than could younger children can be supported in psychological treatment. The practitioner can help the family to acknowledge the empathy that the teenager is expressing as a means of solidifying the bonds between parents and the teenager, and making the teenager feel important to the overall functioning of the family.

The common conflicts about control and independence at this age, however, may make it difficult to involve some teens in treatment in the same way that a younger child could be involved. The family's involvement in the care of the injured parent or sibling may be seen as an intrusion into the teen's drive for independence. The teen, like other family members, is apt to feel frustrated, helpless or depressed by the slow, uncertain course of the survivor's recovery but may not have effective means of expressing these feelings. Research on the reactions of teens to the traumatic brain injury of a family, particularly with respect to the relationship between the teen's involvement in treatment, emotional adjustment, and premorbid relationship with the injured family member, would be beneficial as a guide to treatment intervention and education of parents.

Treatment interventions for adolescents may be in individual or group formats. The importance of peer relationships for the adolescent suggests that they may be more receptive to group treatment in which problems and support can be generated by peers rather than professionals in positions of authority. Again, the school system may be used by the practitioner as a way of providing the teen with education, peer support and emotional outlets. The practitioner should encourage the family to inform the school about the trauma so that teachers and guidance personnel can understand the stress that the teen may be experiencing and the possible effect it will have on school work and activities.

It may be more realistic to encourage the family to seek out psychological services for the adolescent in need outside of the rehabilitation facility, perhaps in the school or the home community. This may give the adolescent a greater sense of independence from the rehabilitation setting and fewer concerns about confidentiality. Despite the possibility that the teen may prefer not to be involved in psychological treatment, it is very important that such services be provided in some format. Their susceptibility to acting out emotional conflicts by antisocial behavior such as drug or alcohol use, or other problems is greater than for younger children. These problems pose a large risk to the adolescent, the family and the society at large and may be avoided through treatment. The issues in working with children and adolescents described in Chapters Two and Five are summarized in Table 5.1.

TREATMENT FOR SPECIAL PROBLEMS OF THE SURVIVOR AND FAMILY

In addition to treatment interventions that focus on particular family members and family structure, psychological treatment also must address specific problems that the survivor is apt to show in a rehabilitation setting. Four general groups of problems will be discussed: problems of behavior control, sexuality, denial, and discharge planning. As discussed in Chapter One, problems in behavior control, sexuality, and denial are commonly noted among survivors of severe traumatic brain injury. It is particularly important that psychological treatment for the family address itself to these groups of problems because they are noted to be the areas of most emotional distress for families over the years postinjury (Brooks, 1984), outweighing the distress associated with physical or cognitive difficulties that the survivor may have.

Discharge planning is also an important issue in psychological treatment. Treatment of the survivor often spans several different treatment settings and different groups of professionals. In order to maintain effective working relationships with the family and to develop the consistency in treatment

Table 5.1 Children's Reactions to Traumatic Brain Injury and Suggested Treatment Interventions

Developmental stage	Key cognitive and emotional changes	Reaction to trauma	Treatment intervention
Infancy and toddler ages 0–2 yrs.	Explore world through senses and motor skills	Curiosity; sensitive to changes in routine, may not notice changes in survivor	Minimize changes, visit and explore rehab unit
Preconceptual ages 2–5	Use language, aware of larger social systems, less dependent on parents, thought is concrete and egocentric	May be fearful, may regress in developmental milestones, difficulty understanding the severity of the trauma	Continue visitation, allow child chance to express feelings in words or action, use stories or other concrete activities
Operational ages 6–12	Able to focus on different dimensions of a problem, aware of larger social system, able to learn through social observation	May see trauma as punishment for own behavior, may resent lack of attention	Give concrete rehab tasks to perform, model ways of interacting with survivor, use verbal and nonverbal expressive therapy tasks
Adolescence ages 13–19	Able to think abstractly, concerned about independence, physical appearance, social issues	May be angry about infringement on own lifestyle, concerns about fairness, may feel distant from survivor or feel the experience is not relevant to own life, may welcome chance to have adult responsibility, and chance to support their family members	Verbal and nonverbal psychotherapy, group therapy, agree on plan for the teen's involvement in rehab treatment

that is important for the survivor, the matter of discharge must be handled well.

Psychological treatment of the family in handling these issues is closely integrated with the psychological treatment provided directly to the survivor. Nevertheless, the focus of this book is not on treatment interventions for the survivor. Individuals interested in treatment programs for survivors with some of these problems are referred to several references on the topic (Howard, 1988; O'Neill & Gardner, 1983; Rehabilitation Institute of Chicago, 1983; Tate, 1987a, 1987b; Wood, 1987).

Although the specific programs for the survivor in these areas will not be discussed, it is essential that the practitioner have specialized and clearly established treatment plans for working with these survivors before treatment with the family can be approached. The family expects the practitioner to be an expert in the psychological treatment of brain injury. Though they may question the decisions of rehabilitation professionals, family members still turn first to the professionals for potential solutions to problem situations with the survivor. The practitioner's credibility with the family in handling specific behavior problems is based on the trusting relationship that he or she has established with them and the degree to which he or she feels in control of the situation at hand.

Behavior Control Problems

Behavior problems of the survivor and their meaning for the family, as described in Chapter One, include: agitation, noncompliance and aggression. Whether these problems are the result of the brain injury, personality, or mood changes, they are all problems in control. The family's emotional reaction to these problems will be affected by the values that the family members place on behavioral control and the controlled expression of emotion in interpersonal relationships.

Because a survivor's behavior problem represents a problem in control, with all of the implications that this may have for the family, the first part of psychological treatment is to help the family to maintain as much appropriate control over the situation as possible. The four levels of psychological intervention described in Chapter Four can all be utilized to help families gain control over the changes caused by the survivor's behavior problems.

Education

Much of the family's emotional distress and feelings of loss of control will stem from their confusion about the behavior problem. The survivor may show uncharacteristic or bizarre behaviors. This is particularly true in the case of survivors in the agitated stage (Rancho IV) of recovery. The practitioner's intervention for families at this stage can focus on providing them with information about this stage of recovery, helping the family to recognize that the behavior problems seen are part of the consequences of a severe traumatic brain injury. The practitioner should help the family recognize that the behavior problems shown by the survivor are the result of physiological, cognitive, and emotional changes that have occurred since the trauma, and are part of the expected stages in recovery from the trauma.

The practitioner should also have a preexisting plan for handling behavior problems that occur during the agitated stage of recovery (Brigman et al., 1983) or at higher levels of recovery. This behavior plan can be explained to the family as part of the educational process. Even if the survivor does not show any behavioral problems, at that time the family should be forewarned that behavior problems may occur and that treatment plans are ready and waiting. An established plan of action gives direction and self-confidence to the professional team and communicates to the family that behavior problems, however extreme they may appear to be, are an expected part of rehabilitation for which an expected treatment is provided.

Educational material, especially in a video format, can be used to great effect in meetings with the family. Contacts with other families who have been through this stage with their injured family member may also be informative. The goal of these interventions is to give the family a sense of control and an idea of what to expect with respect to the behavior problem. In this way the family's emotional reaction is apt to be less disruptive to the survivor when they are with him or her.

Problem-solving

In addition to receiving educational information, families will need to feel involved in the care and control of the survivor's behavioral difficulties. In the case of agitated behavior, families may be frustrated because the survivor's behavior creates a distance between them and the survivor. The agitated individual is not often receptive to social contacts. Small changes in the environment or excessive visitors may exacerbate the agitation (Tate, 1987b). Families may feel isolated and powerless to assist the professional staff in the care of the agitated individual.

To overcome these problems, the practitioner should engage the family in a problem-solving discussion of indirect means of caring for the survivor at this stage. For example, this may be a time for families to assemble materials that can be used in treatment when the survivor comes out of the agitated stage (e.g., family pictures, music, work, or home activity materials). The family may be a resource for identifying techniques or people who are particularly soothing to the agitated survivor. As noted in Chapter One, behavioral problems in the survivor may be related to underlying cognitive difficulties. Families may be able to become involved in some basic cognitive retraining activities with the survivor (Anderson & Parente, 1985) that indirectly address the survivor's behavioral problems. A preexisting treatment plan is also helpful in behavioral problems observed in survivors at higher levels of recovery.

For survivors who show noncompliance or aggressive behavior, the importance of having a treatment plan has been discussed. To be effective, however, this plan must be individualized to meet the particular problems posed by the survivor. Family input is helpful in devising these treatment plans and should be solicited by the psychologist (Greif & Matarazzo, 1982; Howard, 1988; LeBow, 1976). In psychological treatment sessions, families can be asked by what methods behavior problems prior to the traumatic injury have been handled, and what specific activities the survivor would find reinforcing or not reinforcing. This information is incorporated into the behavior management plan as needed. When several options for treatment exist in handling the behavior problem these should be discussed with the family and their decision should guide treatment.

> Case example: After having her injured son home with her for six years, the survivor's mother returned him to a treatment facility. He showed extreme behavioral control problems that included physical threats and destruction of family property. In discussions with the psychologist, the mother was able to provide an extensive list of different techniques she had used while the son was at home in order to gain control. The possibility of medication as a means of controlling her son's behavior was also discussed with her. She was able to provide information on past medications that had been used and discussed her opinions about current use of medication.

Obtaining the family's input with respect to behavior management can be a way of teaching the family about behavior management principles so that they may apply them on their own with the survivor. It also communicates to the family that the family's behavior is an important factor in the development and management of the behavior problem (Prigatano et al., 1986, p. 44).

Including the family's suggestions in the behavioral management plan or allowing families an active part in the implementation of the plan will also alleviate some of their concerns about the role of behavior therapy. For some, behavioral treatment is seen as dehumanizing and subject to ethical questions and value judgments in terms of the target behaviors for treatment and the use of tangible positive and negative contingencies. The practitioner must be prepared to answer the concerns of the family in a manner that reduces their anxiety about behavior management and provides them with more information about the value of behavioral interventions. These concerns and responses to them have been discussed in the general behavior therapy field by Bandura (1969) and Mahoney (1974), and with respect to the field of rehabilitation by O'Neill and Gardner (1983) and Turnbull (1988).

At times behavioral modification techniques are insufficient to manage behavioral disturbances. The family should always be solicited with respect to the use of other treatments such as medication or physical restraints. These measures may be presented and discussed in psychological treatment sessions in a format that emphasizes review of the advantages and disadvantages of various courses of action with the goal of reaching a decision that is agreeable to both family and practitioner.

> Case example: When behavioral guidelines were not sufficient to control the aggressive behavior of a survivor in a long-term residential treatment program, the professional staff decided to have him evaluated for medication. A psychiatrist evaluated the survivor and prescribed a particular medication regimen on an emergency basis because of the survivor's escalating agitation. The psychiatrist recommended that the medication be used in conjunction with behavioral treatment. The family had not been consulted about this intervention. The survivor did not show any behavioral change as the result of the medication intervention. The parents of the survivor later found out about the medication intervention and were angry that they had not been informed about it. The professional team discovered that the family had some strong feelings about the use of medication with their son. It was revealed that he had been seen for psychological treatment as a youngster and had a brief treatment with psychotropic medication. The parents were opposed to use of medication and angry that they had not been consulted in its use.

This example illustrates several important points in behavioral treatment planning with families of survivors. One, is the need to obtain a thorough history from the family with respect to past behavioral problems and how the family had handled them. Because behavioral problems are often seen in traumatic brain-injury survivors, it is incumbent on the practitioner to obtain information in the initial psychological interview of the family about the survivor's past treatment for behavior problems and about the family's values regarding such problems and treatment. Two, the family needs to have the option to be involved in all phases of rehabilitation treatment. Although emergency decisions may need to be made in the course of rehabilitation care, some mechanism needs to be in place to have the family informed and involved in the decision-making process.

The problem-solving approach to treatment is helpful when the survivor continues to show behavioral problems at the time of discharge. The extent of these behavioral problems may affect the choice of discharge placement. Families may wish to have their family member at home but not realize the difficulty in managing the problem behaviors at home. Open discussion of the different discharge options and their relationship to the survivor's behavior is beneficial in this situation. Home visits of the survivor with family are a useful adjunct to these discussions. The visit may provide the family with concrete examples of the behaviors they will face at home. Behavioral guidelines for the family can be developed from these visits. These guidelines may help to structure the family's interactions with the survivor at home in a consistent way.

Emotional Support

Psychological treatment sessions can be used to allow families to ventilate their feelings about the behavior problems shown by the survivor. Families of a survivor in the agitated stage may feel powerless to help their family member. They may benefit from discussion of this feeling and the chance to reflect on past times when they felt unable to comfort their injured family member. The practitioner's goal is to allow families the opportunity for such emotional expression and to support their patience in enduring this very difficult stage in recovery.

The family's anxiety about behavior problems may become more intense as discharge approaches. Problems that could be denied earlier in treatment are less effectively denied at this point. The feelings of loss of control that the family sought to deny are experienced more intensely. The practitioner will need to provide the family with the opportunity to express their feelings at this stage in treatment and support them in their distress.

Resolving Emotional Conflicts and Structural Interventions

The behavioral changes shown by the survivor can be a major source of change in the family structure. The family organization is based on certain expectations for each family member's behavior and contribution to the family system as a whole. When the survivor is unable to behave in the same way as before the injury, the family members must accommodate to this change. This can result in stresses to the family structure that affect the individual family members. Psychological intervention for the family may need to focus on the emotional conflicts that have been spawned by the survivor's behavioral problems and suggest some modifications in the family's structure in order to cope with such conflicts.

> Case example: A 26-year-old woman returned to live with her parents after extensive rehabilitation. She was physically independent and had some cognitive limitations although she was able to obtain a part-time volunteer position. Her most prominent postaccident problem was severe temper outbursts. These would come in response to experiences of frustration when she had difficulty performing certain activities, when she was fatigued, or when someone

disagreed with her. She would not become physically threatening to others during these outbursts but she would break household objects and took about ten minutes to calm down after the outburst. Her parents and sister had been able to manage these outbursts by recognizing what would set them off and trying to avoid these situations. As a result, however, the family felt as though they were walking on eggshells with the survivor. They were angry at her behavior. They felt that she was capable of handling more responsibility at home but avoided bringing it up because of her outbursts. They were reluctant to go out together as a family for fear of an outburst by her, yet they felt guilty going out on their own without her.

In this example, the outbursts that the survivor showed affected the family structure in several ways. One, the sense of cohesion among family members had been disrupted. The family did fewer activities together because of the survivor's outbursts. Two, the responsibilities of family members increased to minimize the burdens to the survivor. Three, family communication was altered. Family members felt reluctant to share their feelings of frustration with the survivor. In their attention to the survivor they may have had fewer opportunities to communicate among themselves.

The practitioner can take such structural factors into consideration in devising psychological treatment interventions. Certainly behavioral management guidelines and emotional support and ventilation were all appropriate treatment interventions for this family. The behavior guidelines helped the family to recognize that they might be reinforcing the disruptive behavior in their attempts to control it. In addition, the parents and sibling of the survivor benefited from treatment that focused on helping them to recognize the importance of taking more time among themselves for their own sense of family togetherness and communication. If they felt a sense of cohesion and understanding between themselves without the survivor, they might be able to be consistent in their treatment of the survivor. Treatment also focused on developing a method of communicating distressing feelings between the survivor and the family members.

The Rehabilitation Professional's Reactions

The rehabilitation professional must also be mindful of his or her own reactions to behavioral problems. The agitated individual often defies efforts to be controlled. The aggressive individual intrudes on the professional's safety and physical integrity. Violations of this kind are extremely inappropriate and subject to sanctions in the rules of everyday society. In the treatment setting, however, the rules are different. The safety and integrity of the brain-injury survivor as a rehabilitation facility resident often appears to be better protected than that of the professional staff. Professional staff may become very angry without any channel for expressing this anger. The professional must control his or her temptation to act out these feelings of anger in nontherapeutic behavior toward the survivor or family. Ideally, the professional should attempt to model self-control for the family so they may learn through observation how to approach the survivor in an effective manner. The psychologist is in an ideal position to assist other rehabilitation professionals to handle their feelings of frustration or anger about the survivor and not to let such feelings interfere with appropriate therapy.

Team cooperation is important in effective behavioral treatment. "To make a behavior management model work, rehabilitation team members must see themselves as teachers in an educational model, with behavior as the focus" (Howard, 1988). Similarly, the effectiveness of behavior management depends on teamwork between the professionals and the families. The practitioner should have a positive therapeutic alliance with the family in treatment prior to instituting any behavioral interventions with the survivor (Liberman, 1976). Different levels of intervention for behavioral problems are summarized in Table 5.2.

Sexuality

Changes in sexual behavior noted after traumatic brain injury were briefly reviewed in Chapter Two. As was noted there, problem sexual behavior in the brain-injury survivor is a subset of general behavioral problems. Therefore, many of the same principles for treatment intervention that were discussed with respect to behavior problems in general apply to sexual behavior problems. As before, this section will illustrate how the four levels of psychological intervention can be applied to work with families in the area of the survivor's sexuality.

Education

In the educational approach to psychological intervention with the family, the practitioner's first job with the family is to help them to differentiate problem and nonproblem behaviors. Family values and the regulations of the rehabilitation facility will affect what behaviors are seen as problematic. The psychological treatment practitioner, as representative of the rehabilitation team, and the family must reach an understanding about which behaviors are judged to be a problem before any treatment for the behavior is initiated.

> Case example: A family had their son placed in an acute rehabilitation facility far from their home. Their injured son was one of five sons. The survivor was observed to make inappropriate gestures, comments, and attempts to become intimate with female nursing staff. In a family conference with the rehabilitation team, the problem was brought to the family's attention. The family did

**Table 5.2   Examples of Different Levels of Psychological Treatment
for Families of Survivors with Behavioral Problems**

1. EDUCATION

   a. Explaining the relationship between behavioral problems and the injury to the brain

   b. Explaining the place and frequency of behavioral problems within the context of TBI recovery

   c. Explaining the principles of behavior theory (For example, reinforcement, shaping and extinction)

2. PROBLEM SOLVING

   a. Identifying problem behaviors, their impact on the survivor and family, and family goals for problem resolution.

   b. Developing a plan of action for handling the problem behaviors and including a role for the family in such plans

   c. Eliciting the family's suggestions for reinforcers and penalties for the survivor in a behavior plan.

3. SUPPORT AND VENTILATION

   a. Discussion of the uncertainty and stress associated with caring for a survivor with a behavior problem.

   b. Trying to reduce family's expectations for rapid improvement so that they can have energy over the long course of rehabilitation

   c. Supporting the family's efforts to set limits on the survivor's behavior and to pursue their own needs.

4. RESOLVING EMOTIONAL CONFLICTS

   a. Helping family to understand the connection between the survivor's loss of behavioral control and their own fears about loss of control over their lives or the survivor's life.

   b. Resolving differences between family members that may arise in terms of differing opinions about how to handle the survivor's behavior problems

   c. Confronting the family's possible unwillingness to allow the survivor freedom of movement because of the demonstrated behavior problem, thereby denying the survivor the opportunity to face new challenges.

---

not perceive the survivor's behavior to be a problem. As the parents of the survivor stated, all of their sons showed this sort of behavior. In fact the parents and the other siblings appeared amused when the staff was telling them about the survivor's behavior. This infuriated the staff and made it difficult for the staff and family to agree on behavioral guidelines for the survivor. Much of the professional intervention with the family was spent on explaining to them the relationship between their son's brain injury and the dyscontrolled behavior he showed. Although much of this behavior was similar to his premorbid behavior, the practitioner tried to help the family recognize that the behavior appeared more extreme after the injury.

Discrepancies between how the professionals and family view the survivor's behavior must be resolved before a treatment program can begin. Psychological treatment may best begin by having the practitioner and family discuss their understanding of the problem behavior and seek to resolve any discrepancies. The education of the family should focus on helping them to recognize that sexual behavior may be an expression of underlying needs for affection and reflect the survivor's self-esteem. This information may be a point from which to discuss how affection is expressed in the family and how other family members react to the survivor's feelings of loneliness and changed life. In such a discussion, family members may indirectly examine with the practitioner how their own communication patterns, needs for affection and self-esteem have been affected by the trauma.

In psychological treatment sessions with parents of a survivor it is often useful to discuss sexual development. There may be a similarity between how the parents handled the survivor's expressions of sexuality at other times in his or her life, and how they currently react to the survivor's behavior. When considering this comparison, parents may be able to reflect on the first time they recognized that their child was becoming an adult. These reflections may facilitate their ability to understand their reactions to their child's present behavior.

Education and discussion with family about the definition of the problem sexual behavior is important in the case where the survivor demonstrates atypical sexual behavior. In such cases the practitioner's goals in educational treatment remain the same. The family should be helped to distinguish between appropriate and inappropriate expression of sexual behavior regardless of the matter of sexual preference.

Case example: A 23-year-old survivor identified himself as a homosexual prior to the traumatic brain injury and was known by friends and family to have had homosexual relationships. In the acute rehabilitation setting, when he was just becoming more independent in daily living activities and showing improved cognitive and orientation, his parents expressed to the psychologist their dissatisfaction with their son's past behavior. They asked the psychologist if this sort of behavior could be discouraged as their son recovered from his injury. For example, they preferred to minimize visits between their son and friends he had prior to his injury.

The matter of sexual preference in the survivor of a traumatic brain injury has received little attention in the clinical research literature on brain-injury rehabilitation. When the issue arises, the family may see the rehabilitation process as an opportunity to remold the survivor. Past emotional conflicts in the family about the issue of homosexuality may be reactivated. Families may feel as though they have failed in some way as family members or worry that the survivor will be unhappy as a homosexual (Sanders, 1980). The practitioner should seek to educate the family about sexual behavior in general and how it represents the survivor's needs for affection and personality style. In this context, homosexual behavior should be treated in the same way as heterosexual behavior. The focus of rehabilitation treatment is to help the survivor gain the maximum level of independence in order to reintegrate into the society at large or to adapt realistically to his or her incapacities. In the case of a survivor who identifies him or herself as homosexual, this preference needs to be respected in the course of helping that person to reintegrate into the community and live independently.

Problem-solving

Should the survivor show problems in the expression of sexual behavior, the practitioner should have a preexisting plan of action for handling the problems. As mentioned earlier, this plan will give direction and confidence to the rehabilitation team, and reassure the family. Such a treatment plan is apt to be general and must be individualized for the survivor's particular needs.

In psychological treatment, the family's ideas should be sought out and incorporated into a treatment plan for sexual behavior problems. In effect the practitioner poses the problem to the family that has been raised by the survivor's behavior and discusses with the family the various means of resolving the problem. The treatment plan should include specific instructions for the family about their role in managing the behavior. These aspects of the plan should be reviewed with the family so they can understand the reasons for the plan and why their role in it is important to the plan's effectiveness.

In seeking out the family's input and including them in this way, the practitioner seeks to remove the social stigma of the behavior. The sexual behavior in question is seen as a specific behavior and not a reason for shame or a reflection of the survivor's upbringing. Rather it is a behavior that is seen after a traumatic brain injury and handled accordingly.

Case example: An 18-year-old survivor was observed by nursing staff to engage in frequent masturbation. He did this in his room and in rehabilitation therapy areas when there was no other person nearby. Because he had memory difficulties and subsequent difficulty appreciating the passage of time, he tended to engage in the masturbation even if he was left alone in a room for a few minutes. He had expressive language difficulties and showed a tendency to grab at staff in order to get their attention. Staff found this behavior very disturbing. The psychologist met with the survivor and the parents separately to discuss the problem. The survivor appeared to feel isolated and sexually frustrated. His masturbation and grabbing were two ways of expressing these feelings. The parents were initially distressed by the report of the behavior problem but were able to recognize that masturbation is common among adolescents. Thus, their son's behavior was not unusual for his age. In discussing the problem of their son's social isolation and difficulties in adjusting to his expressive speech problems, the parents suggested ways in which they could bolster his social activities at home and through visitations of friends. They suggested that a staff member spend individual time with their son in the evenings to alleviate his feelings of isolation. The survivor was also instructed on appropriate times and places for masturbation, as part of a general sexuality education program within the facility.

For survivors who have the opportunity to go out independently into the community, greater sexual options and decisions are presented to them. Therefore, in addition to the general behavior plans described above, the practitioner should have in place plans that include guidelines for dating and sexual relationships with spouse or surrogate.

Case example: A 26-year-old survivor who was never married was preoccupied with the desire to have a sexual experience with a woman. He spent most of the time in individual counseling and in general conversations discussing his need for a sexual experience. He was able to participate in all aspects of the postacute treatment program where he resided. He was observed, however, to be depressed frequently. His family informed the staff that he had lived with a girlfriend prior to his injury but she had left the relationship after the survivor's injury. The psychologist and rehabilitation team discussed the possibility of having this man see a sexual surrogate. It was felt that such an experience might be an emotional release for him. On the other hand, his expectations might be that the surrogate would become a new girlfriend. Because this man was considered legally responsible for his own affairs, the psychologist did not discuss the matter with the family.

The frequency of using sexual surrogates has increased as brain-injury rehabilitation programs have recognized the needs that these fulfill for some survivors. In the case of a survivor who is legally a minor, this decision needs to be discussed with and approved by those who bear legal responsibility for the treatment decisions, usually the family. The practitioner should share with the family some of the ways in which surrogates have been used with survivors, and the advantages and disadvantages of such treatment as a way of educating the family. The practitioner must allow the family to discuss their feelings and values about the matter freely in order to facilitate their decision.

The survivor who is legally responsible for his or her own affairs, however, should make such a decision alone. When the family is not legally responsible for the survivor, the psychologist is under no legal obligation to discuss any treatment intervention with the family. On the other hand, some contact with the family about this matter may be advisable clinically in order to respect their wish to be involved in treatment. In such a situation, it is recommended that the practitioner work with the survivor in order to have the survivor share with the family the treatment plan for contacting a sexual surrogate. The practitioner can facilitate this discussion between family and survivor.

The practitioner will also need to have a plan for confidentiality in this and other matters. The plan should clarify to the survivor, family, and rehabilitation staff what matters are necessary to share with the family and the team about the survivor's psychological treatment.

Ventilation and Support

The privacy with which most people value sexual behavior may make it particularly difficult for families to discuss their feelings about it in psychological treatment sessions. Parents of a survivor may have difficulty accepting their child as a sexual being and allowing sexual feelings to be expressed openly. They may fear losing control of their child. These feelings should be acknowledged by the psychologist and the parents' willingness to express the feelings should be supported.

The spouse of a survivor will experience emotional reactions that are different from those of the parents. The decision about sexual intimacy between the noninjured spouse and the survivor will arouse many different emotions. The spouse may feel isolated and unable to discuss such issues with other family members. The practitioner can provide an opportunity for the spouse to ventilate such feelings in order to understand them and make a decision regarding his or her sexual relationship with the survivor.

Resolving Emotional Conflicts and Structural Interventions

The sexual behavior problems of the survivor will affect the structure of the family particularly in the case of the injured spouse. Because sexual relations are part of the marital relationship, and usually unique to the marital relationship, a change in this aspect of the relationship can alter the structure of the relationship and the family as a whole.

> Case example: The husband of a survivor had difficulty resuming a sexual relationship with his wife when she returned home after four years of various institutional rehabilitation treatments. She made a good physical recovery and he did not feel that she had been physically disfigured although she was weaker and somewhat thinner than she had been prior to her injury. He explained to the psychologist that he had difficulty seeing her as an equal after such a long period of hospitalization when she was dependent on him. They had had sexual relations several times but it was not satisfying for him. She sought out sexual relations with her husband more than he did with her and she felt rejected by him. In fact, this pattern of relating characterized their re-

lationship as a whole. The husband shunned his wife's desires for increased social interaction and togetherness. There was no history of difficulties in sexual relations prior to the wife's brain injury.

In this example, the parity that apparently characterized the relationship between this couple prior to the trauma did not exist after the wife's injury. The husband had difficulty accepting his wife in a different type of relationship and in recognizing changes that she had made from a time when she was more dependent. The injured wife did not appear to be sensitive to the husband's adjustment problems. In terms of the structure of the relationship, the sexual difficulty represented one aspect of an overall structural change. The spouses were less cohesive and communicated differently. They appeared to have different values and beliefs. Each having gone through a unique aspect of the trauma, their different experiences served to separate them rather than draw them closer to each other.

Treatment intervention for this couple focused on helping them to understand the changes that had occurred in their relationship and the place of the sexual problem within the entire structure of their relationship. With this background, they were encouraged to build stronger connections with each other through regular communication and planned activities together. It was hoped that such interventions would facilitate the development of a sense of togetherness that could be a basis for a sexual relationship. In addition, it was felt that the husband's distress about his relationship with his wife was partly the result of feeling an insufficient boundary with her. Therefore, treatment focused on setting boundaries between the spouses with respect to sexuality and some aspects of the husband's work. Rather than setting a goal of sexual intimacy, treatment sought to get a goal of social intimacy and physical affection.

Structural treatment interventions should be based on a structural analysis of the family. Weaknesses or imbalances in the structure of the family may be connected to the emotional distress that the family is experiencing. Treatment interventions should be designed to help the family regain a balance or repair structural aspects that have been stressed or damaged by the trauma. Different levels of intervention for sexual problems are summarized in Table 5.3.

Denial

As described in Chapter One, denial is a common behavioral and emotional reaction to the trauma in the survivor and family members. Denial in families may be expressed in many forms but basically it derives from an unwillingness to acknowledge the implications of the survivor's problems postin-

Table 5.3   Examples of Different Levels of Psychological Intervention for Families of Survivors with Problems in Sexuality

1. EDUCATION

   a. Explaining the normalcy of certain sexual behavior in all individuals regardless of brain injury

   b. Explaining the connection between some sexual behavior problems and the survivor's injury or emotional adjustment postinjury.

2. PROBLEM-SOLVING

   a. Identifying a problem behavior and a goal for treatment.

   b. Enlisting the family's support in developing an appropriate behavioral protocol for the behavior in question.

3. SUPPORT AND VENTILATION

   a. Allowing families to express their uncertainties or fears about the survivor engaging in sexual behavior.

   b. Allowing families to express their shame about certain sexual behaviors and the recognition that such behavior may be different from how they have previously viewed the survivor.

4. RESOLVING EMOTIONAL CONFLICTS

   a. Discussing the difficulties family may have in accepting the survivor as a sexual being.

   b. Discussing values about sexuality and how these may be affecting the family's goals for treatment and their cooperation with treatment protocols for sexual behavior.

   c. Discussing the role that family can take in education of the survivor and other family members in sexuality.

jury. Family denial can be very disruptive to rehabilitation treatment. As noted in Chapter Three, those families that show high levels of denial are particularly difficult to engage in productive rehabilitation treatment. Cases in which the family or survivor have high degrees of denial seem to be most frequently discussed among members of the brain-injury rehabilitation team. The four levels of psychological treatment intervention described in this chapter can give the practitioner a framework for addressing the issue of family denial in the course of psychological treatment.

Education

Some discussion of denial should be included as part of the family education program during the course of rehabilitation. The discussion might be most effective and least threatening to the family if it could take place before the family members showed signs of denial. In educating the family, denial should be explained to families as a reaction to the trauma. The practitioner should emphasize that denial is an adaptive and widely seen emotional reaction to any distressing emotional event. It can help a person cope

with the immeasurable stress of the trauma without becoming overwhelmed. At the same time, however, extreme denial may lead family members to make impractical treatment plans for the survivor or to ignore significant emotional stressors affecting themselves (see Deaton, 1988). The
practitioner might engage family members in discussion of the subject by
giving them a list of behaviors or examples to illustrate adaptive and maladaptive denial. They may be encouraged to identify these behaviors in themselves and others as part of treatment. The family may be more comfortable
discussing the issue of denial with respect to the survivor's behavior. This
discussion may give the practitioner some hints about the family's feelings
about such behavior and how they might react to such behavior being noticed in themselves.

Resolving Practical Problems

When a family is showing denial behavior that is affecting treatment, in addition to providing education the practitioner can approach the subject
from a problem-solving perspective. The practitioner points out how the
family's interpretation of the survivor's behavior or of the rehabilitation
treatment is affecting the course of treatment. The practitioner then discusses the advantages and disadvantages of the family's point of view with
respect to the survivor's course of recovery. Whereas in the educational approach the practitioner presents some general information about the denial,
in the practical approach, it is best if the practitioner deals with specific
and concrete instances or examples. Family members who are experiencing
denial will more readily refute or ignore information that is general in nature than information that is specifically linked to their situation.

> Case example: The wife of a survivor maintained the hope that her husband
> would be able to return to work as manager of a food services office after his
> injury. The wife had worked with her husband in the office and was waiting
> until he recovered in order to return to work herself. The psychologist and re-
> habilitation team felt that the severity of the man's injury and his age, 67
> years, made it unlikely that he would be able to return to the same type of
> work. The team did feel, however, that this man would be able to do some less
> demanding work within the office environment, especially given that he be-
> came very familiar with the workings of the office over the years. The team
> also felt that the wife would benefit emotionally from returning to work her-
> self rather than isolating herself by spending all of her time with her husband.
> The psychologist discussed this issue with the wife in terms of the conse-
> quences she would face if her husband did and did not improve to the point
> where he could return to work. Specific examples of the husband's work ac-
> tivities and his performance on similar tasks within the rehabilitation setting
> were used to illustrate how the man's work performance would likely be in-

adequate. The psychologist did not wish to reject entirely the possibility that the man would recover because such an approach would have undermined the woman's sense of hope. Rather, the psychologist tried to help the woman see that she had something to benefit from setting up alternative vocational plans for herself and her husband in the short-term, while still maintaining the hope that he would recover in the long-term.

Setting short-term goals with families should be part of any treatment program as a means of overcoming denial. By setting short-term goals, the family is focused on what can be expected over a brief period of time. Their long-term expectations are left unchallenged.

At times it may be necessary to allow families to experience the consequences of their denial even though the practitioner may feel that the family will experience failure or disappointment. Relevant to the case example above, Fawber and Wachter (1987) illustrate how such an approach can be used to affect survivors who deny their postinjury vocational potential. Having the family face the direct consequences of their decisions may be the most effective means of helping them to recognize their denial. To allow for such experiences is not irresponsible on the practitioner's part as long as the practitioner remains available to the family for support and counseling in the future.

Emotional Support

Providing emotional support can be an indirect method of addressing the family's denial. The practitioner does not confront the family about their denial but rather focuses on continued emotional support for the family, permitting them to maintain hope that the distressing situation will improve (Caplan & Schechter, 1987). The support that is provided, however, is selective. That is, verbalizations and actions of the family that indicate a realistic acknowledgement of the survivor's status are reinforced by the practitioner. Denial behavior is ignored rather than confronted. In this way, the practitioner seeks to maintain open communication and a positive relationship with the family. Should any confrontation be necessary at some future point, the past support that the practitioner has provided may give the practitioner more leverage in persuading the family of a given point of view.

Resolving Emotional Conflicts

In this approach the practitioner seeks to identify and bring to light what feelings and thoughts may motivate a family member to maintain denial of the survivor's condition. At times, the issue of denial could be addressed indirectly by discussing with the family members how they might feel if the survivor were not to get any better. In this hypothetical discussion, the family members may become aware of some of their feelings that are making it difficult to acknowledge the survivor's status.

Case example: The wife of a 45-year-old survivor discussed with the psychologist her plans to have her husband return home after his recovery. The rehabilitation team felt that this woman was expecting her husband to recover further than he seemed likely to recover. The psychologist had shared this information with the wife in the process of discussing psychological test results and other evaluations from the rehabilitation team, yet the wife seemed to maintain her feeling that her husband would recover further. The psychologist took a different approach and discussed with the woman how she might feel, hypothetically, if her husband didn't recover. The woman was disturbed by this thought. In the course of discussing alternative living arrangements for her husband if he did not go home, she discussed her anxiety about managing alone and her past dependency on her husband in their marital relationship. The psychologist pointed out how her anxiety about being alone may be related to her fervent feeling about her husband's recovery. Though she continued to insist on her husband's full recovery and return home, the psychologist and rehabilitation team felt that she became more receptive to their input about her husband's condition. The psychologist focused on providing her with information about community resources should she need to manage without her husband, and discussed with her some of her anxiety about being independent.

This example illustrates how the denial that is expressed may be motivated by underlying feelings of distress. The practitioner can attempt to address these issues by the questions posed to the family member in counseling discussion. The practitioner seeks to answer questions like: What does it mean to let go of denial? What kind of substitute can be provided? What does the injury symbolize, represent to the family and to a given family member?

At times the practitioner's intervention will focus on the structural changes that have occurred in the context of the injury.

Case example: A brain-injury survivor was injured when he was 18 years old. At the time of his admission to a postacute rehabilitation facility he was 25 years old and severely impaired in his physical mobility and his expressive language. He was wheelchair dependent and able to propel himself independently for only short distances. He ate independently although slowly because of severe limitations in the range of motion in his hands and arms. Neuropsychological evaluation revealed cognitive impairments consistent with a moderate to severe brain injury. He was admitted to a postacute rehabilitation facility in order to receive more intensive physical rehabilitation than he had received at the time of his injury, when the resources for brain-injury rehabilitation treatment were not as prevalent. His mother was very closely involved in his treatment, visiting frequently and making many suggestions to the staff about how treatment should be provided. She was felt to be very suspicious of the treatments provided by staff, questioning many different aspects of the treatment. She antagonized the staff who felt manipulated and controlled by her. The survivor's father accompanied the mother on all visits to the facility but tended to defer to her in discussions with staff. The staff felt that the parents were focusing on small details of their son's care and avoiding facing the larger issues of the severity of the son's deficits and the difficulty of expecting much recovery so late postinjury. In psychological counseling sessions it became evident that their overt behavior masked a marital conflict. The psychologist felt that the parents, especially the mother, were focusing their attention on the survivor in order to avoid facing the difficulties in their own relationship. Based on the parents' behavior in the session, the psychologist hypothesized that the survivor had served as an emotional barrier between the parents prior to his injury, but now that he was not at home and unable to fill this role the parents' sense of marital conflict had increased. In psychological treatment sessions, the psychologist sought to reinforce the father's standing in the family system by encouraging him to speak his thoughts and feelings in treatment sessions and contrasting his comments with those of his wife. When there was a difference of opinion between the spouses, the psychologist backed off and encouraged them to resolve it. This technique had the effect of increasing the conflicts between parents in the treatment session but also forced them, for perhaps the first time, to try to resolve their conflicts directly rather than through their son. As a result, communication between the parents was more direct and their emotional conflicts with staff were reduced because they were no longer working out these conflicts through their son. Unfortunately, the parents discontinued these contacts with the psychologist because they felt that the discussions were not directly pertinent to their son's needs in treatment.

It bears repeating that denial is probably the most difficult problem that the rehabilitation professional will face in the course of brain-injury rehabilitation treatment. Though the cognitive and physical impairments of the survivor are numerous, and the emotional distress of the family and survivor is profound, problems of denial are the most emotionally trying ones for professionals. The treatment framework outlined above will hardly resolve all of the problems that professionals will face with respect to denial. Having a framework on which to base treatment intervention, however, will enable the professional to endure the long struggles of treatment with a family in the throes of denial. Levels of treatment intervention for denial are summarized in Table 5.4.

Discharge and Termination of Treatment

Discharge is an inevitable part of rehabilitation treatment. Because of the long duration of treatment within any one setting, the family and survivor

Table 5.4   Examples of Different Levels of Psychological Treatment for Families with Problems of Denial

1. EDUCATION

a. Explaining denial as a common reaction to emotional distress in all people.

b. Explaining how denial can be expressed in adaptive and maladaptive ways with respect to the trauma and the rehabilitation process.

2. PROBLEM-SOLVING

a. Identifying a problem in the treatment process that may be related to or the result of the family's denial of the trauma.

b. Discussing the possible positive and negative consequences for the survivor and the family of the family's point of view with respect to a particular problem.

c. Setting short-term goals for treatment that do not directly clash with the family's long-term hopes or beliefs for the survivor's recovery.

d. Allowing family to face the consequences of their denial with the understanding that the practitioner is available for continued supportive treatment.

3. SUPPORT AND VENTILATION

a. Supporting the family's statements or actions that indicate a realistic appraisal of the survivor's condition and needs without directly confronting their denial.

b. Being available to family for emotional support regardless of the family's decisions about treatment and the consequences of their actions.

4. RESOLVING EMOTIONAL CONFLICTS

a. Identifying underlying feelings and thoughts that may motivate the family member to express denial and discussing these feelings and thoughts openly with the family.

b. Engaging the family in a hypothetical discussion of their feelings if the survivor's recovery does not meet their expectation.

c. Discussing the purpose that denial may serve in the family structure as it affects the family's cohesion, values, communication and relationship with others outside the family.

---

will have developed a level of familiarity and dependency on professionals in the setting. Transfer to another treatment setting or to home may arouse anxiety in the family because of the uncertainty about the new treatment environment.

The family's anxiety about discharge may be focused on whether staff at a new treatment facility will be able to understand and manage the survivor. If the survivor is to be discharged to his home, the family may be anxious about their ability to manage the survivor without professional support nearby.

Discharge is also interpreted by the family as an indication of success or failure. For example, when a survivor is leaving an acute rehabilitation facility for a more independent treatment setting, discharge may be a reason for joy and satisfaction for the survivor and family. For the less fortunate survivor who had made little progress and is being considered for longer term nursing care facilities, the family may feel that the professional staff is giving up on their family member or that the survivor or family have in some way failed.

The tendency for many survivors and families to interpret the rehabilitation environment as an educational setting often reinforces this notion of success or failure at discharge. It is common for survivors to refer to their therapy activities as "classes" and to the rehabilitation professionals as "teachers." Staff, unwittingly, may reinforce this notion by describing rehabilitation therapy activities as reeducation or relearning, and treating discharges, especially for survivors who have made much progress, as graduations.

The approach to handling discharge with a family in psychological treatment is an extension of the principles that have been discussed previously. By focusing on clearly defined goals for treatment and through regular contacts with the family in psychological treatment, the matter of discharge should not come as a surprise. Rather, it is something that should be discussed throughout the course of treatment sessions. To this end, the overall goals for treatment should be defined at the outset and then redefined at regular intervals during the course of treatment. The therapy meetings with the family then become an occasion for review of treatment goals as well as working on any pressing issues in treatment. The matter of discharge in this format can become something that families are aware of well in advance of the actual time of discharge.

When the time for discharge becomes more clear so that it can be defined in terms of specific date or within a span or weeks (for example, sometime in April; or before Thanksgiving), the practitioner should direct the family to discuss their emotional reactions to discharge. Treatment goals for discussion of discharge should be to help the families gauge their expectations for the future and maintain their hope and energy for future rehabilitation work. As before, education is an important part of discharge discussions. If the survivor is to be discharged to a new treatment site, families may not clearly understand the purpose of the treatment at the new site. This lack of understanding can lead to a disruption in treatment at the next treatment site. Having a clear sense of the family's expectations about treatment at the new treatment site can be particularly informative to the staff at that site.

Case example: The parents and spouse of a survivor were pleased that he was being transferred to a transitional living program from an acute rehabilitation setting. He was Level VII on the Rancho scale at the time of his discharge. In discussing the family's expectations for transitional living, however, the psychologist noted that the family maintained unrealistically high expectations. They saw the transitional living program as a brief interim site where the survivor would only need to stay a period of several weeks before discharge to home. They appeared to have agreed on the transitional living program mainly to give themselves some additional preparation time in order to take the survivor home. They fully expected the survivor to return to home and to work after 4–6 weeks in this transitional program.

Intervention Strategies

Families may expect or wish that the treatment relationship that has developed in one rehabilitation setting will be repeated in other settings. The family needs to understand that the change in setting, personnel, and rehabilitation facility will make the new rehabilitation experience entirely different from the prior one. Particularly difficult is the adjustment from acute rehabilitation to postacute settings such as transitional or home-care settings. Levels of nursing and rehabilitation therapies are different at postacute facilities from acute rehabilitation facilities. Some of the family adjustment problems seen in the postacute settings are the result of inappropriate expectations of the families and the survivors coming from the security and close attention of the acute rehabilitation setting. The amount of dependency that has developed between survivors, families, and professionals cannot be underestimated.

It is important to focus the family on the transition to a new treatment or living environment. It is also important, however, to maintain and support the family's hope and energy for the future. The balance between facilitating the development of realistic expectations and maintaining hope is a fine one, but one that is important to achieve in psychological treatment. Families' hopes and wishes for the future should not be challenged in and of themselves, but only with respect to the short-term decisions they will need to make. For example, family members of a survivor who has responded little to treatment may be able to maintain their hopes and energy during the course of acute rehabilitation treatment. As discharge approaches, however, the reality of the survivor's condition may hit them and they may show signs of more severe emotional distress and depression.

The practitioner should develop a means of presenting these issues without coming across as abrupt or negativistic. One way of presenting the ideas is as follows: "You should never give up hope that your family member will improve. Advances in medical technology make things possible today that we would have never dreamed possible years ago. But it is important for you to think about what type of improvement can be realistically expected over the next 6 to 12 months. If you expect dramatic improvement and plan your life accordingly, you are likely to be disappointed. I would like to help you prevent that from happening. If you go about your daily responsibilities while still maintaining hope you are likely to have more energy to devote to your family member and feel less frustrated."

In addition to these issues, discharge represents termination in a relationship between the practitioner and the family. As in traditional psychotherapy, discussion of termination is an important component of treatment in the rehabilitation setting. The separation from the practitioner that comes with the survivor's discharge may recall for families how they have handled past separations. Understanding these feelings may make the transition to the professionals in the new facility easier. It may also make the family better able to handle their separations from the brain-injury survivor as he or she becomes more independent, or in order to carry out daily life responsibilities rather than spending excessive time at the survivor's bedside. As a rule of thumb, it is recommended that the discussion of termination and its impact on the relationship between the practitioner and the family be discussed at least one month prior to discharge.

These guidelines for discussing discharge assume that there is sufficient time to anticipate and plan the discharge. Often this is not the case. The survivor may need to leave a given rehabilitation facility because of very rapid recovery, extremely severe impairments, medical complications, or funding peculiarities among other reasons. This situation makes discharge planning difficult and complicates family intervention.

In deciding on family intervention for the rapid discharge situation, the practitioner should keep in mind the working relationship that has developed between families and professional staff. When families who have been involved in treatment for a period of several months face discharge, the practitioner should set up a special meeting or series of meetings to discuss the discharge. This may need to be done several times in one week. These discussions are a more intense version of the discussions that might be held over a longer period of time.

With family members of a survivor that has been involved in rehabilitation treatment for only several weeks, the practitioner may have difficulty engaging them in any intense discussion of discharge. The approach in these cases should be more educational and supportive in nature. The goal of psychological intervention should be to prepare the families for what they can expect in the new treatment setting and to encourage them to become involved in obtaining supportive services for themselves.

In sum, the practitioner's role in helping families cope with the survivor's discharge from a rehabilitation facility goes beyond discussion of the family's feelings about terminating treatment with the practitioner. The practitioner also seeks to prepare the family for the discharge placement by helping them to recognize their feelings about the discharge, what it means in terms of the survivor's prognosis for recovery, and how they can accept the changes that occur with discharge while maintaining hope for the future. These points are summarized in Table 5.5.

Table 5.5   Examples of Different Levels of Psychological Treatment
for Families Regarding the Survivor's Discharge from a Treatment Facility

1. EDUCATION
   a. Review of the goals and accomplishments of the survivor within the treatment facility.
   b. Review of the reasons for discharge and the nature of the facility to which the survivor is being sent.
   c. If being sent home, review of the sources of institutional and social support for the family in handling the survivor at home.
2. PROBLEM SOLVING
   a. Developing a behavioral plan that can be used at home by the family, or a list of behavioral interventions that have or have not worked in the past to be sent to the new treatment facility.
   b. Developing a plan for home visits or other activities in order to make the transition from one site to another easier for the family and the survivor.
3. SUPPORT AND VENTILATION
   a. Allowing the family to reflect on the accomplishments or limitations they have recognized in the survivor during his or her treatment.
   b. Allowing the family to express their uncertainties or fears for the survivor in the future.
   c. Helping the family recognize what was most and least helpful to them in the treatment program, in order to use this knowledge in communicating and planning future treatment.
4. RESOLVING EMOTIONAL CONFLICTS
   a. Discussing the different discharge options for family and confronting them about a possible problematic choice for discharge.
   b. Discussing the connection between the family's feelings of success and failure, and their feelings about discharge.
   c. Resolving conflicts among family members in their treatment of the survivor that may affect the survivor in the new treatment facility or at home.

SUMMARY

The structural understanding of the family and the four levels of psychological intervention provide the practitioner with a framework for psychological treatment intervention for the specific problems presented by family members and the survivor. Although specific treatment techniques for the survivor have not been discussed in this chapter, effective family treatment must include an established plan for psychological intervention for the survivor's presenting problems. This plan can be integrated into the plan for family treatment. In providing psychological treatment, the practitioner must work flexibly in the role of family counselor, mediator of the relationship between the survivor and family members, and consultant to the other rehabilitation professionals in their dealings with the family.

A husband speaks
by Robert

This is the story of Bob and Linda. We were a young couple. I was 27. Linda was 24. We knew each other well having been together for five years before marrying. Linda was a hard-working woman with big dreams of raising a family. She had that complete unselfishness necessary to be a good mother, and it was this single trait that I admired most in her. She never forgot birthdays, and enjoyed a reputation as a kind, generous, and cheerful person.

After just three short months of marriage, our lives were violently interrupted by a terrible car accident that left Linda in a coma for 3½ months. Life would never be the same for either of us. We were separated at the accident scene and sent to different hospitals. One week later I signed out of my hospital and made the trip to the hospital where Linda was. The sight of her in the ICU with a half dozen IVs, chest tubes draining her lungs, a respirator hose disfiguring her nose and breathing for her, a bite block in her mouth, her head shaved, two bolts in her forehead connected by wires to constantly beeping monitors, and that rotating bed, complete with head vice, straps and padded restraints, had the feeling of some sick science-fiction movie. I have never been so intimidated nor so challenged.

Our relationship at the hospital was completely one-sided. For two months, I could barely push aside the apparatus to kiss her on the cheek. My conversations with her went unanswered. My roles as her lover, friend, and companion were put aside. All my energy went into being advocate and motivator for her.

Looking back on the experience now eight years after the accident, I see three general stages in our relationship, each with its own problems and adjustments: the first two years after the accident when Linda was actively involved in inpatient and outpatient rehabilitation treatment, the third through sixth years after the accident when we attempted to live together and reestablish our marriage, and the time after that when we agreed to live apart and ultimately became divorced.

The first stage, when Linda was involved in acute-rehabilitation treatment, was a time when things were most consistent and tangible. It was a nonstop crisis, but it was consistent. When Linda did come out of the coma, there were many behaviors that came and went, at times weekly. Nurses and staff usually warned us. These changes didn't last long. I never felt threatened by them nor did I need too much strategy to handle them.

The first big change I noticed was a self-centeredness that had never been there before. Under the circumstances I made nothing of it at first. It seemed quite natural for someone in Linda's situation. At times, though, I felt like a single parent with an unappreciative child. Linda required constant attention and had very little capacity for empathy or compassion towards others. This was a sharp contrast to her former self. I had difficulty tolerating this behavior after a while. She lapsed into self-pity and became bitter and resentful. Her self-centered behavior prevented her from fulfilling her part of our relationship. She could not listen to any complaints of mine without trivializing them in light of her own. I became frustrated because I could not get her to change this behavior even though I saw it as a major roadblock to her recovery. I also felt cheated. I found myself deprived. Dreams were fading. I would have to say that her self-centeredness played a major part in the demise of our marriage.

A second change in Linda during this stage was the inconsistency of her behavior. Amidst totally appropriate behavior there would be periods of inappropriate behavior, and vice versa. At times she would act like a 24 year old; at other times like a 6 year old. I found the early stages of this phenomenon generally more humorous. As she progressed emotionally and intellectually it was less frequent but also more troublesome. I worried as she acquired more freedom and responsibility that her behavior would become more shocking on a social level. Fortunately, this inconsistency diminished about two years after the accident.

In summarizing our marriage during the first two years of Linda's recovery I would say that there was no marriage. The relationship was very paternal and needed to be so. As a spouse I greatly enjoyed her dependence on me, and my importance as her advocate. It played up to my ego and to my parental instincts. It was a novelty and, at times, fun being a parent but underneath great pressure was building. I was suppressing normal needs and desires.

The second stage of our relationship was a time during which Linda was less actively involved in rehabilitation treatment and had returned home with me. I would equate Linda's emotional and intellectual level at this time with that of an adolescent. Her self-centeredness showed itself as jealousy. She felt threatened by most women. She was aware that I had needs and desires, but didn't really know how or didn't have the confidence to try to satisfy them. She was very insecure about sex and didn't like her appearance. I couldn't revive the old romantic feelings. I still felt like her father. I couldn't consider her an equal partner.

I retreated to my work and hobbies and used them to fill the loneliness, to satisfy my need to feel important, and basically to avoid confrontation with Linda. I believe we got through these years because Linda continued to make progress. She had successful surgery to her hip and elbow. This allowed her to be more independent and she started driving. A carpenter by trade, I built our house. I became involved in car racing and raced on a very successful championship team. These accomplishments provided pride, satisfaction, and cameraderie that disguised our festering problems.

I also became aware that we had a tendency to blame our problems on the head trauma. Some of our problems at the time were normal to a marriage and would not be resolved by the natural healing of Linda's brain, nor by blaming her deficiencies. Yet, we could not see past the head trauma. We both thought of ourselves as different even though our ultimate goal was not to be. I was so engrossed in trying to motivate her that I could not even see my own problems. Linda's being the center of my attention had turned from a positive to negative experience.

Six years after the accident we split up on the premise that she would go away to school for a year, and we would reassess things after that. It became clear to me that I was burnt out and that Linda was a new person who needed to shed the ghost of her former self, to explore and learn to love the new person she had become.

The separation was tough on Linda at first. For me, it was like an incredible weight had been taken off me. I fought with guilt for a while, and eventually decided that it was useless and tried to ignore it. Linda became challenged by school and a new social life. She made great strides towards self-esteem and independence. I had an experience with another woman, short-lived, that reminded me of my worth and satified my deprived needs. This initially drove a wedge between Linda and me. She was jealous and I believe that this was the first time that we both entertained the possibility that our marriage might fail.

Although we stayed in contact, Linda filed for divorce in the seventh year. Sometimes I think she did it half as a threat, hoping I would come back. I felt as though the divorce was necessary. If we had a future together it would be under new terms.

It took another year for us to become officially divorced. During that time we saw each other often. I know it was tough on Linda that year and at times I got depressed. But I had a new hope for us. We could make it on our own. Maybe we would get together again, maybe we wouldn't. Marriage didn't seem to be as important anymore. It was important that we be happy. Linda needed to be happy with herself before she could make someone else happy, the same for me. We had both lost ourselves in the course of our ordeal.

Today we are friends. Linda is doing wonderfully on her own. Her work at the day-care center (she had a college degree in child development before the accident) is satisfying and keeps her from too much self-pity. She has a romantic void in her life but I believe that time will fill her void. There is a new person in my life. Although emotions still run too high for the three of us to share time together, I feel that someday we will.

There were times during this ordeal that I related to Robert DeNiro in the movie "The Deer Hunter" wondering how, after the stress and intensity of our experience, we would ever return to everyday life. In fact, everyday life will never be the same as it was. We lost our innocence, and we lost our marriage, but we found ourselves.

6

The Family Self-Help
Movement

The growth of professional and public recognition of traumatic brain injury is due in large part to an active and vital self-help movement. The groups that comprise this self-help movement are involved in political and clinical settings to influence the directions of treatment and research as well as the direction of institutional and governmental policy. The rehabilitation professional working with families of brain-injury survivors must incorporate into his or her treatment plan a means of interacting with the self-help movement. In the present chapter, the traumatic brain injury self-help movement will be examined in terms of the impact that it can have on the psychological adjustment and treatment of families and survivors.

HISTORY OF THE SELF-HELP MOVEMENT

The self-help movement has developed in many different areas of health and mental health work (Gaioni, 1988; Leerhsen, et al., 1989; McCormack, 1981). It is estimated that there are as many as 500,000 self-help groups in existence (NIMH, 1981). The basic principle of self-help groups is that the group can "provide emotional support and practical help in dealing with a problem that is common to all members" (McCormack, 1981, p. 2). Rather than relying entirely on professionals to provide such support, self-help group members seek to provide support to each other. Individuals with conditions as diverse as developmental disabilities, chronic emotional difficulties, specific medical conditions and addictions have established self-help groups.

The development of self-help in general can be traced to several factors. Perhaps the primary factor is the change in society during the last half of the twentieth century. Technological advances in travel and communication have led to changes in the distribution of families and communities. Social supports that used to be available within the extended family and the local community are not as strong (McCormack, 1981). Yet, the individual's need for social support has not changed and has necessitated a replacement for the lack of community. The self-help movement fills this gap.

Institutional and professional treatment does not, and cannot, provide the day-to-day support to counter the isolation and emotional distress that many individuals in crisis and their family members feel. Sharing experiences with people in similar situations or with similar values provides a person with another means of coping with his or her predicament. Gaoini (1988) notes that self-help groups can "have an immense normalizing effect on members . . . such groups seem to go past the pathology to recognize and nurture members's strengths and competence" (p. 31). This aspect of self-help groups may be one reason why they are able to help some individuals who are not helped by professionals.

The lack of personal connections and support within the community at large that stimulated the development of self-help groups also extends to the health care system. Individuals and families have found that the growth in size and technological sophistication of health care institutions, and the proliferation of specialists have created a system of care that is more impersonal, one over which the individual feels little control (see Cousins, 1979). Individuals and families dissatisfied with the treatment available in professional settings and seeking more control over the care provided to them, sought out an independent means of providing treatment. As a result some people may prefer the treatment provided by some self-help groups, such as Alcoholics Anonymous, to professionally based treatments. Even if they do not provide an alternative to professional treatment, self-help groups provide a useful supplementary treatment that "does not intend to replace physicians, therapists, and other skilled professionals" (NIMH, 1981, p. 4) but rather emphasizes peer support and personal rather than professional experience.

Not all individuals choose to be involved in self-help groups because they were dissatisfied with professional treatment. Consolidation into larger self-help groups give the individuals more power in affecting the course of treatment and political decisions with respect to their areas of concern (Gaioni, 1988). The consolidation into such groups is one means of gaining greater control over the treatment within a given treatment setting and over the priorities for treatment funding and research on a governmental level.

The opportunity for education is also a key motivation for the development of self-help groups. The professional services for a given medical or mental health problem may be limited by geographical or financial reasons. Information in professional journals and conferences is not often made available to families or nonprofessionals. The self-help group provides a means of disseminating information about clinical issues and community resources with respect to a given condition. It also provides an opportunity for group members to learn from each others' experiences thereby providing positive role models for the group members (Gaoini, 1988; Yalom, 1985).

SELF-HELP WITH TRAUMATIC BRAIN INJURY

In the field of traumatic brain-injury rehabilitation the self-help movement has led to the development of several different groups with which families of survivors and professionals may be involved. The fulcrum for many of these self-help groups is the National Head Injury Foundation (NHIF). NHIF was developed around 1980 by several families in the Boston area "as a grassroots consumer organization to promote advocacy and public awareness (of traumatic head injury)" (Spivack, 1986, p. 42).

Bush (1988) has outlined some of the issues that NHIF addresses. These include education focused on prevention of traumatic brain injury, increased public awareness of the consequences of it, and efforts to change public attitudes toward the survivors. Education is also provided to families of survivors and to professionals, including consultation regarding research. Efforts are directed toward influencing public policy through legislation at a state and national level. Finally, the NHIF is a forum for the communication between the professionals, families, and survivors who work together in the field of rehabilitation.

Being a relatively young organization, the NHIF does not encompass all traumatic brain-injury support and interest groups. Some state organizations are only loosely affiliated with the national organization or are in the process of becoming more closely affiliated. Other groups such as Mothers Against Drunk Driving (MADD) and Students Against Drunk Driving (SADD) may overlap in their goals and their membership with NHIF.

NHIF is not an accrediting organization. Rehabilitation facilities need to meet standards set by organizations such as the Committee for Accreditation of Rehabilitation Facilities (CARF) or the Joint Commission on Accreditation of Hospitals (JCAH). NHIF does not certify professionals nor organizations, although it does maintain an extensive directory of treatment resources and educational materials.

Much of NHIF's energy is focused on political advocacy and stimulating awareness of and research in brain-injury rehabilitation. In addition to the NHIF and its chapters, smaller support groups exist in rehabilitation facilities, community agencies, and private homes. These groups are focused more directly on peer emotional support and family networking (Rosenthal & Young, 1988; Williams, 1987). Professionals may be involved in these groups as facilitators of group discussion, particularly if the groups are held at rehabilitation facilities offering their own support programs.

NHIF AND THE REHABILITATION PROFESSIONAL

The presence of NHIF and its smaller affilitated groups is an asset to the practitioner working with families of brain-injury survivors. By encouraging families to become part of the organization, the practitioner shows the family his or her concern for their need to be connected with families in similar situations. The practitioner also acknowledges that his or her expertise is limited, and that there are other resources available that can be beneficial to the family's adjustment to the trauma.

The family's participation in support groups and contact with other families of survivors is an important supplement to professional treatment. There are some things that families may only appreciate or understand when they are in communication with other families who have had similar experiences (McKinlay & Hickox, 1988). As has been mentioned, many families are uncertain how to judge professionals' opinions about their family member's treatment prognosis and progress. For example, decisions about locations of treatment facilities, types of treatment, difficult stages in the rehabilitation process or other issues may be more readily made by the family if they have discussed the issues with families who have made similar decisions.

Case example: Parents of a young child who was comatose after a severe brain injury attended their first family support group approximately 3 weeks after their child's injury. The group was organized by family members but also included survivors of brain injury and local rehabilitation professionals. The group began with each member introducing him or herself to the group and explaining some reasons for attending the group. This couple was so distressed and exhausted from the past three weeks that the wife was unable to speak and the husband could offer only a few words of introduction. During the course of the group meeting, a speaker from the state organization provided information about activities, educational information, and accomplishments of the group. Another speaker gave a presentation on family adjustment problems after brain injury. Then there was a general discussion among the participants. The parents of the injured child appeared to become more comfortable during the meeting. They shared with the group some of their concerns about their child's chances for recovery, some of the medical decisions they needed to make, and long-term treatment options for their child. Group members provided them with support and encouragement. Some of the group members were relatives of survivors who had been in coma for longer than three weeks. These family members shared with the couple their experiences in rehabilitation and what the survivors were now able to do. Both speakers gave the parents information in the form of reading material on the subject of brain injury and names of local groups that had additional educational information. At the end of the group meeting, both parents were conversing comfortably with other group members. Though they admitted they were still very distressed, they appeared more energetic and appreciative of the assistance they had received.

As this example illustrates, the education and emotional support provided by support groups complements that which is provided by the professional. This couple had not received any formal psychological counseling so soon after their child's injury. They appeared overwhelmed, confused, and isolated. Their participation in the support group with the opportunity to meet informally with other family members, survivors, and professionals helped to break their emotional isolation and socialize them to the system of care and support that existed for their child and them. Their positive experience with the group meeting made them receptive to further professional psychological treatment not to mention further support group participation.

In addition to the family, the rehabilitation professional benefits from actual participation in the self-help groups. Listening and interacting with the families in the context of a family support group and in the context of the larger organization can give the professional a larger view of the family's experience. With this experience, the professional can be more sensitive and effective in his or her work with the family. Through participation in NHIF conferences the professional can also benefit by keeping up to date on treatment developments in the field of brain-injury rehabilitation.

There are potential pitfalls in the interaction between the practitioner and family self-help groups. These can be avoided if the professional adequately prepares the family for involvement in the support group and if the professional clearly defines his or her role in the group (Williams, 1987). One problem may occur when the family's affiliation with the group exposes them to bad experiences other families have had in the course of rehabilitation. The family may gain valuable information in this way, but the experience can be detrimental to their working relationship with the rehabilitation team if it is not put in perspective by the professional. The professional can accomplish this by explaining to the family that recovery from traumatic brain injury is different for each survivor and family. Rehabilitation technology is not sufficiently advanced to allow professionals to predict adequately who will benefit from what treatments. Training of rehabilitation professionals working in brain injury is quite variable. Thus, it is expected that there will be a range of positive and negative experiences by survivors and families. Often rehabilitation professionals exacerbate this problem by not sharing with families the drawbacks of some treatment interventions.

The professional should recognize that rehabilitation treatment is not a service provided by knowing professionals to ignorant families and survivors. Rather it is a joint process that involves the input of professionals, families and survivors. Seeing the survivor and family as partners with the professional in the treatment process may help the practitioner to manage splits in opinion that may occur between families and professionals without letting them disrupt the overall goals of treatment. Some concrete ways of productively handling the inevitable differences between families and professionals are through regular psychological treatment sessions as described in this book. This approach may be taken further by developing joint educational and political groups within a treatment facility to focus on pressing issues for treatment within the facility and within the surrounding community. Although larger health care facilities have volunteer associations, most do not include families of patients in the higher levels of the organization such as administrative planning boards. Yet, the involvement of families at this level of the health care organization might stimulate the development of treatment programs that more directly meet the family's needs. Involvement of families in larger facility-wide planning boards may help this process. It is more difficult for a family to refute a particular treatment plan for a survivor when the family knows that other families have been involved in the actual design and implementation of such a treatment plan.

Another problem that may occur for families in support groups is that the family avoids the group because the role of group leader is unclear or that the other families in the groups are discussing situations that are not relevant to their own experience.

Case example: A support group at a rehabilitation facility had been meeting regularly with consistent membership for about one year. The group was comprised of family members of brain-injury survivors and a rehabilitation professional who facilitated the group discussion. One woman in this group was very outspoken, at times hostile to treatment professionals and appeared to have difficulty acknowledging the severity of her family member's injuries. After the first year in the group she decided to start her own group out of her home and invited the members of the facility support group to attend. Several members of the original group attended this woman's group, in addition to maintaining membership in the original group. After about three sessions they chose to leave the new group. They told the professional who facilitated the original group that they found the new group unproductive, and that various family members brought up emotional concerns and the group was uncertain about how to handle the discussion. Several years later the rehabilitation professional felt the group had achieved a true level of autonomy and sought to leave the group. A similar scenario occured in which the group members were uncertain about how to handle the group discussion and requested professional involvement.

This example illustrates several important points about the organization of support groups and the roles of family members and professionals. Effective group experiences require someone to facilitate group discussion and to serve as an objective participant in the group. The rehabilitation professional can fill such a role with the goal of helping family members to learn the basic skills of group dynamics including effective ways of listening to, supporting, and confronting other group members. As mentioned several times before in this book, the family members of brain-injury survivors enter rehabilitation treatment involuntarily under tremendous emotional stress. It is expecting a lot of such a family member to identify and experience his or her own areas of emotional distress and to manage the dynamics of a group of individuals in similar predicaments. The goal of the rehabilitation professional in such a group must be to facilitate rather than lead the group and to educate the family members so that they can participate in the group experience independently.

The self-help movement as a whole, and particularly within the field of brain-injury rehabilitation, has generally been unstudied by clinical researchers. Yet, the movement is prominent and growing in influence. The self-help movement in brain-injury rehabilitation can be a valuable asset to psychological treatment of the brain-injury survivor and family if incorporated into treatment properly. A useful direction for research would be to discover the actual impact of self-help on family members' emotional adjustment to the survivor's injury. Also of interest would be the impact of the professional's involvement in such groups on the professional's treatment efficacy.

SUMMARY

Families need the opportunity to interact with other families who share similar experiences. Such interactions between families provide emotional support that supplements the support provided by professionals. By joining together in family groups and participating in some of the community awareness and political activities of such groups, family members may also exercise more control over the treatment provided to their family members. Professionals may assist families in self-help activities but must recognize that their role is as a consultant to such activities rather than a director. Self-help groups provide a means of increasing interactions and building bridges between professionals and families in ways that may not occur within the confines of standard rehabilitation treatment.

A daughter speaks
by Judy

My name is Judy. I'm 39-years-old and single. I'm going to try to express my feelings and thoughts after a traumatic change in my life occured. My mother, Maria, suffered a closed head injury this past summer.

Before this injury, Maria was independent. She lived alone in her own house in the Bronx and worked long hours at a job and at home. Our relationship was strong and close. I helped her with her housekeeping and in taking care of her grandchildren (my nieces and nephews). She had quite a load on her hands. Of course, as in any mother and daughter relationship, we argued. Since I did not live at home I would usually just ignore her. Maria is a strong woman set in her ways and by no means would she give an inch when we disagreed on a topic. By the same token, so am I. But anytime we needed each other we would let bygones be bygones and supported each other.

In August 1989 everything changed. I had just come home to my own apartment from shopping. I still remember; it was a sunny Sunday afternoon. As I turned the corner to my building three transit police cars were waiting for me. I knew immediately that something was really wrong, but I kept myself from thinking the worst. I just assumed that my mother had been mugged. It had happened twice before. I just prayed that she was fine.

The detectives were nervous and evasive. They would not elaborate on what happened, just that I had to accompany them to Brooklyn. I was taken to a hospital where the Chief of Detectives and my mother's immediate supervisor were waiting for me. By the expression on their faces I suddenly realized that this was more than a mugging. I asked, "What happened?" They explained as best as they could that my mother was beaten up. She was in surgery; a life or death matter. I panicked. I froze, and then kicked, went berserk and asked how could such a tragedy happen. I could not hear any explanations; I was numbed. I wanted to run but did not even have the strength. It was as though I was a zombie in a trancelike state. The only thing that kept ringing in my mind was "She is critical . . . might not make it." I never felt so useless, alone, and inadequate. I was so emotionally messed up that the emergency doctor wanted to sedate me. That's when I screamed my head off. No way was I going to be under sedation in case something happened to my mom.

I finally made it to the emergency room. I waited there for hours, crying and praying until I felt that I had no tears left. I wanted to see my mother but was not allowed in. One of the staff doctors realized that I was alone. He asked for my immediate family but I could not remember any numbers. He then took my purse and called my uncle. I think he must have broken speed limits driving to the hospital, he was at my side so quickly. He also brought with him another uncle. I was too upset to speak to my uncles. They had to talk to the detectives to find out what had happened. I never saw men cry like babies, but both of them did. Since I would not be sedated or tranquilized, coffee was brought to me. That only made matters worse. I got sick. I kept hoping that it was a nightmare and I would wake up and call my mother and everything would be fine. But no, to my dismay it was reality.

The nurses were kind and tried again to explain what had happened to my mother. I still could not understand. I did not want to know anything, I just wanted to see my mother. What would happen to me if she died? I could hardly bear to think about it.

After several hours my mother came out of surgery, still in critical condition and in a coma. They told me that she had a less than four percent chance of making it through the night. I pleaded with them, I wanted to see her. I finally did but not alone. My God!!! I can still see all those tubes, all the blood. She was swollen. She looked like a monster, and I could not do anything to help her. I felt anger. At that instant I felt I could have killed the person who did this to my mother with my bare hands and no remorse, just an eye for an eye. It took him less than an hour to do so much damage and he changed my mother's life forever. I knew it would take the rest of my life to cope with it. I just wanted to know why? How come? No answers were available.

I knew then that I could never deal with this tragedy by myself. I could not for the life of me bear this alone so I did what I thought was best. I asked for a priest. I received some kind of comfort at that time from him, but honestly that was not enough. I needed a miracle. I could not lose my mother. I promised that I would change everything that was possible for me to do, even give up my own life, only if she lived. I kept on saying to myself that she could not leave me, not all alone.

I stayed with her for nine consecutive days while she was in a coma. I never went home. I did not eat, sleep or even think in a normal way. In the intensive care unit, I slept next to her. They had mentioned to me that people in a coma can be brought out of it by familiar songs. I sang to her. I played her favorite songs. I tried everything. I begged her and even pinched her. I just wanted her to open her eyes.

Finally, after nine long days she opened her left eye slightly. I noticed right away and called the doctor. She was trying to come out of it. I knew

then that, no matter what, I would have her back. I did not let her go back
to sleep. I worked with her and with her therapists and made her move
slowly each day. I learned so much about her treatments, that I was even offered a job at the hospital. I had lost 16 pounds and looked like hell. My
employer asked me to come back to work just so that I could keep my mind
occupied. He knew that it was just a matter of time before I would collapse.
I finally went back to work with the understanding that I would set my own
hours and stay at the hospital for as long as I was needed.

As my mother progressed and came out of her coma completely I realized that there would be a long, hard, painful recovery path for her. She did
not recognize me. I cried every time she would tell me to leave because she
did not know me. I had to slowly explain to her who I was. I had to teach
her how to cough and eat. All she kept saying was, "Leave me alone." I handled this by just leaving the room everytime she would stare blankly at my
face and ask me "Who are you? Why are you here?"

To this day I do not know where I got all the strength, but I stuck by her.
I would not give up. She was going to be fine. No matter what it took or how
long I would do it. It is hard to express my feelings. I was just emotionally,
physically, and mentally stressed out.

Everything seemed to be closing in on me. I suddenly became a house
owner, a guardian to the kids, my mother's sole support, and everything
else, including caretaker of my mother's cat. I wanted to run, scream. I had
no one to help me. No one to lend me a hand. It was all up to "Judy." I
would go to work, to the hospital, to my apartment, to my mother's house,
and then, only if I could, back home to sleep.

At times I wanted to die and even thought of committing suicide. I was
irritable, unbearable to be with. All my friends pitied me. I could not believe that I even felt guilty and did not know why. My poor friends tried everything from flowers to music. Nothing seemed to help. I just fought with
them, and cried all the time. This went on for months. Then I said, enough
was enough, I needed help. I started therapy, first in Albany where my
mother had been transferred for treatment. It really helped. I could talk
about my feelings to someone who at least understood what I was going
through. He told me I had to let my anger and frustrations out, and not bot-
tle it up inside. With help I started smiling again.

I thought no one in this world could imagine what a family member of a
head-injured person goes through. But I spoke to families that had gone
through similar tragedies and I did not feel so alone anymore. I felt that I
was not the only person who was going through this. Each case is unique.
Each person is affected differently. Everyone hurts and the hurting does not
go away. Time just eases the pain but even today I still hurt everytime I see
the confused look in my mother's eye. I now deal with it differently, thanks
to therapy, but it still hurts.

Since this tragedy my mother is very dependent on me. She is overemotional and sensitive now. She has a lot of fears. I have moved back to her home. I make all the important decisions. In other words we have reversed roles. I'm still in therapy but not as often. I include my mother in everything and everyday tasks. I hope that every time I make a decision it is for her best. But, I realize that for the rest of my life I will have to be there for her. As I mentioned in the beginning, what took an hour to do, has changed my life completely.

I do not regret my decisions. I will take care of her for as long as she needs me. I would never dream of leaving her. I love her too much and I almost lost her. Some people say that I am sacrificing a lot, but I just say I love my mother. I thank God she is alive. She understands my position now and is a joy to be with. She helps as much as she can and adores me.

So I feel no matter how dark the tunnel seems to be, there is always a ray of hope at the other end. Patience, love, faith, and understanding from those who know what head injuries are about eases the pain. I would have never made it alone and for that reason I am willing to share these thoughts and feelings with you. I hope I can be of some assistance to someone out there who is going through a similar experience. I wish that I did not have to write this and that no family ever has to experience these things, but that's wishful thinking. I just hope that at least I was some comfort in some way. I know firsthand how hard it is. It's unbearable.

7

The Emotional Impact
of Family Treatment
on the Professional

Psychological treatment will arouse certain emotional reactions in the individuals providing such treatment. These reactions have been described in the field of psychotherapy (Weiner, 1975; Bugenthal, 1987) as countertransference. In this book, psychological treatment has been described as a joint process between the professional and the family. Thus, it is expected that the emotional status of the professional will have as important an impact on treatment as the emotional status of the family. "Every therapist has, whether he is aware of it or not, an attitude toward each of his patients. This is inescapable. . . . The important thing is that the therapist be alertly aware of his attitude as he carries out his role (in therapy). The therapist always should be observing himself as well as the patient" (Chapman, 1978, p. 171). How some of the professional's reactions to the families of brain-injury survivors are expressed in rehabilitation treatment will be examined in the present chapter.

Work in a traumatic brain-injury rehabilitation setting, no matter how satisfying or stimulating, creates emotional stress for the professional. He or she is confronted with the tragedy and suffering that has befallen the brain-injury survivors. The medical conditions that led to hospitalization highlight to the professional how instantaneously and uncontrollably life can be changed. "Staff and patient (in a rehabilitation setting) are placed in a situation of accelerated intimacy" (Horowitz & Hartke, 1988). Some survivors may be close in age or life situation to the professional, leading him or her to identify intensely with the survivors' predicaments.

The emotional impact on the professional also extends to his or her work with the families of the brain-injury survivors. The close relationship between families and the professional over the long course of rehabilitation creates intense emotions. The professional may identify with the family in their grief and outrage over the tragedy of the trauma. Discussions of difficult treatment decisions are emotionally draining for the family and the professional.

These reactions to the survivor and the family do not necessarily indicate that the professional is at fault in his or her work. On the contrary, the lack of an emotional reaction to brain-injury rehabilitation work would suggest that the professional is too distant or emotionally detached from the experiences of the survivor and family to be empathic and helpful to them. The intensity of these emotional reactions, however, may affect the professional's treatment interventions with the family. Therefore, the professional must be mindful of these reactions in working within the rehabilitation environment.

Three common emotional reactions will now be discussed: denial, anger, and exhaustion. An attempt will be made to describe how these reactions are seen in the professional's behavior and the positive and negative effects of such reactions on treatment.

DENIAL

As has been discussed in Chapters One and Two, denial of physical and emotional difficulties is a problem that is seen in survivors of brain injury and in families. As mentioned, however, denial in general is a natural human reaction to stressful events. All people, regardless of their experience, utilize denial in some manner as part of their strategy for coping with daily events. As such, the rehabilitation professional will experience denial and this can have a major impact on treatment. Therefore, in order to manage the denial in the survivor and family, it is vital that the professional recognize and understand his or her own experience of denial.

The definition of denial used earlier in this book emphasized how denial involves the development of a fantasy by which the individual seeks to minimize a distressing aspect of reality. The rehabilitation professional may express his or her denial of the painful emotions generated by rehabilitation work in the form of a fantasy that minimizes the painful emotions. In illustrating the effects of denial in professionals and amelioration of problems that result from denial, three such fantasies will be described and discussed (Sachs, 1987).

Fantasy I: "I'm Different"

The rehabilitation setting provides many opportunities for the professional to identify with or feel something in common with the survivors and families. One way to minimize the pain that such identification can cause is to create a distance between oneself and the survivor or family. In the "I'm different" fantasy the professional maintains the belief that he or she is different from the survivor, that there is not much in common between them. Many ideas or events are used to bolster this fantasy. The professionals may emphasize or think about the differences between him or herself and the survivor. These differences may be in family background, education, or life experiences. Indeed, the entire structure of a rehabilitation setting encourages this distinction between professional and patient, or professionals and families. Professionals wear uniforms and have privileges within the facility that are not open to survivors and families. If the professional is able to feel that the loss or suffering of the survivor and family is not necessarily relevant to the professional's own experience it becomes easier to tolerate the survivor's loss and suffering.

Sometimes the "I'm different" fantasy may be expressed in a tendency to blame the survivor for his or her difficulties. The survivor is worthy of blame because of certain characteristics the survivor has (e.g. drinking a lot, driving above the speed limit, not wearing a helmet), characteristics that the rehabilitation professional can claim not to have. As Kushner (1988) has stated, "blaming the victim is a way of reassuring ourselves that the world is not as bad a place as it may seem, and that there are good reasons for people's suffering" (p. 39).

Fantasy 2: "I'm in Control"

The experience of work in the rehabilitation setting may highlight to the professional just how little control a person at times has over his life. In response to this realization, the professional may adopt the "I'm in control" fantasy. He or she may believe that he or she can actually control every aspect of his or her life.

Here again the rehabilitation facility environment serves to support this fantasy. Procedures for routine care, therapy schedules, and other regulations help all rehabilitation staff to control their time and control the patients and families with whom they work. Psychologists in particular are often called upon by the administration or other rehabilitation staff to use their skills to help control behavior in survivors. Haley (1976) has cogently described the nature of the psychotherapist's role as an agent of social control rather than to help distressed individuals.

The belief that life is under control allows the professionals to feel that disabling injuries can be avoided. In this way the feeling of fear that is aroused by working with the survivors and families is reduced. Yet the professional's desire for and belief in control can create problems in therapeutic treatment if the professional attempts to be too controlling of the survivor and family. By "emphasizing dependent, compliant behavior in the patient while simultaneously promoting the ethic of maximal independence" (Horowitz & Hartke, 1988, p. 3), the professional may appear to contradict him or herself in treatment. Taking responsiblity for the welfare of the patient or family may also communicate to them that the professional does not "believe in (their) capacity to be a competent person" (Whitaker & Bumberry, 1988, p. 43).

Fantasy 3: "The Survivor Will Recover"

The rehabilitation period is one of great anxiety for the survivor and family because of the uncertainty of recovery and the threat of long-lasting disability. Professionals who find themselves closely identifying with the survivors and families may adopt the fantasy that "the survivor will recover." By believing that the survivor will recover completely from the injury, the professional may avoid facing the sadness that would be felt if the survivor does not recover.

This fantasy often finds support in the documentation policies required by a facility or a third party payer. Some patients may not remain in the rehabilitation facility unless they show evidence of benefit from treatment. Rehabilitation professionals are encouraged to seek out and make the most of signs of recovery in order to document the value of continued treatment for the survivor. Such behavior may also be expressed directly toward the survivor when professionals give them unrealistic, inaccurate, or less critical feedback about their performance (Hatsdorf et al., 1979).

Although the idea of a denial fantasy has a negative connotation, denial is not a harmful phenomenon per se. If a professional were unable to deny some of his or her pain through fantasy, that person would be overwhelmed by emotions and quickly unable to function effectively in the work setting. Likewise the survivor and family that are unable to deny some of the distress they experience would be unable to pursue treatment activities and other life experiences to their fullest satisfaction.

However, rehabilitation professionals, like some survivors and families, are susceptible to excessive amounts of denial. When a professional's denial is extreme, it can be disruptive to the therapeutic treatment program. The distinction between appropriate and excessive denial is difficult to make. To a large extent, the distinction will depend on personal and institutional values. One way to draw the distinction is by focusing on the fact that denial is appropriate to the extent that it helps the professional to adapt effectively to the work situation.

Effective adaptation involves many things. This book has emphasized the importance of establishing a working relationship with families, as well working effectively within a transdisciplinary rehabilitation team. The professional should also be able to relate to the survivors and families in a sensitive yet objective manner, to be emotionally flexible and creative, and able to learn new procedures and treatment tasks. The professional should also be able to pursue satisfying relationships and activities outside of work, and to maintain a balance between the two worlds.

When denial is adaptive, it enables the professional to withstand the stress in the workplace and to work in the manner described above. Maladaptive denial, however, will interfere with the professional's ability to relate to survivors, families, and co-workers; to cope with change; and to maintain a balance between work and home lives. Table 7.1 shows how each of the denial fantasies can be expressed adaptively and maladaptively.

Maladaptive denial in a professional may be relatively easy to identify but much more difficult to overcome as illustrated in the following example.

Case example: A rehabilitation professional in a postacute rehabilitation center was observed by other members of the rehabilitation team to be particularly involved in the care of one brain-injury survivor. The survivor was an attractive, single woman in her twenties judged to be at Level VII on the Rancho scale five years postinjury. Although her physical recovery was quite good, cognitive and behavioral difficulties remained that interfered with her ability to enter the workforce and to live independently. The professional, married with young children, would spend time after work hours talking to the survivor and assisting her with cognitive rehabilitation exercises. The professional had invited the survivor to his house on weekends to socialize with his family. In team meetings, other staff felt that the professional was resistant to some of the rehabilitation treatment plans. The team felt that this woman would need structured living and working arrangements, and were attempting to help the woman to accept her limitations in order to make plans for such arrangements. The professional felt that the woman had more potential and argued that the other staff was giving up on her. Staff also felt that the professional was sabotaging treatment by encouraging the woman to reject the treatment plans. It was decided that the team leader would confront the professional in question to state that he appeared to be overly involved with this survivor in a way that was disruptive to treatment. In the meeting between the professional and the team leader, the professional admitted that he had strong feelings about the woman. He stated that the woman reminded him of a cousin who had suffered a head injury and that he thought about the woman frequently after work hours, occasionally having dreams about her. The professional reiterated, however, the points he had made in the team meetings. He genuinely believed that the team was giving up on the woman and that his extra involvement with her treatment was an expression of his commitment to his work rather than any untoward emotional reaction to the woman.

Table 7.1 Adaptive and Maladaptive Expressions of the Three Denial Fantasies

Denial fantasy	Adaptive expression	Maladaptive expression
I'm different	Able to maintain professional distance from patient, to be objective yet empathic	Distant and unempathic with patient, becomes inordinately demanding or critical of patient
	Able to enjoy life outside of work, to participate in family and social activities	Inflexible in time commitments to job duties, not cooperative with coworkers
I'm in control	Able to complete job duties without losing emotional control, able to maintain objectivity without excessive emotional interference	Concerned about job duties at the expense of patient' needs, seeks to control patient's decisions, intolerant of change, unable to think creatively, humorless
	Able to retain emotional energy for family and friends	Concern with control pervades all aspects of life, interfering with spontaneous interaction with family and friends
	Recognizes importance of discussing upsetting feelings and can do so in a productive way	Unable to admit or discuss upsetting feelings, denies the importance of such feelings
The patient will recover	Able to maintain hope for patient and family while still providing appropriate treatment and information, inspires coworkers	Hopeful attitude maintained at expense of attention to practical treatment issues, creates unrealistic expectations in patient and family, disrupts confidence of patient and family in coworkers, overinvolved in patient's care

Sachs, P. R. (1987, August). Denial in rehabilitation professionals. Paper presented at the meeting of the American Psychological Association, New York.

Recognizing denial in oneself is the most important step toward using it effectively in treatment. Every rehabilitation professional should recognize that denial is a common human reaction to stress and very often it is a valuable coping strategy. By its very nature, denial is difficult for a person to detect. As this example illustrates, denial may be easier to spot in a co-worker than in oneself. Therefore, rehabilitation professionals must work together to assist each other in recognizing denial when it occurs and to determine if it is adaptive. The rehabilitation psychologist is in a unique role to assist other rehabilitation professionals in this task. Staff meetings, educational programs, and informal contacts between people can be times for the psychologist to facilitate discussions about denial and the distressing feelings that cause it among the other rehabilitation professionals.

Adaptive denial should be reinforced. Simple praise and support for a professional who is able to handle stressful job duties can be one way of doing this. Keeping the three denial fantasies in mind suggests other recommendations. Professionals should be encouraged to feel that they are different in some way from the survivors and families. Private working and studying areas, and leisure and educational activities exclusively for professionals are all ways of bolstering an adaptive sense of difference among professionals.

Separation between professionals, survivors, and families should not be so extreme as to make it difficult for them to develop working relationships. The role of family self-help groups and of cooperation between families and professionals have been emphasized in the previous chapter. Policies and procedures within the rehabilitation facility, however, should recognize the importance of this cooperation and the need for professionals to have some distance from the recipients of their professional care.

Regular schedules for handling patients and predictable staffing patterns can instill a sense of control that will enable professionals to better carry out their work. Procedures that detail which staff members are to be involved in a given activity and how it is to be handled are reassuring to the professionals even if such procedures are not precisely followed. Particular attention should be given to procedures for handling survivors and families that lose control.

A hopeful attitude among professionals is helpful to the survivors and families and gives the professional team a sense of purpose. This may be difficult for the professional to communicate to the survivors and families. The professional may feel uninformed about a given clinical condition and reluctant to say anything to a family or survivor that may be misunderstood or inaccurate. He or she may also be unsure of the most effective way to express what he or she does know. Thorough staff education about clinical issues provides useful information to families. Procedure manuals may be expanded to include specific ways in which information can be communicated, such as actual phrases that have been found useful. In this book examples of phrasing for some difficult clinical issues to families have been provided. In any case, professionals should recognize that hope is not only communicated by good news. The professional who appears well-informed and responsive to the survivor and family will be perceived as trustworthy. Having someone to trust is the foundation of the family's hope.

The professional who is able to express adaptive denial can be effective in helping the family and survivor to overcome their own problems with denial. By understanding his or her own emotional state, the professional will be able to educate the family about denial and its impact on treatment. The professional's behavior becomes a model for the family. The difficulties that are caused by the family's denial may be much easier for the professionals to tolerate and work with when they are able to recognize similar reactions in their own experiences.

ANGER

There are numerous ways in which anger is expressed and confronted during the course of a survivor's rehabilitation program. As has been described earlier, families are likely to experience anger about the injury that occured to the family member and to express this anger directly or indirectly in psychological treatment. The professional's identification with and empathy for the family and its predicament may lead the psychologist to feel emotions that parallel those of the family. Also a family's argumentative or noncompliant behavior may pose obstacles to treatment that cause professionals to feel frustrated or angry about their inability to work effectively. The long course of rehabilitation treatment and the inevitable fluctuations in mood that both families and professionals experience will lead professionals to find even the most likable and compliant families difficult to manage. In extreme, this may result in professionals developing a feeling of hate toward the patients and families (Gans, 1983).

The professional, like the family, is in conflict with respect to expressing angry feelings. Professional protocol indicates that the professional remain patient, tolerant, and sensitive to even the most trying family and survivor. Yet the emotional stress of suppressing angry feelings may be difficult for the professional to contain. The professional may express anger indirectly by becoming argumentative, noncompliant, sarcastic, or socially isolated. Such behavior will quickly disrupt psychological and general rehabilitation treatment for the family and for the survivor.

Case example: A rehabilitation counselor was observed to be excessively sarcastic with the patients and families during casual contacts outside of scheduled treatment sessions. Family members generally were taken aback by this behavior and disturbed by it. Given the cognitive difficulties of many survivors it was questioned to what extent the counselor's comments were properly understood by the survivors. The counselor's co-workers found such behavior to be inappropriate for professional work. In discussion between the department head and the psychologist a treatment plan was developed in which educational information was provided to all staff regarding emotional distress in professionals and how this might be expressed to patients. In particular it was mentioned how anger may be expressed indirectly by sarcasm or cynicism. In addition, the supervisor spoke directly with the counselor about her behavior with a particular family. During the supervision session, the counselor stated that she was trying to make the families feel more at ease and thus adopted this sarcastic manner. She was able to acknowledge how such comments might be confusing to the survivors and disturbing to families and staff members. Over time, she was observed to be able to change her behavior in accordance with the expectations of the facility and other staff. She was able to express humorous comments to the family without appearing to be sarcastic or angry and did so more selectively based on the particular family and patient with whom she worked.

Effective supervision and feedback from peers is of great importance to the professional in coping with angry feelings. Co-workers and supervisors are a source of emotional support and an appropriate outlet for frustration. Moreover, some of the behaviors that represent an indirect expression of anger may not be noticed by the professional alone. Feedback from other professionals is important to help the professional recognize this behavior and ameliorate the problem that has caused it. A "therapist support system" (Haley, 1980, p. 62) is useful for this and many other emotionally difficult issues that the professional may face in work with families.

It is a delicate matter to confront a co-worker on a question of such behavior or to be the recipient of such feedback. It is more tolerable, however, to learn about the problem in this way than to have the family bring the behavior to the professional's attention, with the subsequent disruption in treatment that could be caused. Gans (1983) has noted the importance of helping the professional to recognize that his or her emotional reactions are normal reactions to the stressful work of the rehabilitation setting (see also Prigatano et al., 1986).

Unfortunately, within the active schedule of the rehabilitation unit, there may be little time for discussing such behavior. It may seem easier to ignore the problem in the hopes that it will disappear. In doing so, professional staff demonstrate the same approach to problems that they are quick to criticize when observed in clients or families.

Regular team conferences and peer review groups might be an opportunity to ventilate such feelings and discuss ways of coping with them. It is important that staff have a place in which to discuss these matters free from contact with survivors and family. Facilities might consider including a section on how employees handle distress in the routine employee education programs and annual evaluations to assure that these issues are discussed among professionals. Some psychological treatment interventions including assertiveness training (Rimm & Masters, 1974) may be helpful to the professional in learning how to express difficult feelings directly to patients and families in a productive rather than destructive manner.

EXHAUSTION

"There is continuous tension and emotional pain for patients, their families, and staff in a rehabilitation setting. Patients and their families are overwhelmed, and in trying to care for them, staff at times, will be overwhelmed also" (Gans, 1983, p. 179). The identification that professionals feel with the families and survivors leads them to experience intense emotions that often tax the professional's ability to cope effectively with work responsibilities. The impact of such emotional and physical exhaustion as it affects health care professionals has been given increasing attention in the general psychological and vocational literature under the heading of burnout (Freudenberger & Richelson, 1980).

The characteristics of the brain-injury rehabilitation unit make it a prime breeding ground for burnout. The emotional stress created by work with the brain-injury survivors and their families has been described throughout this book. Employees in the rehabilitation setting often feel that they have little control over or certainty about the outcome of their work with the survivors. The relationship between burnout and the sense of loss of control has been documented in rehabilitation counselors (Maslach & Florian, 1988) and it probably holds for other rehabilitation professionals. As evidence, some areas of professional staff within the rehabilitation setting experience high degrees of turnover indicating the possibility that emotional factors as well as economic ones are affecting individuals' feelings about their jobs.

Case example: A rehabilitation professional from a traumatic brain-injury rehabilitation program sought out individual psychotherapy because of symptoms of anxiety and depression. His supervisor had noted he appeared depressed and sullen on the job. Although his supervisor had been very pleased with the professional's work, lately the professional had shown reduced initiative and creativity, and tardiness with documentation. The professional was also heard to be critical of the rehabilitation facility and of some of the staff in the presence of patients and families. The professional reported to the psychotherapist symptoms of sleep disturbance with frequent dreams about patients and staff from the workplace, irritability with his family, reduced sexual drive, and anxiety about driving in a motor vehicle. He described his work activities as basically interesting and stimulating but felt he had become burdened by a large case load and too much documentation to complete. He usually worked through lunch and often worked 50 to 60 hours per week. He spent so much time at work that he did not wish to socialize with other people from the workplace after hours and felt socially isolated. He found himself feeling resentful and angry toward the demands of patients, families, and administrators. Psychotherapy intervention spanned several levels of intervention. The professional was encouraged to ventilate his feelings of anger and sadness. Yet he was also informed by the psychotherapist that many of his frustrations at work such as the burdens of paper work, and conflicts between demands of patients and administration and the clinician's abilities, were very common to the health care workplace. He was asked to identify the aspects of his work activities that were satisfying to him and to think of ways in which he could set more effective limits on his less satisfying work activities. The psychotherapist sought to point out that underlying feelings of fear of loss of control and overidentification with the patients and families may have stimulated the development of his current predicament. The professional found the psychotherapeutic intervention to be helpful. Many of his symptoms were reduced and he was able to redirect his energies at work and at home in order to attain a better balance of time and emotions. Though he still experienced symptoms of emotional stress, he did not become as alarmed by them as he had in the past and made efforts to control their impact on his professional and personal life.

Treatment intervention for staff burnout incorporates the ideas that have already been described with respect to problems of denial and anger. First, education of the professional staff should include information about the notion of burnout. Supervisors and co-workers should be alert to behaviors that might indicate a reduction or withdrawal of energy in work activities indicative of burnout. The goal of these educational programs would be to heighten awareness of the issue so that problems can be identified early when treatment interventions may be helpful, rather than too late for treatment to be effective.

The structure of the rehabilitation setting can facilitate a sense of emotional support and control to minimize the likelihood of burnout. Some examples of changes in the rehabilitation setting were mentioned in the previous section on denial. Some attention might be given to this in initial employee orientations and employee evaluations.

Beyond interventions done within the rehabilitation facility, the question of burnout should be raised with respect to the training and selection of individuals who do rehabilitation work. An individual who shows signs of reduced energy for work and feelings of lethargy or loss of control might choose to withdraw from rehabilitation work. This is not necessarily a bad occurrence. It is possible that some intervention might help the individual to accomplish the work tasks more effectively. However, it is also possible that the person came to a realization that rehabilitation work was not his or her preference. Therefore, recruitment for rehabilitation professionals should include some information about the potential employee's expectations of work activities. An individual's expectations that are grossly out of line with the practicalities of work in a brain-injury rehabilitation setting need to be confronted before the individual begins work. The intervention might begin prior to the time of job application in incorporating programs relating to emotional stressors in rehabilitation work as part of training in the rehabilitation specialty programs.

SUMMARY

The rehabilitation professional cannot isolate him or herself from the emotional experiences of the families and the survivors in a brain-injury rehabilitation setting. Feelings of denial, anger, or exhaustion are expected and common among brain-injury rehabilitation professionals. Sometimes, the solution to these problems is as simple as taking a break from work or balancing rehabilitation work with other activities. At other times, more intensive intervention and supervision may be needed. In any case, the professional can deepen his or her understanding of the survivors and families, and the professional connection with them by identifying and sharing their emotional experiences. In doing so, the professional goes beyond seeing the survivor and family as recipients of rehabilitation care or as victims, but rather appreciates them as fellow human beings.

8

Conclusions and
Future Directions

SUMMARY

This book has presented a framework for psychological treatment of the families of brain-injury survivors. Although specific techniques and case examples have been described throughout the book, the focus has been on describing the general principles that the practitioner should follow in designing psychological assessment and treatment for the families. These principles will be briefly summarized.

1. The practitioner must be knowledgeable in traumatic brain-injury rehabilitation. Effective family intervention requires the involvement of a professional who is well-versed in the sequelae of traumatic brain injury, the course of recovery, common family reactions to the trauma, and the system of care in which rehabilitation treatment is provided. Certainly such a practitioner should first be trained and experienced as a general clinician in psychological assessment and treatment techniques. Such general training, however, is not sufficient. As this book has emphasized, general psychological techniques cannot be directly transferred and applied to the families of brain-injury survivors. Moreover, in order to establish a working relationship with the practitioner, the family must be able to trust the practitioner as a person and as an experienced practitioner in the field of brain-injury rehabilitation.

2. The practitioner must consider the family's structure and development in designing treatment for them. The family of a brain-injury survivor is first and foremost a family. The assessment and treatment interventions for the family must be based on a thorough knowledge of the family. This means an understanding of how the family operated as a organizational unit before the injury, how the injury has affected the family's operations, the role of the survivor in the family system, and the meaning of the various aspects of the rehabilitation program for the family.

3. The practitioner must be flexible. Traditional treatment techniques must be modified to meet the needs of the family. These modifications should be based on understanding the needs of the people with whom the

practitioner works. The brain-injury rehabilitation setting also requires the practitioner to modify his or her role to meet the needs of the survivors, the families, and the other rehabilitation professionals. A thorough grounding in basic psychological assessment and treatment techniques is essential. The practitioner must be flexible, however, in modifying these techniques within the rehabilitation setting and make such modifications based on clinical judgment rather than on whim.

4.   The practitioner must establish a close working relationship with the family. Establishing and maintaining an effective working relationship is the primary goal of psychological intervention with the family of a brain-injury survivor throughout the course of rehabilitation treatment. A relationship means more than regular communication or correspondence. It means an ability of all parties to express feelings openly without fear of judgment, to discuss all sides of an issue, and to meet on a regular basis according to established ground rules.

Most important in the working relationship is that the family be able to trust the practitioner and to derive a sense of inspiration from him or her. Cousins (1979) has stated this aptly, "The central question to be asked about hospitals — or about doctors for that matter — is whether they inspire the patient with the confidence that he or she is in the right place; whether they enable him to have trust in those who seek to heal him; in short, whether he has the expectations that good things will happen" (p. 154). To be inspired does not mean to be blindly hopeful, but rather to believe in oneself and one's decisions.

5.   The practitioner is a member of a treatment team. The practitioner must work effectively with that group of professionals that constitute the rehabilitation treatment team. The role of the psychologist within a brain-injury rehabilitation setting is very different from the role in a mental health or psychiatric setting. The psychologist must recognize the limits of his or her expertise and influence over the survivors and families. The psychologist should have a clear understanding of his or her unique contribution to the rehabilitation treatment team while being able to respect and utilize the expertise of other rehabilitation professionals on the team.

6.   The practitioner must be mindful of his or her personal values as they affect treatment. As with other types of psychological intervention, work with brain-injury survivors and their families is emotionally demanding. However, the combination of physical and emotional changes that a brain-injury survivor presents challenges the psychologist to examine his or her values and beliefs more so than does an individual presenting with only emotional difficulties. Values cannot be excluded from psychological treatment. It is the practitioner's responsibility to be aware of his or her values and of the impact that these values may have on clinical work with families. The practitioner must also accept that his or her values may be different

from those of the families of survivors. Acceptance of the family's values in psychological treatment means helping the family to be aware of their own values and how they affect their emotional well-being, and not to impose the practitioner's values on the family.

In speaking about the work of a psychiatrist, DeNour and Bauman (1980) have nicely summarized the aforementioned points, "(the practitioner) . . . must be well-versed and flexible in different techniques of treatment. He must feel secure and unthreatened when taking a variety of roles. He must be ready to work outside the isolation of his consultation room and above all must be keenly aware of his own reactions" (p. 33).

FUTURE DIRECTIONS

Research

The discussion of family treatment and the unique role for the mental health professional in such treatment suggests several areas for research that would be worthwhile for the practicing clinician and for the field of traumatic brain injury research in general. Some of these are described below.

1.   Research identifying the relationships between family structure, the family's emotional reaction to the trauma, and the survivor's status. The present book has attempted to describe the impact of the trauma on the family structure and what treatment interventions can be developed to repair the damage to that structure. Implied in this discussion is that the family's emotional reaction to the trauma will be mediated by the type of structure that exists in the family and what aspects of it are changed by the trauma. Research that more clearly identifies the connection between these variables would provide direction for developing treatment interventions for families and for identifying which families may be at risk for severe emotional disruption as the result of the trauma. It should be noted that such research must balance an individual and group emphasis. Grouping families together in order to assess aspects of family structure may be expedient and yield some general findings. Each family, however, is unique in its structure and adaptive abilities. Therefore, single case studies may also be valuable in examining family structure and adjustment.

2.   Research on the relation between family emotional reactions and their explanation for the survivor's behavior. During the course of rehabili-

tation the family seeks to explain the behavior of the survivor by attributing the behavior to a variety of factors in the individual survivor, the treatment personnel, and the treatment environment. It is felt that the family's emotional reaction to the survivor's behavior will be affected by the types of attributions that the family members make. Research that identifies the connection between the family's cognitive interpretation of the survivor's behavior, their subsequent emotional reaction to the behavior, and their ability to change their interpretation of the survivor's behavior would help clinicians to develop appropriate educational and psychological treatment techniques for this problem.

3.   Research on what families know about traumatic brain injury and the effectiveness of educational programs. It is generally recognized that education is a vital component to traumatic brain injury treatment for the families and the survivors. Usually such treatment is provided without a clear assessment of the family's level of understanding about the concepts of brain-injury rehabilitation and their ability to benefit from the educational information presented to them. Some attention has been given to the general conceptions and misconceptions about brain injury (Gouvier et al., 1988). A standardized way of assessing this knowledge and a standardized curriculum for education of families is needed for the clinical setting. Such a program should address the extent to which professional, paraprofessional, and peer education are valuable in educating families.

4.   Research on the differences between family members in their adjustment to the trauma and their response to treatment intervention. Recognizing the importance of family structure means also recognizing that each family member has a different part in the family system. Thus, treatment interventions for these family members should be modified to meet the different needs of family members. Identification of what types of treatment are particularly helpful with which family members would assist professionals in treatment planning. In addition, it would be important to identify the relation between the emotional status of different family members, the family's overall emotional status, and the survivor's outcome. It is anecdotally known that certain family members have a greater impact on some survivors. It would be useful to know if there were any patterns to this influence that could direct treatment planning.

Training

Increased sophistication of assessment and treatment of families and survivors in the field of traumatic brain injury necessitates the development of proper training programs for professionals in the area. In the field of psychology two divisions of the American Psychological Association, Rehabilitation Psychology and Neuropsychology, whose membership encompasses most of the psychologists working in the field of traumatic brain-injury rehabilitation, have examined the question of a formal training curriculum for the field (INS-Division 40, 1987).

This book has emphasized that the psychologist must have general clinical background but also be specifically familiar with the sequelae of brain injury and with the structure and development of the family. Therefore, specialization is beneficial for the psychologist but should not be taken so far that the psychologist loses sight of general concepts. It is felt that training programs for psychologists working with the traumatic brain-injury population be offered at the postdoctoral level as a specialization after general training has been completed.

In developing a training program for psychologists in this area, clinical experience with the brain-injury survivors as well as didactic training is recommended. Some of the areas that might be included in the didactic training are listed below.

1. Medical sequelae of Traumatic Brain Injury
2. Neuropsychological sequelae of Traumatic Brain Injury
3. Psychosocial sequelae
4. Rehabilitation treatment: a review of PT/OT/Speech Therapy and Nursing contributions
5. Cognitive rehabilitation
6. Behavior management and psychiatric treatment options
7. Family issues and family therapy
8. The role of advocacy and self-help in Traumatic Brain Injury recovery
9. The role of the professional's values in Traumatic Brain Injury recovery
10. Disability legislation and rights in the community and workplace

Field placement in a brain-injury rehabilitation setting with supervised experience in assessment and treatment techniques is a necessary supplement to classroom learning.

The Social Context of Traumatic Brain-Injury Rehabilitation

In addition to research and training, the rehabilitation professional working in the field of brain-injury rehabilitation must come to terms with his or her role as an advocate for the survivors and families that he or she treats, the beliefs that underlie his or her treatment techniques, and the social system in which treatment is provided.

Prevention

The prevention of traumatic brain injuries is the most effective method of treatment. "Many patients suffer preventable disabilities. Rehabilitation practitioners may have a moral responsibility to lobby for education, air bags, seat belt and helmet laws, gun control, and good nutrition and medical care for pregnant women" (Haas, 1986, p. 271). Professionals need to ask themselves to what extent they will take the responsibility to prevent traumatic brain injuries, an activity that goes beyond their duties in a treatment facility and therapy session.

Quality of Life and Allocation of Services

The cost of traumatic brain-injury rehabilitation can run into the hundreds of thousands of dollars for direct services and into the millions when the cost of disability to the person over a lifetime is calculated. The fortunate individual with sufficient health care coverage is able to receive the variety of treatment services that are available. There are many, however, that do not receive such services because of limitations in insurance coverage or other financial limitations or the lack of sufficient services to be allocated.

Even those who receive the services may not recover to the point where they are able to be independent in any sense of the word. "Part of the price paid for the good recoveries, of which there are many, is that some others will be left so badly crippled that sensitive observers may judge their survival a greater disaster than if they had died" (Jennett, 1976, p. 597). The brain-injury rehabilitation professional must assess his or her values about the problem of allocation of treatment services and the quality of life of brain-injury survivors (Flanagan, 1982). There are sound personal and financial reasons for treating individuals who have resources to pay for rehabilitation services. Nonetheless, the professional may need to consider to what extent he or she, or the facilities in which the professional is employed, have an obligation to survivors without such resources.

Cultural Factors

The system of brain-injury rehabilitation is closely tied to the society and culture in which it operates. These cultural factors may be less apparent to the professional than are the physical and emotional problems presented by the family and the survivor. Yet there are several aspects to this matter that need to be considered in the course of one's professional work.

One, contemporary American culture places a high emphasis on independence and free will. This cultural value makes the goal of independence a particularly strong one for professionals to expect of their clients and patients, and for the families and survivors to expect of themselves. Yet, this emphasis may become a problem as stated nicely by Zola (1982), "I was always told to push myself to the maximum of my physical capability. Yet I was never given any advice as to what to do when my capability reached its limits . . . By living according to someone else's definition of physical independence, I contributed to the demise of my own social and psychological independence" (p. 394). These comments about physical capabilities are also apropos to the development of treatment for the brain-injury survivor. Our culturally mandated emphasis on independence may conflict with the individual's actual abilities creating emotional distress for the individual.

Two, as society changes, the family that must accommodate to society must also change (Minuchin, 1974). Notions of what constitutes a family and what the family should provide to its members have changed in the past decade. In setting goals for families in psychological treatment the practitioner must be mindful of the cultural expectations of what the family is and is not able to provide for its members. The practitioner must try to maintain this broad view throughout the course of the survivor's rehabilitation treatment: one that encompasses the survivor, his or her family members, the family as a whole, personal values, the goals of rehabilitation treatment, and the cultural environment in which the family lives.

Epilogue

Traumatic brain injury is a tragedy that changes forever the survivor and the family who experience it. The tragedy of the trauma is one reason why many families feel they can never "accept" the trauma but only "adapt" to its consequences. Professionals cannot extinguish the feelings of grief, outrage, and uncertainty that families experience but rather must help family members to hold the feelings and use them. If it is possible to "salvage something positive" (Bettelheim, 1952) from the experience of traumatic brain injury, it would seem to be embodied in the personal statements of family members, of which only four of thousands are included in this book. These statements show that, despite the enormity of their distress and the destructiveness of the trauma, family members of brain-injury survivors are still able to feel and to create. The very feelings that overwhelm family members may be the same ones that inspire them to create new lives for themselves, to "transmute the tragedy into an achievement" (Frankl, 1969, p. 72). However confusing or upsetting they may at times be to professionals, the feelings and creativity of family members are the raw material of the family's rehabilitation. It is on the understanding of their feelings and the nurturing of their creativity that the foundation of the family's life after a traumatic brain injury can be built.

References

Ackerman, N. W. (1958). *The psychodynamics of family life*. New York: Basic.

Adamovitch, B., Henderson, J. A., & Auerbach, S. (1985). *Cognitive rehabilitation of closed head injured patients: A dynamic approach*. San Diego, CA: College Hill.

Alexander, M. P. (1984). *Neurobehavioral consequences of closed head injury (Neurology and neurosurgery update series Vol. 5)*. Princeton, NJ: CPE Center.

Alves, W. M., Coloban, A. R. T., O'Leary, T. J., Rimel, R. W., & Jane, J. A. (1986). Understanding post-traumatic symptoms after minor head injury. *Journal of Head Trauma Rehabilitation, 1*, 1–12.

Anderson, J., & Parente, F. (1985). Training family members to work with the head injured patient. *Cognitive Rehabilitation, 3*, 12–15.

Bandura, A. (1969). *Principles of behavior modification*. New York: Holt, Rinehart & Winston.

Barrer, A. E. (1988, August). *A systems approach to working with families*. Paper presented at the meeting of the American Psychological Association, Atlanta, GA.

Bettelheim, B. (1952). *Surviving and other essays*. New York: Random House.

Bishop, D. S., & Miller, I. W. (1983). Traumatic brain injury: Empirical family assessment techniques. *Journal of Head Trauma Rehabilitation, 3*, 16–30.

Blanck, G., & Blanck, R. (1974). *Ego psychology: Theory and practice*. New York: Columbia.

Bond, M. R. (Ed.). (1988). Families of the brain injured. (Special issue, J2712). *Journal of Head Trauma Rehabilitation, 3*.

Bond, M. R. (1990). Standardizing methods of assessing and predicting outcome. In M. Rosenthal, E. R. Griffiths, M. R. Bond, & J. D. Miller (Eds.), *Rehabilitation of the adult and child with traumatic brain injury* (rev. ed.) (pp. 59–74). Philadelphia, PA: F. A. Davis.

Bowen, M. (1978). *Family therapy in clinical practice*. New York: Jason Aronson.

Braswell, L., & Kendall, P. C. (1988). Cognitive-behavioral methods in children. In K. S. Dobson (Ed.), *Handbook of cognitive-behavioral therapies* (pp. 167–213). New York: Guilford.

Brigman, C., Dickey, C., & Zegeer, L. J. (1983). The agitated aggressive patient. *American Journal of Nursing, 83*, 1409–1412.

Brody, J. (1983, March 23). Head injuries and the "silent epidemic." *New York Times*, p. C11.

Brooks, N. (Ed.). (1984). *Closed head injury: Psychological, social and family consequences*. New York: Oxford.

Brooks, N. (1984). Head injury and the family. In N. Brooks (Ed.), *Closed head injury: Psychological, social and family consequences* (pp. 123–147). New York: Oxford.

Brooks, N., Campsie, L., Symington, C., Beattie, A., & McKinlay, W. (1987). The ef-

197

fects of severe head injury on patient and relative within seven years of injury. *Journal of Head Trauma Rehabilitation, 2,* 1–3.

Bugenthal, J. F. T. (1987). *The art of the psychotherapist.* New York: W. W. Norton.

Burke, M. (1984). Reflections of a brother. *Cognitive Rehabilitation, 2,* 10–11.

Bush, G. W. (1988). The National Head Injury Foundation: Eight years of challenge and growth. *Journal of Head Trauma Rehabilitation, 3,* 73–77.

Caplan, B., & Schechter, J. (1987). Denial and depression in disabling illness. In B. Caplan (Ed.), *Rehabilitation psychology desk reference* (pp. 133–170). Rockville, MD: Aspen.

Chamovitz, I., Chorazy, A. J. L., Hinchett, J. M., & Mandella, P. A. (1985). Rehabilitative medical management. In M. Ylvisaker (Ed.), *Head injury rehabilitation: Children and adolescents* (pp. 117–140). Boston, MA: Little Brown.

Chance, P. (1986, October). Life after head injury. *Psychology Today,* pp. 62–69.

Chapman, A. H. (1978). *The treatment techniques of Harry Stack Sullivan.* New York: Brunner-Mazel.

Clark, M., & Zabarsky, M. (1981, October 21). Hope for coma victims. *Newsweek,* p. 111.

Corrigan, J. D., & Mysiw, W. J. (1988). Agitation following traumatic head injury: Equivocal evidence for a discrete stage of cognitive recovery. *Archives of Physical Medicine and Rehabilitation, 69,* 487–492.

Cousins, N. (1979). *Anatomy of an illness as perceived by the patient.* New York: W. W. Norton.

Deaton, A. V. (1988). Denial in the aftermath of traumatic brain injury: Its manifestations, measurement, and treatment. *Rehabilitation Psychology, 31,* 231–240.

De-Nour, A. K., & Bauman, A. (1980). Psychiatric treatment in severe brain injury: A case report. *General Hospital Psychiatry, 2,* 23–34.

Duggan, M. (1984). *The effects of parental/sibling head injury on children in the family.* Southborough, MA: National Head Injury Foundation.

Durgin, C. T. (1989). Techniques for families to increase their involvement in the rehabilitation process. *Cognitive Rehabilitation, 7,* 22–25.

D'Zurilla, J. D. (1988). Problem-solving therapies. In K. S. Dobson (Ed.), *Handbook of cognitive-behavioral therapies* (pp. 85–135). New York: Guilford.

Eames, P. (1988). Behavior disorders after severe head injury: Their nature and causes and strategies for management. *Journal of Head Trauma Rehabilitation, 3,* 1–6.

Eames, P., Haffey, W. J., & Cope, D. N. (1990). Treatment of behavioral disorders. In M. Rosenthal, E. R. Griffiths, M. R. Bond, & J. D. Miller (Eds.), *Rehabilitation of the adult and child with traumatic brain injury,* (rev. ed.), (pp. 410–432). Philadelphia, PA: F. A. Davis.

Eisenberg, H. M., & Weiner, R. L. (1987). Input variables: How information from acute injury can be used to characterize groups of patients for studies of outcome. In H. S. Levin, J. Graffman, & H. M. Eisenberg (Eds.), *Neurobehavioral recovery from head injury* (pp. 13–29). New York: Oxford.

Erickson, G. D., & Hogan, T. P. (1976). *Family therapy: An introduction to theory and technique.* New York: Jason Aronson.

Evans, R. L., Bishop, D. S., Matlock, A., Stranahan, S., Smith, G. G. G., & Halar,

E. M. (1987). Family interaction and treatment adherence after stroke. *Archives of Physical Medicine and Rehabilitation, 68,* 513–517.

Ewing-Cobbs, L., Fletcher, J. M., & Levin, H. S. (1985). Neuropsychological sequelae following pediatric head injury. In M. Ylvisaker (Ed.), *Head injury rehabilitation: Children and adolescents* (pp. 71–90). Boston, MA: Little Brown.

Fawber, H. L., & Wachter, J. R. (1987). Job placement as a treatment component of the vocational placement process. *Journal of Head Trauma Rehabilitation, 2,* 27–33.

Felker, K. (1988). Guiding parents toward helpful resources: A role for professionals. *Rehabilitation Psychology, 33,* 185–189.

Flanagan, J. C. (1982). Measurement of quality of life: Current state of the art. *Archives of Physical Medicine and Rehabilitation, 63,* 56–59.

Flavell, J. H. (1977). *Cognitive development.* Englewood Cliffs, NJ: Prentice Hall.

Fleck, S. (1985). The family and psychiatry. In H. I. Kaplan & B. J. Sadock (Eds.), *Comprehensive Textbook of Psychiatry* (4th ed.), (pp. 273–294). Baltimore, MD: Williams and Wilkins.

Frank, J. D. (1974). *Persuasion and healing.* New York: Schocken.

Frankl, V. (1969). *The will to meaning.* New York: New American.

Freudenberger, H. J., & Richelson, G. (1980). *Burnout: the high cost of high achievement.* Garden City, NY: Doubleday.

Freudenheim, M. (1987, December 29). Rehabilitation in head injuries. *New York Times,* p. D2.

Friedman, W. A. (1983). *Head injuries.* Summit, NJ: CIBA-Geigy.

Gaioni, K. (1988, July-August). ℞: Self-help. *The New Physician,* pp. 31–32.

Gans, J. S. (1983). Hate in the rehabilitation setting. *Archives of Physical Medicine and Rehabilitation, 64,* 176–179.

Ginsberg, H., & Opper, S. (1979). *Piaget's theory of intellectual development* (rev. ed.). Englewood Cliffs, NJ: Prentice Hall.

Goolsby, E. L. (1976). Facilitation of family-professional interaction. *Rehabilitation Literature, 37,* 332–334.

Gouvier, W. D., Prestholdt, P. H., & Warner, M. S. (1988). A survey of common misconceptions about head injury and recovery. *Archives of Clinical Neuropsychology, 3,* 331–343.

Graffman, J., & Salazar, A. (1987). Methodological considerations relevant to the comparison of recovery from penetrating and closed head injuries. In H. S. Levin, J. Graffman, & H. M. Eisenberg (Eds.), *Neurobehavioral recovery from head injury* (pp. 43–54). New York: Oxford.

Grant, I., & Alves, W. (1987). Psychiatric and psychosocial disturbances in head injury. In H. S. Levin, J. Graffman, & H. M. Eisenberg (Eds.), *Neurobehavioral recovery from head injury* (pp. 232–261). New York: Oxford.

Greif, E., & Matarazzo, R. G. (1982). *Behavioral approaches to rehabilitation: Coping with change.* New York: Springer Publishing Co.

Haas, J. F. (1986). Ethics in rehabilitation medicine. *Archives of Physical Medicine and Rehabilitation, 67,* 270–271.

Haas, J. F. (1987). Ethical and legal aspects of psychotropic medications in brain injury. *Journal of Head Trauma Rehabilitation, 2,* 6–17.

Haley, J. (1976). *Problem solving therapy.* San Francisco, CA: Jossey Bass.

Haley, J. (1980). *Leaving home.* New York: McGraw Hill.

Hastorf, A. H., Northcraft, G. B., and Picciotto, S. R. (1979). Helping the handicapped: How realistic is the performance feedback received by the physically handicapped. *Personality and Social Psychology Bulletin, 5,* 373–376.

Heilman, K. M., Bowers, D., & Valenstein, E. (1985). Emotional disorders associated with neurological disease. In K. M. Heilman & E. Valenstein (Eds.), *Clinical neuropsychology* (rev. ed.) (pp. 377–402). New York, Oxford.

Heilman, K. M., Watson, R. T., & Valenstein, E. (1985). Neglect and related disorders. In K. M. Heilman & E. Valenstein (Eds.), *Clinical neuropsychology* (rev. ed.) (pp. 243–294). New York: Oxford.

Horowitz, M., & Hartke, R. (1988, August). *Transference and countertransference with older adults in a rehabilitation setting.* Paper presented at the meeting of the American Psychological Association, Atlanta, GA.

Howard, M. E. (1988). Behavior management in the acute rehabilitation setting. *Journal of Head Trauma Rehabilitation, 3,* 14–22.

International Neuropsychology Society, Division 40. (1987). Guidelines for doctoral training programs in clinical neuropsychology. *The Clinical Neuropsychologist, 1,* 29–34.

Jacobs, H. E. (1985). The Los Angeles head injury survey: Procedures and initial findings. *Archives of Physical Medicine and Rehabilitation, 69,* 425–431.

Jennett, B. (1976). Resource allocation for the severely brain damaged. *Archives of Neurology, 33,* 595–597.

Jennett, B. (1990). Post-traumatic epilepsy. In M. Rosenthal, E. R. Griffiths, M. R. Bond, & J. D. Miller (Eds.), *Rehabilitation of the adult and child with traumatic brain injury* (rev. ed.) (pp. 89–93). Philadelphia, PA: F. A. Davis.

Jennett, B., & Teasdale, G. (1981). *Management of head injuries.* Philadelphia, PA: F. A. Davis.

Jones, E. E., Kanouse, D. E., Kelley, H. H., Nisbett, R. E., Valins, S., & Weiner, B. (1977). *Attribution: Perceiving the causes of behavior.* Morristown, NJ: General Learning.

Joynt, R. J., & Shoulson, J. (1985). Dementia. In K. M. Heilman & E. Valenstein (Eds.), *Clinical Neuropsychology* (rev. ed.) (pp. 453–477).

Kalisky, Z., Morrison, D. P., Meyers, C. A., & Von Laufen, A. (1985). Medical problems encountered during rehabilitation of patients with head injury. *Archives of Physical Medicine and Rehabilitation, 66,* 25–29.

Kalsbeek, W. D., McLaurin, R. L., Harris, B. S. H., & Miller, J. D. (1980). The national head and spinal cord injury survey: Major findings. *Journal of Neurosurgery, 53,* 519–531.

Kay, T. (1986). *Minor head injury: An introduction for professionals.* Southborough, MA: National Head Injury Foundation.

Kay, T., Ezrachi, O., & Cavallo, M. (1988). *New York University head injury family interview.* New York: New York University Medical Center.

Kozloff, R. (1987). Networks of social support and outcome from severe head injury. *Journal of Head Trauma Rehabilitation, 2,* 14–23.

Kushner, H. S. (1981). *When bad things happen to good people.* New York: Schocken.

Langs, R. (1973). *The technique of psychoanalytic psychotherapy* (Vols. 1–2). New York: Jason Aronson.

Lasden, M. (1982, June 27). Coming out of coma. *New York Times Magazine,* pp. 28–33, 39–40, 54.

Lazarus, A. A. (Ed.). (1972). *Clinical behavior therapy.* New York: Brunner Mazel.

LeBow, M. D. (1976). Behavior modification for the family. In G. D. Erickson & T. P. Hogan (Eds.) *Family therapy: An introduction to theory and technique.* (pp. 347–376). New York: Jason Aronson.

Leehrsen, C., Lewis, S. D., Pomper, D., Davenport, L., & Nelson, M. (1990, February 5). Unite and conquer. *Newsweek,* pp. 50–55.

Levin, H. S., Benton, A. L., & Grossman, R. G. (1982). *Neurobehavioral consequences of closed head injury.* New York: Oxford.

Levin, H. S., Graffman, J. & Eisenberg, H. S. (1987). *Neurobehavioral recovery from head injury.* New York: Oxford.

Levin, H. S., O'Donnell, V. M., & Grossman, R. G. (1979). The Galveston orientation and amnesia test. *Journal of Nervous and Mental Disease, 167,* 675–684.

Lezak, M. D. (1978). Living with the characterologically altered brain injured patient. *Journal of Clinical Psychiatry, 39,* 592–598.

Lezak, M. D. (1986). Psychological implications of traumatic brain damage for the patient's family. *Rehabilitation Psychology, 31,* 241–250.

Lezak, M. D. (1988). Brain damage is a family affair. *Journal of Clinical and Experimental Neuropsychology, 10,* 111–123.

Liberman, R. (1976). Behavioral approaches to family and couple therapy. In G. D. Erickson & T. P. Hogan (Eds.), *Family therapy: An introduction to theory and technique* (pp. 120–137). New York: Jason Aronson.

Lidz, T. (1976). *The person.* New York: Basic.

Livingston, M. G. (1990). Effects on the family system. In M. Rosenthal, E. R. Griffiths, M. R. Bond, & J. D. Miller (Eds.), *Rehabilitation of the adult and child with traumatic brain injury* (rev. ed.) (pp. 225–235). Philadelphia, PA: F. A. Davis.

Mahoney, M. J. (1974). *Cognition and behavior modification.* Cambridge, MA: Bollinger.

Malec, J. (1985). Personality factors associated with severe traumatic disability. *Rehabilitation Psychology, 30,* 165–172.

Malkmus, D., Booth, B. J., & Kodimer, C. (1980). *Rehabilitation of the head injured adult: Comprehensive cognitive management.* Downey, CA: Rancho los Amigos Hospital.

Maslach, C., & Florian, V. (1988). Burnout, job setting, and self-evaluation among rehabilitation counselors. *Rehabilitation Psychology, 33,* 85–93.

McCormack, N. (1981). *Plain talk about mutual self-help groups.* Rockville, MD: National Institute of Mental Health.

McKinlay, W. W., & Hickox, A. (1988). How can families help in the rehabilitation of the head injured? *Journal of Head Trauma Rehabilitation, 3,* 64–72.

McLaughlin, A. M., & Schaffer, V. (1985). Rehabilitate or remold?: Family involvement in head trauma recovery. *Cognitive Rehabilitation, 3,* 14–17.

Mesulam, M. M. (Ed.). (1985). *Principles of behavioral neurology.* Philadelphia, PA: F. A. Davis.

Mesulam, M. M. (1985). Attention, confusional states and neglect. In M. M. Mesulam (Ed.), *Principles of behavioral neurology* (pp. 125–168). Philadelphia, PA: F. A. Davis.

Miller, B. L., Cummings, J. L., McIntyre, H., Ebers, G., & Grade, M. (1986). Hypersexuality as altered sexual preference following brain injury. *Journal of Neurology, Neurosurgery and Psychiatry, 49,* 867–873.

Miller, J. D., Pentland, B., & Berrol, S. (1990). Early evaluation and management. In M. Rosenthal, E. R. Griffiths, M. R. Bond, & J. D. Miller (Eds.), *Rehabilitation of the adult and child with traumatic brain injury* (rev. ed.) (pp. 21–51). Philadelphia, PA: F. A. Davis.

Minuchin, S. (1974). *Families and family therapy.* Cambridge, MA: Harvard.

Minuchin, S., & Fishman, H. C. (1981). *Family therapy techniques.* Cambridge, MA: Harvard.

Moore, B. E., & Fine, B. D. (1968). *A glossary of psychoanalytic terms and concepts.* New York: The American Psychoanalytic Association.

National Head Injury Foundation. (1986). *What to look for when selecting a rehabilitation facility: A working guide.* Southborough, MA: National Head Injury Foundation.

National Head Injury Foundation. (1990). *National directory of head injury rehabilitation services.* Southborough, MA: National Head Injury Foundation.

National Institute of Handicapped Research. (1982). Working with brain injured clients. *Rehabilitation Brief, 5,* 1–4.

National Institute of Handicapped Research. (1984). Disability and families: A family systems approach. *Rehabilitation Brief, 7,* 1–4.

Napier, A. Y. & Whitaker, C. A. (1978). *The family crucible.* New York: Harper & Row.

Narayan, K. K., Gokasian, Z. L., Bontke, C. F., & Berrol, S. (1990). Neurologic sequelae of head injury. In M. Rosenthal, E. R. Griffiths, M. R. Bond, & J. D. Miller (Eds.), *Rehabilitation of the adult and child with traumatic brain injury* (rev. ed.) (pp. 94–106). Philadelphia, PA: F. A. Davis.

Oddy, M., Humphrey, M., & Uttley, D. (1978). Stresses upon the relatives of head injured patients. *British Journal of Psychiatry, 133,* 507–513.

O'Neill, G. W., & Gardner, R. J. (1983). *Behavioral principles in medical rehabilitation: A practical guide.* Springfield, IL: Charles Thomas.

Pang, D. (1985). Pathophysiologic correlates of neurobehavioral syndromes following closed head injury. In M. Ylvisaker (Ed.), *Head-injury rehabilitation: Children and adolescents* (pp. 3–70). Boston, MA: Little Brown.

Papp, P. (1981). Paradoxes. In S. Minuchin and H. C. Fishman, *Family therapy techniques* (244–261). Cambridge, MA: Harvard University Press.

Piaget, J. (1952). *The origins of intelligence in children.* M. Cook (trans.). New York: International Universities.

Prigatano, G. (1987). Psychiatric aspects of head injury: Problem areas and suggested guidelines for research. In H. S. Levin, J. Graffman, & H. M. Eisenberg

(Eds.), *Neurobehavioral recovery from head injury* (pp. 215–231). New York: Oxford.

Prigatano, G., Fordyce, D. J., Zeiner, H. K., Roveche, J. R., Pepping, M., & Wood, B. C. (1986). *Neuropsychological rehabilitation after brain injury.* Baltimore, MD: Johns Hopkins.

Rao, N., Jellinek, H. M., & Woolston, D. C. (1985). Agitation in closed head injury: Haloperidol effects on rehabilitation outcome. *Archives of Physical Medicine and Rehabilitation, 66,* 30–34.

Rapp, D. (1986). *Brain injury casebook.* Springfield, IL: Charles C. Thomas.

Reiss, D. (1981). *The family's construction of reality.* Cambridge, MA: Harvard.

Rehabilitation Institute of Chicago. (1983). *A manual of behavior management strategies for traumatic brain injured adults.* Unpublished manuscript.

Reitan, R. M., & Wolfson, D. (1985). *Neuroanatomy and neuropathology.* Tucson, AZ: Neuropsychology Press.

Rimel, R. W., Jane, J. A., & Bond, M. R. Characteristics of the head injured patient. In M. Rosenthal, E. R. Griffiths, M. R. Bond, & J. D. Miller (Eds.), *Rehabilitation of the adult and child with traumatic brain injury* (rev. ed.) (pp. 8–16). Philadelphia, PA: F. A. Davis.

Rimm, D. C., & Masters, J. C. (1974). *Behavior therapy: Techniques and empirical findings.* New York: Academic.

Rogers, C. R. (1951). *Client-centered therapy: Its current practice, implications and theory.* New York: Houghton Mifflin.

Romano, M. (1974). Family response to traumatic head injury. *Scandinavian Journal of Rehabilitation Medicine, 6,* 1–4.

Rosenthal, M. (1984). Strategies for intervention with families of brain injured patients. In B. A. Edelstein & E. T. Couture (Eds.), *Behavioral assessment and rehabilitation of the traumatically brain-damaged* (pp. 227–246). New York: Plenum.

Rosenthal, M. (1989). Response to "Psychotherapeutic interventions with traumatically brain injured patients." *Rehabilitation Psychology, 34,* 115–116.

Rosenthal, M., Griffiths, E. R., Bond, M. R., & Miller, J. D. (Eds.). (1990). *Rehabilitation of the adult and child with traumatic brain injury.* Philadelphia, PA: F. A. Davis.

Rosenthal, M., & Young, T. (1988). Effective family intervention. *Journal of Head Trauma Rehabilitation, 3,* 42–50.

Sachs, P. R. (1984). Grief and the traumatically brain injured adult. *Rehabilitation Nursing, 9,* 23–27.

Sachs, P. R. (1986). A family guide to evaluating transitional living programs for head-injured adults. *Cognitive Rehabilitation, 4,* 6–9.

Sachs, P. R. (1987, August). *Denial in rehabilitation professionals.* Paper presented at the meeting of the American Psychological Association, New York.

Sachs, P. R., Bell, E., Berger, M., Carroll, R. C., Davidson, K., Heavener, W., Peters, S., Schaffer, V., & Stabene, F. (1986). A six-factor model for treatment planning and cognitive retraining of the traumatically head-injured adult. *Cognitive rehabilitation, 4,* 26–30.

Sanders, D. (1980). A psychotherapeutic approach to homosexual men. In J. Marmor (Ed.), *Homosexual behavior: A modern reappraisal* (pp. 342–356). New York: Basic.

Sbordone, R. J., Kral, M., Gerard, M., & Katz, J. (1984). Evidence of a Command Performance syndrome in the significant others of victims of severe traumatic head injury. *Clinical Neuropsychology, 6,* 183–185.

Schwentor, D., & Brown, P. (1989). Assessment of families with a traumatic brain injury relative. *Cognitive Rehabilitation, 7,* 8–20.

Sherman, R., & Fredman, N. (1986). *Handbook of structural techniques in marriage and family therapy.* New York: Brunner Mazel.

Signoret, J. L. (1985). Memory and amnesias. In M. M. Mesulam (Ed.), *Principles of behavioral neurology* (pp. 169–192). Philadelphia, PA: F. A. Davis.

Simon, R. (1985). Family therapy. In H. I. Kaplan & B. J. Sadock (Eds.), *Comprehensive textbook of Psychiatry* (4th Ed.) (pp. 1427–1432). Baltimore, MD: Williams & Wilkins.

Sparadeo, F. R., & Gill, D. (1989). Effects of prior alcohol use on head injury recovery. *Journal of Head Trauma Rehabilitation, 4,* 75–82.

Spivack, M. P. (1986). Advocacy and legislative action for head injured children and their families. *Journal of Head Trauma Rehabilitation, 1,* 41–47.

Strickland, B. R. (1978). Internal-external expectancies and health related behaviors. *Journal of Consulting and Clinical Psychology, 46,* 1192–1211.

Sullivan, H. S. (1940). *Conceptions of modern psychiatry.* New York: Norton.

Sullivan, H. S. (1953). *The interpersonal theory of psychiatry.* New York: Norton.

Symington, D. C. (1984). The goals of rehabilitation. *Archives of Physical Medicine and Rehabilitation, 65,* 427–430.

Tate, R. L. (1987a). Issues in the management of behaviour disturbance as a consequence of severe head injury. *Scandinavian Journal of Rehabilitation Medicine, 19,* 13–18.

Tate, R. L. (1987b). Behavior management techniques for organic psychosocial deficit incurred by severe brain injury. *Scandinavian Journal of Rehabilitation Medicine, 19,* 19–24.

Teasdale, G., & Jennett, B. (1974). Assessment of coma and impaired consciousness. *Lancet, 2,* 81–84.

Teasdale, G., & Mendelow, D. (1984). Pathophysiology of head injuries. In N. Brooks (Ed.), *Closed head injury: Psychological, social and family consequences* (pp. 4–36). New York: Oxford.

Turnbull, A. P., Summers, J. A., & Brotherson, M. J. (1984). *Working with families with disabled members: A family systems approach.* Lawrence, KS: University of Kansas.

Turnbull, J. (1988). Perils (hidden and not so hidden) for the token economy. *Journal of Head Trauma Rehabilitation, 3,* 46–52.

Uomoto, J. M., & McLean, A., Jr. (1989). Care continuum in traumatic brain-injury rehabilitation. *Rehabilitation Psychology, 34,* 71–79.

Walsh, F. (1982). Conceptualization of normal family functioning. In F. Walsh (Ed.), *Normal family processes* (pp. 3–42). New York: Guilford.

Walsh, K. W. (1978). *Neuropsychology: A clinical approach.* Edinburgh: Churchill Livingstone.

Warrington, J. M. (1981). *The Humpty Dumpty syndrome*. Winona Lake, MN: Light and Life Press.

Weiner, I. B. (1975). *Principles of psychotherapy*. New York: John Wiley.

Whitaker, C. A., & Bumberry, W. M. (1988). *Dancing with the family*. New York: Brunner Mazel.

Willer, B., Arrigali, M., & Liss, M. (1989). *Family adjustment to the long term effects of traumatic brain injury of husbands*. Technical report 89-2. Buffalo, NY: Rehabilitation Research and Training Center.

Willer, B., Vullo, V., Jain, N., & Skretny, M. (1988). *Behavioral sequelae of traumatic brain injury: An annotated bibliography*. Technical report 88-1. Buffalo, NY: Rehabilitation Research and Training Center.

Williams, J. (1987). *Head injury support groups*. Southborough, MA: National Head Injury Foundation.

Williams, J. (1988). Families: The line between hope and reality. *Trends in Rehabilitation, 3*, 14–18.

Williams, S. E., & Freer, C. A. Aphasia: Its effect on marital relationships. *Archives of Physical Medicine and Rehabilitation, 67*, 250–252.

Wood, R. Ll. (1987). *Brain-injury rehabilitation: A neurobehavioral approach*. Rockville, MD: Aspen.

Wood, R. Ll. (1988). Management of behavior disorders in a day treatment setting. *Journal of Head Trauma Rehabilitation, 3*, 53–61.

Woodruff, M. C. & Baisden, R. H. (1986). Theories of brain functioning: A brief introduction to the study of brain and behavior. In D. Wedding, A. M. Horton, & J. Webster (Eds.), *The Neuropsychology Handbook* (pp. 23–58). New York: Springer Publishing Co.

Yalom, I. (1985). *The theory and practice of group psychotherapy*. New York, Basic.

Ylvisaker, M. (Ed.). (1985). *Head-injury rehabilitation: Children and adolescents*. Boston, MA: Little Brown.

Zasler, N. (1988). Sexuality issues after traumatic brain injury. *Sexuality update, 1*, 1–3.

Ziegler, E. A. (1987). Spouses of persons who are brain injured: Overlooked victims. *Journal of Rehabilitation, 53*, 50–53.

Zola, I. K. (1982). Social and cultural disincentives to independent living. *Archives of Physical Medicine and Rehabilitation, 63*, 394–397.

Index